The Pre-Raphaelite Art of the Victorian Novel

The Pre-Raphaelite Art of the Victorian Novel

Narrative Challenges to Visual Gendered Boundaries

SOPHIA ANDRES

The Ohio State University Press
Columbus

Library of Congress Cataloging-in-Publication Data

Andres, Sophia, 1950–
   The pre-Raphaelite art of the Victorian novel : narrative challenges
to visual gendered boundaries / Sophia Andres.
      p. cm.
   Includes bibliographical references and index.
   ISBN 0-8142-0974-2 (cloth : alk. paper) — ISBN 0-8142-5129-3
(pbk. : alk. paper) — ISBN 0-8142-9049-3 (CD-ROM)
   1. English fiction—19th century—History and criticism. 2. Art and
literature—Great Britain—History—19th century. 3. Pre-Raphaelitism—
Great Britain. 4. Visual perception in literature. 5. Pre-Raphaelitism in
literature. 6. Narration (Rhetoric) 7. Women in literature. 8. Women in
art. I. Title.
   PR878.A7A53 2004
   823'.809357—dc22
                                                   2004012887

Cover design by Dan O'Dair
Type set in Goudy
Printed by Thomson-Shore, Inc.

9 8 7 6 5 4 3 2 1

To Kitty and John Dunagan

Contents

List of Illustrations

Preface and Acknowledgments

Triumphant yet saddened, defiant yet withdrawn, the gaze of the woman who rescues her husband from prison in John Everett Millais's *Order of Release, 1746* polarized critics when it first appeared in the Tate Gallery in 1853. Whereas some of them applauded the poignant expression of the emotional conflict registered in the rescuer's face, others decried the transgression of conventional gender boundaries in this Pre-Raphaelite representation of a narrative scene in one of Walter Scott's novels. The critic of *Fraser's Magazine,* for instance, affirmed, "the picture is entitled to unqualified praise for the subtilty [*sic*] with which it seizes upon the conflict of feelings engaged in the moment of profound emotion it embodies. We still see in her eye the fear that has harassed her—she is not quite sure of his liberty—we read the whole story of her struggles, and sorrows, and heroic endurance, in that hectic flush mounting upon the pallid cheek."[1] John Eagles's objections, on the other hand, echo those of contemporary critics who voiced anxieties over the Pre-Raphaelites' destabilizations of gender constructs: "Instead of the eye dimmed even with a tear," he protested, "it looks defiance, as if she had contested at some previous time the matter with the jailer, and looks a triumph, as much as to say, 'I've won, and so pay me.' " Instead of displaying feminine tenderness, "she is the hardest looking creature you can imagine: Her under lip . . . is thrust out to a very disagreeable expression." In conclusion, he regretted the reversal of conventional gender roles the painting represents: "[I]t is wrong so to exhibit the released man. The painter should have considered that he should be shown worthy a reprieve—that he was, after all, a fine manly fellow."[2]

Millais's reconfiguration of a narrative scene into a painting is representative of the Pre-Raphaelites' ability to express in pictorial form gender issues that continue to preoccupy us. Simultaneously *The Order of Release,* like numerous other Pre-Raphaelite paintings, depicts the coalescence of the verbal and the visual and the extension of temporal and spatial boundaries. The convergence of the verbal and the visual was not limited to Pre-Raphaelite painting or poetry but also transpired in yet another important genre—the Victorian novel. *The Pre-Raphaelite Art of the Victorian Novel* explores the coalescence of the visual and the verbal, that is, the reconfigurations of notable Pre-Raphaelite paintings within the Victorian novel and examines some of the most significant gender issues this convergence involves.

During the last four decades, we have witnessed a great deal of work in the area of gender. This work has taken place on political, legal, social, and cultural fronts. Among the many questions raised during this period is the question of definition. Many authors, scholars, activists, and reformers have argued that gender should not be defined once and for all. Rather, it should be rethought and renegotiated. *The Pre-Raphaelite Art of the Victorian Novel* joins this argument but substantiates it historically and aesthetically. It shows that a great deal of what we have witnessed in recent decades has significant antecedents in the art of the Victorian period, specifically in the paintings of several prominent Pre-Raphaelites and the fiction of renowned Victorian novelists.

Very early versions of parts of the chapters that follow (in a completely different form) can be found in *The Journal of Pre-Raphaelite Studies* (chapters 2 and 4), *The Victorians Institute Journal* (chapter 4), *The Companion to the Victorian Novel*, ed. William Baker and Kenneth Womack, and *The Victorian Newsletter* (chapter 3). I am grateful to the editors concerned for giving me the permission to rewrite the material.

The Pre-Raphaelite Art of the Victorian Novel would not have been possible without the generous support of the Dunagan Foundation, whose grant enabled me to devote an entire year exclusively to the research and writing of this book. Yet another grant by the same foundation has covered the color production cost of the images. I am grateful to the Dunagan Foundation for enabling me to make tangible what might have remained impalpable scholarly notions. I am also grateful to the administrators of the University of Texas of the Permian Basin (UTPB), who granted me a year's Faculty Development Leave and awarded me a grant for the permissions of the reproductions of the images in this book.

I owe a great deal to the staff of the following galleries for their courteous and invaluable assistance: Tate Gallery, the Ashmolean Museum, the Fitzwilliam Museum, the Birmingham Museum and Art Gallery, the Manchester City Art Galleries, the Merseyside County Council Lady Lever Art Gallery, Port Sunlight, St. Paul's Cathedral, the National Portrait Gallery, the Victoria and Albert Museum, the William Morris Gallery, the Metropolitan Museum of Art, the Yale Center for British Art, and the Delaware Art Museum.

Others have contributed to the development of this book at various phases of its composition. Anita Voorhies, the Interlibrary Loan Librarian at UTPB, has been remarkably helpful in locating at times obscure Victorian sources, and I deeply appreciate her wonderful assistance. My effusive thanks to my brother, John Poulakos, who has spent and continues to invest countless hours in our discussions of the Pre-Raphaelites and Victorian novelists. I am also grateful to Bill Baker, Joseph Kestner, and Julie Codell, who found time in their busy lives to read a draft of this book and offer their valuable suggestions. I would like to express my appreciation of The Ohio State University Press staff, especially Heather Lee Miller, Acquisitions Editor, and Eugene O'Connor, Managing Editor, for their ourstanding work. And my thanks are due to those students who served as my research assistants: Maureen Page, Clark Moreland, Christy Tynes, and Sean-Pierre Wilson.

I would also like to thank my mother, Anastasia Poulakou, my children, Dimitri and Elza Andres, and David Barnett, who have lived with the Pre-Raphaelites as long as I have. Finally, my deepest debt is to my brother, Takis Poulakos, whose enthusiasm and passion for my work, through the years, have fuelled wondrous insights.

Introduction

When it comes to a sense of excitement, to making the heart beat faster, Pre-Raphaelitism ranks high among cultural phenomena and certainly has no equal in Victorian art. . . . It is a story with a strong element of romance, of youthful enthusiasm, opposition overcome, success beyond the wildest dreams of the original exponents. . . . The heady mixture of beauty, poetry, intellectual challenge and personal magnetism appeals today every bit as powerfully as it did during the movement's ascendancy, with the added edge that only nostalgia for a vanished age can give.[1]

John Christian's succinct and exuberant comments on Pre-Raphaelitism explain only part of the fascination, excitement, and exquisite appeal that Pre-Raphaelite art generated in the past, continues to emanate in the present, and no doubt will stimulate in the future. Despite an initially hostile reception, that "heady mixture of beauty, poetry, intellectual challenge" gradually spread to all aspects of Victorian popular and high culture, including the novel. Reconfigured in diverse modes such as the sensation novels of Elizabeth Mary Braddon or the intellectual works of George Eliot, Pre-Raphaelite art became an integral part of most Victorian novels, conveying contemporary anxieties over various sociopolitical issues and capturing multiple perspectives on constructions of gender.

The Pre-Raphaelite Art of the Victorian Novel explores the ways in which the Victorian novel was shaped by Pre-Raphaelite art. It focuses on the work of four prominent novelists, Elizabeth Gaskell, Wilkie Collins, George Eliot, and Thomas Hardy, all successful in reaching a wide audience of diverse classes and therefore of varied educational achievement, aesthetic sensibility, and intellectual sophistication. The novels of these four authors reveal the rich and multifaceted complexity of the art of the Victorian novel, attested by innumerable scholarly works devoted to its interpretation. This book elucidates yet another facet of the exquisite intricacy of the Victorian novel, the narrative reconfigurations of Pre-Raphaelite paintings, understood and appreciated by Victorian readers in ways lost to us. Entries in the journals of these writers on Pre-Raphaelite art, as well as letters addressed to prominent Pre-Raphaelite artists or to other contemporary intellectuals, express these novelists' great interest in and glorious delight over Pre-Raphaelite art. Although their comments differ considerably in scope and intensity, they all point to a common sense of excitement and awe at the sight of Pre-Raphaelite masterpieces. In a letter to Charles Norton in 1859, for instance, Elizabeth Gaskell, who crafted the intense emotions of her characters, is at a loss for words to express the overwhelming emotions and startling thoughts that William Holman Hunt's and Dante Gabriel Rossetti's paintings had stimulated in her: "I am not going to define & shape my feelings & thoughts at seeing either Rossetti's or Hunt's pictures into words; because I *did* feel them deeply, and after all words are coarse things."[2]

Like Elizabeth Gaskell, Wilkie Collins was deeply affected by Pre-Raphaelite art throughout his career. Shortly after viewing Hunt's exhibit in 1889, he burst into effusive praise in a letter to him, not merely admiring the beauty and splendor of his paintings but simultaneously underscoring his enormous appreciation of Hunt's unique expression of human emotion, one of the principles that propelled the Pre-Raphaelite revolution against preestablished aesthetic notions: "As a painter of human expression, the most difficult of all achievements in your Art, there is not a man among your living English Colleagues . . . who is fit to be mentioned in the same breath with you."[3] As we shall see in chapter 3, Collins turned some of the most important Pre-Raphaelite painterly techniques he discusses in this letter into narrative strategies in his most successful novel, *The Woman in White*.

George Eliot's response to the Pre-Raphaelites was even more complex than that of other Victorian novelists, the subject of chapter 4. "Art works for all whom it can touch," she writes to Edward Burne-Jones after visiting his studio in 1873. "And I want in gratitude to tell you that your work makes life larger and more beautiful to me."[4] Fascination pervades a short entry in Thomas Hardy's journal following his visit to the Grosvenor Gallery in 1878: "June 8. [1878]— To Grosvenor Gallery. Seemed to have left flesh behind, and entered a world of soul."[5] As these few short entries suggest, Pre-Raphaelite art captivated literary artists, inspired them, and compelled them to reconfigure some of the most notable and popular Pre-Raphaelite paintings in their own ways into narrative images of intense emotions, emotions that reflected multifarious cultural and social issues.

But besides these letters, contemporary reviews of Pre-Raphaelite paintings disclose the complexity of the issues Pre-Raphaelite art involved and generated in British culture and society. Seemingly objections to the Pre-Raphaelites' defiance of the preestablished principles of art upheld by the Royal Academy, derogatory comments in these reviews often conceal and reveal anxieties about the Pre-Raphaelites' transgressions of conventional gender boundaries. Referring to the Pre-Raphaelite paintings exhibited at the Royal Academy in 1850, the critic of *Athenaeum*, for instance, protested: "Abruptness, singularity, uncouthness are the counters with which they play for fame. Their trick is to defy the principles of beauty and the recognized axioms of taste."[6] In this respect this review was typical in interweaving without distinction aesthetic principles with representations of gender, subsumed under aesthetic categories such as beauty and taste.

In addition to new ways of representing gender, the revolutionary and innovative spirit of Pre-Raphaelite art initiated new approaches to perceptual and psychological realism, new ways of seeing, of feeling, of expressing emotions. By evoking popular Pre-Raphaelite paintings that readers had seen either in galleries or in engravings of illustrated magazines and newspapers, Victorian novelists established a common ground with them, interweaving the fictional with the actual in ways that often blurred the borderline between the two realms. At the site of these reconfigurations, where the fictional merged with the actual, readers were drawn into not merely hypothetical issues but also into questions confronting them in their quotidian lives.

In her recent work, *Realism, Representation, and the Arts in Nineteenth-Century Literature*, Alison Byerly discusses several reasons for the nineteenth-century literary artists' fascination with the visual arts. By comparing landscapes to works of art, she points out, Romantic writers attempted to validate the status of poetry as art; by alluding to works of art, realist novelists established "an imaginative space where the fictional world and the real world came together" (121). Byerly's discussion of the relation of literature to the visual arts may explain one of the reasons for the Victorian novelists' tendency to reconfigure Pre-Raphaelite paintings in their novels.

Over the years the relation of literature to the visual arts has been extensively discussed.[7] Yet the particular intersection of Pre-Raphaelite art and the Victorian novel has been noted in only a few brief studies.[8] *The Pre-Raphaelite Art of the Victorian Novel* focuses on this intersection exclusively, providing several reasons for this phenomenon, one of which is that the Pre-Raphaelites' aesthetic and sociopolitical concerns neatly dovetailed with those of the Victorian novelists. Rather than relying merely on ekphrasis, the novelists discussed in this book reconfigured popular Pre-Raphaelite paintings and in the process engaged their readers in contemporary debates on cultural and sociopolitical issues, more specifically on aesthetics, class, and gender.

A brief overview of Victorian reviews of literature or painting points to the contemporary bias for the amalgamation and expansion of the temporal and spatial arts rather than their separation and limitation, which Lessing had championed in his seminal Laocoön.[9] In her recent work, *The Victorians and the Visual Imagination*, Kate Flint shows that Victorian critics of painting tended to "read" paintings, relying mostly on verbal rather than on visual terms.[10] This intersection of the spatial and temporal arts, however, was not limited to critical responses to painting but was also a common occurrence in reviews of the novel. Whereas reviewers early in the century drew rather general affinities between the novel and painting, later on they often sought in narratives techniques employed in the visual arts. Referring to the controversial subject of Gaskell's *Ruth*, for instance, a critic contends that "the extent of the canvas should bear some proportion to the dimensions of the picture."[11] Yet another, speaking about the novelist's obligation to represent life truthfully, applauds Gaskell's realistic treatment of Ruth's story: "The sadder you say the world is, the sadder I must paint it. Woe be indeed unto me, if for the paltry sake of artistical effect, I tamper with its sadness, darken its shadows, exaggerate its miseries, so that the original shall no more be recognized from the portrait."[12] In an article on Wilkie Collins, published in *Fortnightly Review* at the end of the century, A. C. Swinburne compares Collins's novels to those of his godfather's pictures: "All the works of Wilkie Collins which we remember with pleasure are works of art as true as his godfather's pictures, and in their own line as complete."[13]

What often strikes us as paradoxical in some of these reviews is the critics' objection to the novelists' tendency to "merely" write, which is exactly what we assume they were to do. R. H. Hutton, for instance, reviewing *Daniel Deronda* in 1876, criticizes George Eliot for devoting a great part of her novel to studying rather than painting Daniel Deronda's character: "[S]o much pain has been expended on *studying* rather than on *painting* him."[14] Similarly, W. H. Mallock objects to Eliot's disinclination to "paint" her novel, protesting that she "has ceased to use her brush at all, and has left the whole in the condition of shadowy sketches."[15] A. V. Dicey further elaborates on this point, conjecturing that even Eliot herself was unhappy with her heavy reliance on a verbal rather than a visual representation of Daniel Deronda: "The author, too, is dissatisfied, and, returning again and again to the hero's character, retouches a portrait which the very painter seems hardly to consider a likeness. When dealing with minor characters, or carried away by the stress of the drama, George Eliot falls back on artistic instinct and paints with a bold hand."[16]

From the beginning of his career, Thomas Hardy drew attention to the relation between the novel and the visual arts through his novel *Under the Greenwood Tree* with the subtitle "A Rural Painting of the Dutch School." Certainly the reviewers followed his lead. *The Saturday Review*, for instance, notes that "the author has produced a series of rural pictures full of life and genuine colouring."[17] In a review of *Far from the Madding Crowd*, the *Spectator* questions the verisimilitude of the novel, for it lacks a "picture of the scenery and ways of life" and a "picture of the human beings who give the chief interest to that scenery and those ways of life."[18] At the end of the century *The Savoy*, reviewing *Jude the Obscure*, discussed Hardy's ability to paint nature and morals: "[I]t is clear how the artist who has trained himself to the finest observation of Nature cannot fail, as his art becomes more vital and profound, to paint morals. The fresher and more intimate his vision of Nature, the more startling his picture of morals."[19]

Clearly, contemporary reviews of the Victorian novel point to a set of pictorial demands placed on novelists, expected not only to be masters of the art of narrative but also to be familiar with the visual arts. Knowledge of classical or contemporary art was not enough; they were additionally expected to understand painterly techniques to such an extent as to be able to employ them in their narratives or, even further, to transform pictorial into narrative techniques. Under the circumstances, then, it was impossible for any writer to disregard the initial turmoil the Pre-Raphaelites engendered in British culture. Apart from their notoriety and later their popularity, which attracted critical and popular attention, the Pre-Raphaelites initiated unorthodox techniques and unconventional subjects extending aesthetic and social boundaries and creating a magnificent realm of beauty and splendor. Simultaneously they offered various ways to meet the contemporary demand and satisfy the longing for the visual in the verbal.

From the very beginning, Pre-Raphaelite art involved the interplay of poetry and painting, the verbal and the visual. The short-lived, Pre-Raphaelite publication, *The Germ*, highlighted its interdisciplinary nature in its subtitle, *Thoughts Towards Nature in Poetry, Literature, and Art*. After the first two issues, the new title emphasized its intertextual nature: *Art and Poetry, Being Thoughts Towards Nature, Conducted Principally by Artists*. If we consider the critical response to the change of the original title, Lindsay Smith suggests, we may perceive the new title as an attempt to destabilize the categories of art and poetry: "It [the title] is a blatant advertisement for a radical intertextuality that presents the journal as questioning its categorization as discourse. And in this sense it may be regarded as, in effect, a self-parodic intervention into the rigidity of genre division, and into the sister arts analogies of reviewers."[20] The Pre-Raphaelites then from the beginning of the movement had emphasized the extension and intersection of spatial and temporal boundaries. In essays on history, aesthetics, literature, and art, as well as in poems that translated pictorial into verbal texts, *The Germ* thoroughly explored the relationship between visual art and literature. Rossetti's compositions in this journal, particularly his "Sonnets for Pictures," reflect his early attempts to translate painting into poetry and thus achieve not only a destabilization of hitherto established boundaries between visual and verbal texts but also new syntheses of the spatial and temporal arts.

The intertextual nature of subjects continued to distinguish Pre-Raphaelite paintings from the beginning of the movement to its very end. The Lady of Shalott, for instance, made her first appearance in the Moxon edition of Tennyson's poetry and continued to inspire Pre-Raphaelite painters like Waterhouse even as late as the beginning of the twentieth century. It was the "common enthusiasm" for John Keats's poetry, William Holman Hunt recalls, that brought the three founders of the Pre-Raphaelite Brotherhood together and later served as the inspiration for several paintings.[21] Contemporary critics such as John Ruskin and David Masson described the Pre-Raphaelites as poetical painters. Twentieth-century critics, like Stephen Spender, continued to see the Pre-Raphaelites as literary painters whose inspiration was mainly "verbal, literary, poetic, rather than painting."[22] Although Spender's interpretation is quite restrictive, as Elizabeth Prettejohn has recently demonstrated, it is quite applicable to a large corpus of Pre-Raphaelite art.[23] Vibrant, sensuous paintings such as Millais's *Mariana* and *Lorenzo and Isabella,* Arthur Hughes's *April Love,* Rossetti's *Blessed Damozel,* Holman Hunt's *Lady of Shalott,* to name but a few, originated in poetry and illustrated the Pre-Raphaelite painter's vision of a moment, a scene, or a theme. Such literary paintings may be seen as attempts to make palpable and tangible impalpable and intangible verbal expressions or as challenges to ideological representations of gender.

Yet Pre-Raphaelite art was not limited to the well-known and extensively documented amalgamation of the poetic and the painterly. The Pre-Raphaelite convergence of the verbal and the visual transpired in yet another significant contemporary genre—the Victorian novel. Novelists as diverse as Elizabeth Gaskell, Wilkie Collins, Mary Elizabeth Braddon, George Eliot, and Thomas Hardy, whose philosophical and literary perspectives differed considerably, were all fascinated by the Pre-Raphaelites, corresponded with them, visited their studios, and frequently commissioned them to illustrate their novels. But beyond explicit visual illustrations that accompanied the text, the Pre-

Raphaelites entered the Victorian novel in more subtle and implicit ways. It is interesting to note that the relationship between Victorian novelists and Pre-Raphaelite artists was reciprocal. Paintings such as Holman Hunt's *Rienzi* and *The Awakening Conscience* were inspired respectively by Bulwer Lytton's *Rienzi, the Last of the Tribunes* and Charles Dickens's *David Copperfield.*

The affinities of the Victorian novel with the sister arts have been the subject of extensive scholarship, particularly that devoted to William Thackeray, George Eliot, and Thomas Hardy.[24] *The Pre-Raphaelite Art of the Victorian Novel* extends this kind of scholarship and concentrates primarily on representations of Pre-Raphaelite paintings in the Victorian novel. In textual redrawings of these paintings, novelists often engaged readers in questions over restrictive, conventional gender boundaries. Simultaneously, readers became involved in contemporary debates on gender issues, seeing the sociopolitical contradictions that governed constructions of gender in Victorian England.

Never just a sympathetic or mildly antagonistic response but intense emotions, ranging from anger or anxiety to praise or enchantment have governed the critical reception of the Pre-Raphaelites' representations of gender through the years. Since its inception Pre-Raphaelite art has been the locus of impassioned debates. Vituperative critical attacks reached their culmination in 1850, when the meaning of the monogram PRB became known and the Pre-Raphaelite Brotherhood was seen by a few critics as yet another religious or political group with a subversive agenda at a time of tumultuous sociopolitical activities.[25] That year, Charles Dickens's sarcastic denigration of the Pre-Raphaelites in general and John Everett Millais's *Christ in the House of His Parents* in particular is representative of the hostile reception the first Pre-Raphaelite paintings received: "Wherever it is possible to express ugliness of feature, limb, or attitude, you have it expressed. Such men as the carpenters might be undressed in any hospital where dirty drunkards, in a high state of varicose veins, are received. Their very toes have walked out of Saint Giles's."[26] Aesthetics and gender politics were involved in the critical reception of Pre-Raphaelite art from its very beginning and continue to be the controversial subject of critical studies.

Over one hundred years after its inception, the Pre-Raphaelites' representations of gender constructs once again elicited emotionally charged responses. In "Patriarchal Power and the Pre-Raphaelites," Deborah Cherry and Griselda Pollock berate the art historians' responses to the 1984 Pre-Raphaelite Tate exhibit, the first major Pre-Raphaelite exhibit since the 1961 exhibition at the Maas Gallery: "The exhibition at the Tate and its accompanying publications offer no suggestion that such work [on the constitution and culture of the British bourgeoisie] will even be intimated in its procedures. Indeed, class, race and gender are systematically erased from a discourse which none the less provides an affirmation of bourgeois, sexist and racist ideologies."[27] Cherry and Pollock's emotionally charged response is reminiscent of the emotional upheaval that Pre-Raphaelite paintings generated in their earliest viewers.

Ironically, the Pre-Raphaelites have recently been censured not for their subversion but for their endorsement of Victorian gender constructs. Instead of upbraiding the Pre-Raphaelites for their unorthodox representation of gender constructs, as some of the early reviewers had done, critics such as Cherry and Pollock have decried their stereotypical depictions. Similarly, critics like Jan Marsh in *Pre-Raphaelite Women: Images of Femininity* have often discussed Pre-Raphaelite images in terms of feminine stereotypes. Most likely, the Pre-Raphaelites, especially the early ones, who perceived themselves as rebels fighting the artistic and sociopolitical establishment, would have winced at such accusations. These recent responses to the Pre-Raphaelites as well as hundreds of books devoted to their art demonstrate the lasting quality of Pre-Raphaelite art, which has survived the centuries and is still as dazzling and bewildering today as it was in its very beginning.

Today the controversy surrounding the Pre-Raphaelites has not subsided but has taken on our own sociopolitical preoccupations. Class, race, and gender are the primary lenses through which recent critics scrutinize Pre-Raphaelite paintings. Such perspectives, however, are as steeped in ideological battles now as they were more than a hundred years ago. Yet, as Elizabeth Prettejohn in her recent *Art of the Pre-Raphaelites* contends, most often recent perspectives on the Pre-Raphaelites

> have shifted the responsibility for patriarchal bias, comfortingly, away from ourselves and on to the Pre-Raphaelite pictures. By unmasking the misogynistic implication of Pre-Raphaelite pictures of women, we can rail against Victorian patriarchal presuppositions with a complacent sense of our own superiority. Indeed the case with which we find ourselves able to decode the misogynistic meanings of Pre-Raphaelite pictures seems to prove that misogyny is their problem, not ours. (297)

By projecting our own anxieties onto the Pre-Raphaelites, Prettejohn claims, we tend to distance ourselves from our own complicity with gender inequities. In the process, Prettejohn points out, we tend to overlook the Pre-Raphaelites' astonishing contribution to art and culture, not only in Great Britain but also throughout the world. Yet even those writers embroiled in controversial responses to Pre-Raphaelite representations of gender, I believe, would agree that the Pre-Raphaelites expanded the limits of rigid Victorian morality and transgressed established gender boundaries.

The Pre-Raphaelites' resistance to conventional gender constructs was quite often interwoven with an astute understanding of human psychology, at times captured in representations of subjects in emotional turmoil. Their treatment of psychological subjects in turn is reflected in the multifarious interpretations their paintings to this day have received. Recent art historians have unraveled the nuances of meaning that Pre-Raphaelite images convey, they themselves transgressing interpretive boundaries that confine their meaning within racist and misogynist classifications. In just the last few years critics such as J. B. Bullen, *The Pre-Raphaelite Body*, Elizabeth Prettejohn, *The Art of the Pre-Raphaelites*, Kate Flint, *The Victorians and the Visual Imagination*, and Christine Poulson, *The Quest for the Grail: Arthurian Legend in British Art 1840–1920* have pioneered discoveries moving our understanding beyond the hitherto established parameters of psychoanalysis, feminism, poststructuralism, and deconstructivism. Dominated by the forces of the marketplace, the Pre-Raphaelites, like Victorian novelists, quite often hovered over the hazy borderline between the conventional and the unconventional. The belligerent response to their first paintings compelled them to adjust the choice of their subjects to the expectations of their spectators. Nevertheless the Pre-Raphaelites remained throughout their careers more progressive and liberal than their contemporary counterparts. Chapter 1 explores this hazy borderline between the stereotypical or conventional and the unconventional or progressive. In the conflation of the sacred and the profane, the pure and the fallen, the Victorian binary opposites governing conventional representations of femininity, Pre-Raphaelites achieved the extension of gendered boundaries and simultaneously revealed the inherent contradictions in prevailing norms. In chapter 1 I also examine the affinities the Victorian novel and Pre-Raphaelite art shared, specifically in perceptual, psychological, and poetic realism. This chapter concludes with the gender politics governing ekphrasis.

Like the Pre-Raphaelites who challenged prevailing subjects of representation, Elizabeth Gaskell chose Ruth, an unmarried, teenaged woman, for the heroine of her eponymous novel. Most Pre-Raphaelite paintings in the early years of the movement were unorthodox representations of conventional subjects. In her textual redrawings of popular Pre-Raphaelite paintings, Gaskell explores this convergence of the unconventional with the conventional in her contentious *Ruth*, the subject of chapter 2. Her representations of Ruth, like those of the Pre-Raphaelites, involve the conflation of and challenge to a specific contemporary binary—the fallen woman and the Virgin Mary. In her reconfigurations of Pre-Raphaelite paintings of idealized versions of feminine beauty, Gaskell demonstrates that prevalent notions of ideal femininity sustain conditions for victimization. Her concern with the social conditions of victimization may explain her reconfiguration of a notable Pre-Raphaelite painting such as *Ophelia*, which displays the tragedy of an innocent victim, blending youthful features and vibrant female beauty with the fragility of a tragically premature death. Her own representation of the relationship between innocence and victimization, however, does not focus so much on inevitable tragic fate as on social conditions that are situational and as such ought to be changed.

In Pre-Raphaelite art, Wilkie Collins found a unique amalgamation of two quintessential and distinctive qualities of his work—realism and sensationalism. In chapter 3 I explore Collins's new modes of perception developed in *The Woman in White*, initiated by Pre-Raphaelite art, in connection to landscapes, identity formation, and the extension of conventional gender boundaries. In addition to themes for his novel, Collins found in Pre-Raphaelite paintings his primary narrative technique—the treatment of light and shade. This chapter presents a brief overview of early reviews of Pre-Raphaelite exhibits concerned with the Pre-Raphaelites' departure from traditional perspective and treatment of light and shade. The Pre-Raphaelite naturalistic and egalitarian, rather than artificial and hierarchical, representation of life made new demands on spectators, compelling them to see what traditional modes of perception concealed. To Collins, the Pre-Raphaelites were engaged in new ways of seeing, knowing, and understanding the world. In *The Woman in White* Collins develops these new ways of interacting with the world. In particular he situates his characters in Pre-Raphaelite scenes partially lit and partially darkened, in the process-evoking states of consciousness between waking and dreaming and forms of knowledge between the real and the imaginative. *The Woman in White* orients us toward a new perspective on Collins's challenge to gender constructs, inextricably bound with modes of perception initiated by his Pre-Raphaelite friends.

In chapter 4 I argue that the Pre-Raphaelites' impact on George Eliot's *Daniel Deronda* is significantly different from that on her earlier novels. As with her previous novels, in *Daniel Deronda* Eliot derives from Pre-Raphaelite pictorial techniques sources for her narrative strategies and from their subjects inspirations for her literary portraits. I maintain, for instance, that while she initially was more interested in developing the Pre-Raphaelite notion of the germ into an aesthetic theory of narration, she gradually developed it into an aesthetic that integrated narrative technique with social critique. What is new about this stage of her writing is the level of complexity she introduces to her already successful ways of merging literature and painting. The new direction Eliot's reconfigurations of Pre-Raphaelite paintings takes in her last novel may be partly explained by the fact that she met Dante Gabriel Rossetti and Edward Burne-Jones just a few years before the composition of her last novel. A letter occasioned by her visit to Burne-Jones's studio in 1873 records the new perspective she began to form toward his work, the relation between great drama and historical understanding. Thus, I argue, Eliot's understanding of Pre-Raphaelite art at the time affected her previous interest in the relation between literature and painting and extended it toward history. Edward Burne-Jones's *Wheel of Fortune*, I demonstrate, is the locus of the Pre-Raphaelite presence in *Daniel Deronda*, a vibrant illustration of her critique of the British Empire. As the novel progresses, we become aware that Gwendolen's gambling and the sense of supremacy it fuels in her is paradigmatic of the colonialist ideology dominating the mid-Victorian years.

Daniel Deronda reveals that Eliot was aware that the contemporary interest in classical Greece and Rome dovetailed with colonialist and patriarchal ideologies. At a time when women's status was gradually improving through the women's movement and legislative measures, the turn to classical gender constructs expressed the contemporary resistance to women's evolving roles. Unlike contemporary, classical subject painters like Frederic Leighton, Rossetti questioned patriarchal interpretations of classical figures like Pandora, Proserpine, and Astarte Syriaca through the sonnets he wrote for these paintings. Eliot reconfigures Rossetti's representations of these goddesses and further questions her culture's insistence on the universal and natural status of woman as man's inferior. In her notebooks for her last novel we find records of the sensational accounts of African explorers in the 1860s dwelling on "superstition," "bewitchery," and "childish passion." As it happens, Eliot implies, such are the qualities we may also find in Rossetti's and Burne-Jones's Pre-Raphaelite stunners of the 1860s and 1870s, which she reconfigured into images of Gwendolen in *Daniel Deronda*. In images of beauty, evil, and magic, Eliot, like Rossetti and Burne-Jones, blends images of the primitive and the demonic with the civilized, blurring the demarcation between categories considered distinct. But her goal in her last novel differs from that of the Pre-Raphaelites. Through the contradictory representations of Gwendolen, George Eliot articulates and criticizes contemporary anxieties over crucial events, namely the question of women's suffrage and the expansion of the British Empire, which determined conflicting attitudes toward women, often seen as the other. In her last novel Eliot saw otherness as a critical domain from which to refigure the self.

In the latter part of the nineteenth century even hostile critics recognized the Pre-Raphaelites' remarkable contribution to British art. Ironically, what early critics had decried as a distorted, unhealthy depiction of reality, those in the later part of the century lauded as the healthy, Pre-Raphaelite principles that they often contrasted with the decadent aestheticism of the second phase of Pre-Raphaelitism. Chapter 5 includes an overview of the critical reception of the second phase of Pre-Raphaelitism, the aesthetic movement, led by Edward Burne-Jones. Here I focus on prevailing apprehensions over the destabilization of established gender boundaries that his paintings generated during the second part of the nineteenth century. Like the reviewers of the early Pre-Raphaelite pictures, some critics of Edward Burne-Jones's paintings relied on pathological terms to protest his representations of unconventional gender constructs, particularly his recurrent representation of androgyny. In his hazy distinctions of gender Burne-Jones engaged his viewers in more problematic and puzzling ways of understanding gender constructs than did his Pre-Raphaelite predecessors, in whose paintings gender identity was readily understood. In seductive dreamscapes that seem completely removed from the gender politics of his era, Burne-Jones problematized gender constructs in representations of indeterminate androgyny.

Through subtle reconfigurations of Edward Burne-Jones's androgynous figures such as Nimue and Merlin, Cupid and Psyche, Thomas Hardy, I contend in chapter 5, participates in contemporary debates on the "new woman," often labeled "the bachelor girl," who distinguished herself in that era by her rejection of marriage and her demand for equal rights. Like Burne-Jones, who places his androgynous figures in dreamscapes that appear to be removed from the sociopolitical sphere, Thomas Hardy experimented with the suspension of gender boundaries in the "dreamy paradise" Sue and Jude conjure, until crass reality completely annihilates their dreams and their lives, compelling them to seek shelter within the enclosure of conventional gender boundaries they had once spurned. Nevertheless, unlike Burne-Jones, who destabilized gender constructs by representing men and women as androgynous, Hardy, in his reconfigurations of Burne-Jones's paintings, represented only Sue as androgynous. Through the representation of Sue's intellectual power and her depiction as an androgynous figure, Hardy sustained feminism; yet, in her stereotypically feminine breakdown and eventual capitulation to convention, he thoroughly subverted it. Hardy's contradictory perspective on Sue and Jude captured unresolved and puzzling questions about constructions of gender that are characteristic of the Victorian era.

I have limited the scope of *The Pre-Raphaelite Art of the Victorian Novel* to four prolific Victorian novelists, Elizabeth Gaskell, Wilkie Collins,

George Eliot, and Thomas Hardy, and to the four, most prominent Pre-Raphaelite artists, Dante Gabriel Rossetti, John Everett Millais, William Holman Hunt, and Edward Burne-Jones. The works of these literary and painterly artists were widely disseminated and as such represented and shaped salient aspects of Victorian culture.

CHAPTER ONE

The Pre-Raphaelites and the Victorian Novel

Mary Elizabeth Braddon's Pre-Raphaelite portrait of Lady Audley in volume one of *Lady Audley's Secret* (1863) exhibits a curious amalgamation of high and popular culture and exemplifies the Victorian novelists' reliance on Pre-Raphaelite visual art to engage their readers in complex ways. On this occasion the narrator at once endorses and repudiates Pre-Raphaelite art, in the process gaining common ground with both its advocates and detractors. The exquisite appeal of Braddon's Pre-Raphaelite portrait is intensified by its sharp contrast with mainstream art ornamenting the antechamber leading to Lady Audley's boudoir, where her recently painted, full-length portrait still stands on the easel. Looking at notable and valuable masterpieces by artists such as Philips Wouvermans, Nicolas Poussin, and Salvator Rosa, Robert Audley nods his head and, addressing his friend George Talboys, remarks with boredom, "there are our friend's eternal white horses . . . ha—hum."[1] But when he first looks at Lady Audley's portrait, he is transfixed by its splendor, exclaiming to George, "it's an extraordinary picture." No doubt by then the reader is anxious to "see" the portrait that has attracted the unperturbed bachelor's attention.

> Yes; the painter must have been a pre-Raphaelite. No one but a pre-Raphaelite would have painted, hair by hair, those feathery masses of ringlets with every glimmer of gold, and every shadow of pale brown. . . . No one but a pre-Raphaelite could have given to that pretty pouting mouth that hard and almost wicked look it had in the portrait. . . .
>
> Her crimson dress, exaggerated like all the rest in this strange picture, hung about her in folds that looked like flames, her fair head peeping out of the lurid mass of colour, as if out of a raging furnace. Indeed,

1

the crimson dress, the sunshine on the face, the red gold gleaming in the
yellow hair, the ripe scarlet of the pouting lips, the glowing colours of
each accessory of the minutely-painted background, all combined to
render the first effect of the painting by no means an agreeable one.
(70–71)

Like Robert, George is struck by the portrait though he does not
acknowledge the reason to either Robert or Alicia. Yet the reader knows
at this point that George has recognized his former wife. Emotional intensity, one of the characteristics of Pre-Raphaelite art, not only pervades this
picture but also consumes its immediate viewers, Robert and George, and
in turn the reader. By 1861, when *Lady Audley's Secret* first appeared in
the magazine *Robin Goodfellow,* Braddon's readers could have imagina-
tively matched this portrait to an array of Pre-Raphaelite femmes
fatales—Dante Gabriel Rossetti's *Bocca Baciata* (1859) and Edward
Burne-Jones's *Sidonia von Bork* (1860) (the most notorious)—that they
had seen in galleries or in engraved reproductions in illustrated magazines
or papers. In drawing this intertextual portrait, the narrator establishes a
common ground with the reader, grounding the fictional in the real, the
sensational in the actual. The attention to the nuances of details, each
hair painted with "every glimmer of gold," the unorthodox treatment of
light and shadow, their interplay captured in her hair rather than harmoniously distributed throughout the entire portrait, the brilliancy of color-
ing in the features of her face, the pouting lips (which caused an outrage
when Rossetti exhibited *La Bocca Baciata*), her beautiful yet fiendish
expression, the minute details in the objects of the background, all salient
features of Pre-Raphaelite art, outraged or delighted contemporary
reviewers.[2] Replete with signifiers, Lady Audley's Pre-Raphaelite portrait
adumbrates future events. For example, the crimson dress with folds "that
looked like flames" foreshadows her later attempt at setting on fire the
hotel where Robert stays when she discovers that he suspects her of being
instrumental in George Talboys's disappearance.

In the same scene, when Robert avers, his initial enthusiasm having
subsided, "But I don't like the portrait; there's something odd about it,"
Alicia, his cousin and Lady Audley's stepdaughter, brings up yet another
salient feature of Pre-Raphaelite art, the depiction of idiosyncratic
expression congruent with the subject's psychology:[3] " ' I've a strange fancy
on that point, I think that sometimes a painter is in a manner inspired,
and able to see, through the normal expression of the face, another
expression that is equally a part of it, though not to be perceived by common eyes' " (73). While Alicia alludes to the Pre-Raphaelites' preference
for the depiction of expression over beauty, she affirms the readers' aware-

ness of the plot and knowledge of Pre-Raphaelite art. In the process read-ers are invited to collaborate with the writer by contributing their own knowledge to the construction of the narrative. Yet such invitation is not an attempt simply to establish a rapport with the reader on aesthetic grounds but also to involve the reader in sociopolitical constructions of gender. Lady Audley's infantile face, which proves irresistible to everyone, for example, is representative of the Victorian culture's worship of the child-woman, the Angel in the House who in Braddon's case turns into a self-aggrandizing "fiend." As the narrator identifies and distances herself from Lady Audley's Pre-Raphaelite portrait, she both conceals and reveals contemporary anxieties over Pre-Raphaelite transgressions of gender con-structs.

By no means can we overlook the paradoxical perspective governing Lady Audley's Pre-Raphaelite portrait. By extending her power beyond the traditional domestic constraints, the narrator seems to empower her, yet at the same time to weaken her by casting her as a stereotype, a femme fatale, "a beautiful fiend." And though undoubtedly modern, the portrait, we are told, exudes an aura of "quaint medieval monstrosities." In this respect, then, this portrait is also representative of the paradoxical per-spectives embodied in Pre-Raphaelite art from the very beginning of the movement in 1848 till the end, in the early 1900s. Such seemingly incon-gruous concepts as revivalism and modernity, realism and sensationalism, "perverse ugliness" and excessive beauty, eroticism and spiritualism, sci-entific accuracy and symbolism generated vituperative responses in the early years. Victorian spectators, particularly of early Pre-Raphaelite exhibits, were often repulsed, perplexed, and unsettled by the fears and anxieties the unorthodox Pre-Raphaelite vision disclosed. Transgressing aesthetic, social, and gender boundaries, the Pre-Raphaelite avant-garde gaze revealed hitherto unexplored perspectives as, for instance, uncon-ventional beauty in conventional ugliness, feminine fragility in mas-culinity, and masculine strength in conventional femininity.[4]

Lady Audley's striking portrait captures contradictory perspectives, adding richness and complexity to the novel, extending its narrative boundaries, and involving the reader in its fictional construction. Certainly this sort of complexity was also appealing to famous novelists such as Elizabeth Gaskell, Wilkie Collins, George Eliot, and Thomas Hardy, subjects of this work. A letter to Edward Bulwer-Lytton reveals yet another reason for Braddon's redrawing of Pre-Raphaelite art in her nov-els: "I have learned to look at everything in a mercantile sense, and write solely for the circulating library reader whose palette [*sic* for palate] requires strong meat, and is not very particular as to the quality. . . . Now your kind interest arouses an ambition which was . . . utterly dead. . . . I want to be artistic and to please *you*. I want to be sensational, and to please Mudie's subscribers. . . . Can the sensational be elevated by art, and redeemed from all its coarseness?"[5] Other novelists as well as reviewers would have agreed that the connection of the novel with the visual arts would enrich and elevate it. On several occasions in her bestseller *Lady Audley's Secret*, Braddon did not hesitate to make conspicuously clear the connection between the sensation novel and Pre-Raphaelite art.[6] By contrast, Elizabeth Gaskell, George Eliot, Wilkie Collins, and Thomas Hardy preferred subtle and inconspicuous allusions to the Pre-Raphaelites, complicating even further the intertextual and contextual connections in which they engaged their readers. Pre-Raphaelite art, which Braddon explicitly addresses in *Lady Audley's Secret*, is intricately embedded in the subtext of these writers' novels. This chapter explores the most significant affinities Victorian novelists shared with the Pre-Raphaelites and the predominant reasons that compelled them to redraw Pre-Raphaelite paintings in their novels.

The Pre-Raphaelite Revolution

Three decades after the Pre-Raphaelite Brotherhood caused a maelstrom in Victorian society, Oscar Wilde, with characteristic wit and verve, described its important role in British culture: "The Pre-Raphaelites were a number of young poets and painters who banded together in London . . . to revolutionize English poetry and painting. They had three things which the English public never forgive—youth, power and enthusiasm. . . . Their detractors blinded the public, but simply confirmed the artists in their convictions. To disagree with three-fourths of all England on all points is one of the first elements of sanity. . . . This Pre-Raphaelite revolution was not only of ideas, but of creations."[7] Twice in this brief passage Oscar Wilde emphasizes the revolutionary spirit of the Pre-Raphaelite movement and the adverse criticism it generated. The Pre-Raphaelites' repudiation of the aesthetic principles of the Royal Academy, on which mainstream British art was founded, caused an uproar, virtually alienating them from mainstream art circles and reviewers in the early years of the movement. In these early hostile reviews, as we shall see, we detect cultural biases Victorian novelists also repudiated and thus identified early with the Pre-Raphaelites.

Founded in 1848 by Dante Gabriel Rossetti, John Everett Millais, and William Holman Hunt, the Pre-Raphaelite Brotherhood was spurred by a youthful rebellious spirit against the established aesthetics of the Royal Academy.[8] Anthony Harrison presents a brief overview of the political chaos in the continent in 1848, the year the Pre-Raphaelite Brotherhood was formed: "Revolutionary activity had rocked Sicily in January, Paris in late February, Germany and Italy in March. The fall of Austria's once powerful chancellor, Clemens Metternich, on March 13 had signaled political disintegration. In April hostilities had erupted between Germany and Poland. At the same time, Russia had prepared for war to preserve its hold on Poland."[9] With the depression of the 1830s and the Chartist riots of 1842, the stability of the British system was also threatened. As Poulson observes, "the late 1830s and the 1840s were years of instability and discontent and middle-class fear of the mob."[10] At a turbulent time when revolutions raged in Europe, the Pre-Raphaelite Brotherhood initiated a revolution in British culture with far-ranging effects. As such they were seen as a subversive, conspiratorial group, perhaps involved in yet another political upheaval, and were assailed by contemporary critics.

Dante Gabriel Rossetti, John Everett Millais, and William Holman Hunt were determined to infuse youthful vitality and novelty into contemporary art, which, they believed, had been stifled by the prevailing conventions of the Royal Academy, beginning with Raphael's successors and established by the eighteenth-century renowned artist and first president of the Royal Academy, Sir Joshua Reynolds.[11] From the very beginning the Pre-Raphaelites rebelled against Sir Joshua Reynolds's idealism, discussed in his highly acclaimed *Discourses on Art*. In the third discourse Reynolds encourages prospective artists to idealize, universalize, and generalize when painting portraits or landscapes: "[G]reat perfection and beauty," he declares, "are not to be sought in the heavens but upon the earth. . . . All the objects which are exhibited to our view by nature, upon close examination will be found to have their blemishes and defects." However, it was the artist's responsibility, according to Reynolds, to depict "Ideal Beauty," that is, to remove the perceived flaws of a composition; the great artist "corrects nature by herself—her imperfect state by her more perfect." Ideal beauty, Reynolds taught, could be achieved through summary finish, which the Pre-Raphaelites labeled "slosh" and nicknamed the great master, Sir Sloshua.[12] To Reynolds's concept of ideal beauty the Pre-Raphaelites countered their aim "to sympathise with what is direct and serious and heartfelt in previous art, to the exclusion of what is conventional and self-parading and learned by rote."[13] Instead of "ideal beauty," they expressed the idiosyncratic uniqueness of their subjects; instead of idealized permanence, they attempted to capture realistic change. For this reason, instead of excluding "particularities," they accurately displayed minute details—even "blemishes." Their "uncompromising egalitarianism," that is, a painstaking attention to every single object in their pictures, further distinguishes their paintings from those of the old

Plate 1. John Everett Millais, *Christ in the Carpenter's Shop* (*Christ in the House of His Parents*), 1849–1850. Oil on canvas, 34 x 55in (86.4 x 139.7 cm), Tate Gallery. Reproduced by permission.

masters and their contemporaries as well (Prettejohn 186). Thus Pre-Raphaelite techniques from the very beginning were inextricably bound with sociopolitical concerns.

Indeed, Millais's revolutionary representation of the Holy Family in *Christ in the House of His Parents* (1849–1850) (plate 1) became a target in the critical battleground between idealism and realism.[14] Derogatory reviews of this painting reflect contemporary concerns and apprehensions that the Pre-Raphaelite revolution involved not only a resistance to established aesthetic precepts but also the repudiation of social and gender hierarchies as well. In this respect, then, the goals of the Pre-Raphaelites and Victorian novelists, who often questioned established class and gender boundaries, dovetailed. It is worth briefly considering the techniques of this early painting, for they are paradigmatic of the revolutionary changes the Pre-Raphaelites sought to implement and in turn the Victorian novelists frequently adopted.

To begin with, Millais's painting violated all precepts of art that Sir Joshua Reynolds established in his *Discourses*, particularly his injunction in the fourth discourse to young artists to draw divine figures with "great nobleness" and "dignity" and to follow a hierarchical subordination of less to more important parts in their artistic compositions. Instead of the "ideal perfection," which Raphael employed in his representations of the Holy Family and Reynolds upheld as laudatory representations to be emulated, Millais relied on intricate realism in his representation of the Virgin and child, choosing for their models ordinary people of the lowest classes. Instead of representing Mary in a conventionally graceful pose, he depicted her in a hitherto inconceivable position, kneeling as the Christ child kisses her on the cheek and Joseph leans over them inspecting the child's injured hand. Millais's picture combines scientific accuracy with symbolic realism. The objects in the painting in all their details, captured in naturalistic accuracy, can be interpreted both literally and symbolically. The wood and nails in Millais's painting, for instance, remind us of Christ's death on the cross, "elaborating on the idea by showing Christ as having cut himself on a nail and spilt a drop down on to his foot. St. John is shown bringing a bowl of water to bathe the wound, which acts as a kind of attribute identifying him as the Baptist." The sheep in the background stand for the Christian flock; the dove on the ladder, for the Holy Spirit (Warner in Parris, *The Pre-Raphaelites,* 78).

Instead of an artificial arrangement of light and shadow, with the central figures in the light, the subsidiary figures and objects in the shadow, as Reynolds would have dictated, the sunlight through the open windows illuminates figures and objects equally, during a fleeting moment that will change the minute the Christ child moves, the Virgin stands up, or

Joseph puts aside the piece of wood on which he is working. Though biblical characters, these figures appear quite modern. Yet the modern aspect of the picture appears incongruous to the archaic style of the picture, that is, the flat perspective, its lack of depth, the awkward poses. Millais, however, chose such a style deliberately in order to emphasize expressiveness and to distinguish his painting from contemporary genre paintings.[15] In this respect the painting displays yet another salient paradox of Pre-Raphaelite art: historicism and modernity or revivalism and realism (Barringer 10).

Considering the sociopolitical context and the threat the establishment saw in the purportedly subversive paintings of the Pre-Raphaelite Brotherhood, it is not surprising that mainstream reviewers responded vehemently, choosing Millais's *Christ in the House of His Parents* as their target. Millais's stark realism and egalitarian treatment of his subject raised fears and anxieties in upper- and middle-class viewers, who sought in artistic representations confirmation of the hierarchical social structure they endorsed. The *Times* articulates such anxieties in a scathing commentary: "Mr. Millais's principal picture . . . is, to speak plainly, revolting. The attempt to associate the Holy Family with the meanest details of a carpenter's shop, with no conceivable omission of misery, of dirt, and even disease, all finished with the same loathsome minuteness, is disgusting."[16] The *Athenaeum* echoes the outrage: "Mr. Millais . . . has been most successful . . . in giving to the higher forms, characters and meanings a circumstantial Art-language from which we recoil with loathing and disgust. There are many to whom his work will seem a pictorial blasphemy."[17]

Other reviews, also permeated with pathological terms, interweave objections to new aesthetic principles with transgressions of gender boundaries. Ralph Wornum of the *Art Journal*, for example, beginning with hostile comments against the representation of the Holy Family as common people, continues with remarks on gender: "The physical ideal alone can harmonize with the spiritual ideal: in *Art*, whatever it may be in Nature in its present condition, *the most beautiful soul must have the most beautiful body;* lofty sentiment and physical baseness are essentially antagonistic; even in the lowest sinks of poverty in the world, the purest mind will shine transcendent."[18] Wornum's categorical statements, "the most beautiful soul must have the most beautiful body" and "sentiment and physical baseness are essentially antagonistic" reveal hierarchical gender and class biases that exclude a majority of people from the privileges enjoyed by the selected few who meet contemporary standards of beauty. Likewise the critic of *Blackwood's Edinburgh Magazine* denigrates the Pre-Raphaelites for their proclivity for representations of ugliness and "diseased aspects. . . . Ricketty children, emaciation and deformity constitute their chief stock in trade." Referring to Millais's picture, he continues, "we can hardly imagine anything more ugly, graceless, and unpleasant."[19] Both of these critics employ pathological terms not just to describe Pre-Raphaelite violations of traditional aesthetic standards but also to interconnect aesthetics with transgressions of conventional gender boundaries.

Charles Dickens amplifies the censure of these critics in his notorious "Old Lamps for New Ones," published in his journal *Household Words*, where he disparages the Pre-Raphaelites in general for their retrogressive techniques and Millais's *Christ in the House of His Parents* in particular for transgressions of the established conventions associated with the representation of the Holy Family, especially for a conspicuous and offensive lack of "ideal beauty." William Michael Rossetti recorded in the *P.R.B. Journal* that Dickens's "attack on Millais has been most virulent and audacious" (Fredeman 70). Clearly the fundamental premise of Dickens's argument is related to the Pre-Raphaelites' egalitarian methodology, their refusal, that is, to abide by the hierarchical standards of an artistic composition canonized by Sir Joshua Reynolds. If the Holy Family stands at the top of the hierarchy, as Dickens and most reviewers believed, it should not be connected with its lowest rungs, the urban poor. Paradoxically, such vehement protest came from the champion of the underprivileged and the dispossessed. "In the foreground of that carpenter's shop," Dickens points out, "is a hideous wry necked, blubbering, red-headed boy, in a bed-gown; who appears to have received a poke in the hand, from the stick of another boy with whom he has been playing in an adjacent gutter, and to be holding it up for the contemplation of a kneeling woman, so horrible in her ugliness, that . . . she would stand out from the rest of the company as a Monster, in the vilest cabaret in France, or the lowest ginshop in England."[20] Like other contemporary critics, Dickens here interweaves objections to aesthetic standards with violations of established class and gender categories. As Tim Barringer has already asserted, "gender and class are the chosen terms of Dickens's attack: the Christ child is not sufficiently manly; the Virgin is too vulgar in her physiognomy, too coarse in comparison with the sweet features of the Raphaelesque Madonna. Her hardened face appears working class" (40).

The belligerent critical reception of *Christ in the House of His Parents* illustrates the Pre-Raphaelites' blow against artistic, class, and gender hierarchies. Religious figures lack the dignity and grandeur of the aristocratic physiognomy traditionally representing the Holy Family, which by extension endorsed and justified the social hierarchy. Whether it be in the background or in the foreground, every object and figure receives equal attention; thus in political terms a democratic perspective replaces a traditionally hierarchical one. In this respect the Pre-Raphaelites were attuned to contemporary sociopolitical and legislative changes moving England from a stratified nation to an increasingly democratic one. The most revolutionary techniques that characterize the Pre-Raphaelite revolt against the Royal Academy then disclosed their commitment not just to aesthetic but also to social reform as well—an egalitarian society accepting of unconventional gender constructs. Like the Pre-Raphaelites, Victorian novelists such as Elizabeth Gaskell, Wilkie Collins, George Eliot, and Thomas Hardy advocated social reform, particularly the acceptance of a wider range of gender roles.

Pre-Raphaelite Perceptual, Psychological, and Poetic Realism

Like the Pre-Raphaelites, who rejected idealistic representations sanctioned by the Royal Academy, Victorian realist novelists often castigated ideal representations as distorted views of life and truth. Idealism, realist novelists believed, deviated from the novel's most crucial goal, that is, to extend the readers' sympathies and thus accomplish much-needed social reform. For the Victorian novelists as well as the Pre-Raphaelite artists, especially in their early years, realism was the philosophical foundation and the most significant achievement of their art. George Eliot, a pioneer and leader of literary realism, was, like other Victorian novelists, preoccupied with realistic representation and on numerous occasions in her essays, notebooks, and novels defined realism in terms of truth and morality. Her well-known statement on Dutch painting in chapter 17 of *Adam Bede* has often been quoted as the quintessential statement on realism. Though referring to Dutch art, it is entirely possible, I believe, that Eliot is describing the realism of Pre-Raphaelite art, which resisted and repudiated the idealistic principles of the Royal Academy, expressed in Reynolds's discourses on art.

> So I am content to tell my simple story, without trying to make things
> seem better than they were; dreading nothing, indeed, but falsity, which,
> in spite of one's best efforts, there is reason to dread. Falsehood is so easy,
> truth so difficult. . . . It is for this rare, precious quality of truthfulness
> that I delight in many Dutch paintings, which lofty-minded people
> despise. . . . I turn without shrinking from cloud-borne angels, from
> prophets, sibyls, and heroic warriors to an old woman bending over her
> flower-pot, or eating her solitary dinner. . . . "Foh!" says my idealistic
> friend, "what vulgar details! What good is there in taking all these paints
> to give an exact likeness of old women and clowns? What a low phase of

life!—clumsy, ugly people." . . . Therefore let Art always remind us of them [common, coarse people]; therefore let us always have men ready to give the loving pains of a life to the faithful representing of common-place things—men who see beauty in these commonplace things, and delight in showing how kindly the light of heaven falls on them.[21]

In these remarks Eliot captures contemporary debates on idealism versus realism. Contemporary reviewers of Pre-Raphaelite art, as we have seen, were embroiled in such debates, condemning Pre-Raphaelite paintings for their lack of idealism. Indeed, Eliot's defense of realism resonates with the comments of early hostile reviewers of Pre-Raphaelite paintings who defined their scrupulous realism as a perverse tendency to represent "ugliness." Simultaneously, her association of realism with truth resembles that of Ruskin's defense of the Pre-Raphaelite art in terms of truth—"truth to nature" is his most famous motto. As early as 1852 Eliot had noted the Pre-Raphaelites' contribution to art in a letter to John Chapman: "I have noticed the advertisement of the British Q[uarterl]y this morning. . . . They have one subject of which I am jealous—"Pre-Raphaelitism in Painting and Literature."[22]

In his discussion of Eliot's realism, specifically its emphasis on the representation of the ordinary, George Levine explains that in her view "representing the world adequately means representing its very ordinariness, and the moral project of realism is—in resistance to conventional art—to dramatize the value of the ordinary."[23] This resistance to idealism, which Eliot recognizes as the moral basis of realism in the earlier passage, was also the most significant force that propelled Pre-Raphaelite art. Representations of "clumsy and ugly people," associated with those of the lower classes, though relevant to Dutch painting, are also recurrent subjects in Pre-Raphaelite paintings, often denigrated by mainstream reviewers. Since the Pre-Raphaelite controversy was still raging in 1859, when *Adam Bede* was first published, it is entirely possible that Eliot did not want to be identified with a controversial group at a critical time in her career. Hence, she articulated some Pre-Raphaelite principles in terms of the already established and accepted Dutch art.

Eliot's tendency to reconfigure Pre-Raphaelite paintings in her novels is evident even in her first work, *Adam Bede,* which opens with "The Workshop," a carpenter's and builder's, Mr. Jonathan Burge's, shop, where we see "the slanting sunbeams [that] shone through the transparent shavings." When the narrator focuses on Adam Bede, who works there as a carpenter, we are made aware of "the sleeve rolled up above the elbow," showing "an arm that was likely to win the prize for feats of strength" (5–6). It is very likely that this scene, focusing on Adam's muscular arm below the rolled-up sleeve and on the wood shavings, is a narrative recon-figuration of Millais's controversial *Christ in the House of His Parents*. Though Millais had his father sit for Joseph, he chose a carpenter to pose for his body in order to accurately represent his arm (revealed below his sleeve).[24]

Eliot's focus on the "transparent shavings" also recalls Millais's attention to the accurate representation of the wood shavings, which became the focus of ridicule by contemporary reviewers. When discussing this paint-ing, Ruskin notes that derisive critics came to call it *The Carpenter's Shop*.[25] No doubt Eliot's workshop partakes of the qualities of *The Carpenter's Shop* and shares Millais's qualities of symbolic realism. Though it is impossible to ascertain whether Eliot had seen the painting by the time she wrote *Adam Bede*, we know through her numerous references in her letters to the *Times* and the *Athenaeum* that she was aware of the controversy the paint-ing had raised. Even if Eliot herself had not seen the painting, she would have been able to reconstruct it through the extensive and detailed descriptions of the reviewers or of friends who had seen it.

Throughout her career George Eliot, like other Victorian novelists, was deeply preoccupied with new modes of realistic representation. Even before the writing of her fiction, as a contributor to and editor of the influential journal *Westminster Review*, George Eliot in several of her reviews emphasized realism and identified it with the artist's most crucial, moral obligation. In her review of Wilhelm Heinrich von Riehl's works on social history, "The Natural History of German Life," published in *Westminster Review* in 1856, for example, she extols Riehl's realistic rep-resentation of common people and elaborates on the artist's moral oblig-ation to the truthful representation of reality:

> Art is the nearest thing to life; it is a mode of amplifying experience and extending our contact with our fellow-men beyond the bounds of our per-sonal lot. All the more sacred is the task of the artist when he undertakes to paint the life of the People. Falsification here is far more pernicious than in the more artificial aspects of life. It is not so very serious that we should have false ideas about evanescent fashions—about the manners and conversation of beaux and duchesses; but it *is* serious that our sym-pathy with the perennial joys and struggles, the toil, the tragedy, and the humour in the life of our more heavily-laden fellow-men, should be per-verted, and turned towards a false object instead of the true one.[26]

It is interesting to note here, as on various occasions in her prose and fiction, that Eliot elides the distinction between painting and prose, blending visual and verbal boundaries: Riehl "paints the life of the people."[27] Thus it was inevitable that novelists like her, who were interested in the "visually" realistic representation of life, would adopt innovative, Pre-Raphaelite approaches to the representation of realism. In the earlier passage she moves swiftly through the social hierarchy and focuses on the lower classes aligning realism with the representation of the common people, a goal also depicted in early Pre-Raphaelite paintings such as Millais's *Christ in the House of His Parents*, which repudiates hierarchies by representing divine figures as common people.

Earlier that year Eliot had also published in *Westminster Review* her review of John Ruskin's third volume of *Modern Painters*, in which she upheld realism as the most important concept Ruskin conveyed: "The truth of infinite value that he teaches is *realism*—the doctrine that all truth and beauty are to be attained by a humble and faithful study of nature, and not by substituting vague forms, bred by imagination on the mists of feeling, in place of definite, substantial reality."[28] As we have already seen, she reiterates these remarks in her defense of realism in *Adam Bede*. Ruskin's allusions to the Pre-Raphaelites and their truthful representation of reality would also have been of interest to her.

Ruskin's writings were of interest to critics, literary and pictorial artists alike.[29] As George Eliot observed in her review of the third volume of *Modern Painters*, "every one who cares about nature, or poetry, or the story of human development—every one who has a tinge of literature, or philosophy, will find something that is for him."[30] Ruskin's authority could not be ignored. All the novelists included in this study had read *Modern Painters*, published in five volumes from 1843 to 1860, and highly esteemed Ruskin's theories on aesthetics and realism. In the process of seeking out his theories, novelists discovered his exaltation of the Pre-Raphaelites. Thus Ruskin validated the shared goals of realist novelists and Pre-Raphaelite painters.

Ruskin articulated his initial support of the Pre-Raphaelites in two letters to *The Times*, on May 13 and May 25, 1851, in which he emphasizes the innovative means through which the Pre-Raphaelites achieved realistic representation.[31] No doubt his letters attracted the attention of those Victorian novelists already stirred by his own work and by the controversy these young artists had generated. In his review of Collins's *Convent Thoughts* and Hunt's *Two Gentlemen of Verona*, Ruskin calls attention to details hitherto overlooked by artists, praising Collins for his accurate and minute representation of the *Alisma Plantago* and Hunt for his depiction of "the trodden grass and broken fungi" in the foreground of *The Two Gentlemen of Verona*, which registers "the momentary struggle of Proteus and Sylvia just past" (*Works* 12:321, 325).[32] Even in later reviews Ruskin attributed the Pre-Raphaelites' exquisite appeal to naturalism. In a letter

Plate 2. William Holman Hunt, *The Light of the World*, 1851–1853. Oil on canvas, over panel, arched top, 49$^1/_2$ x 23$^1/_2$ in (125.5 x 59.8 cm), Warden and Fellows of Keble College, Oxford. Reproduced by permission.

to the *Times* on May 5, 1854, where he effusively praises Hunt's *Light of the World*, (1851–1853) (plate 2) at a time when most critics denigrated it, he underscored Hunt's sensitive and accurate representation of nature and took this painting as an occasion to distinguish the realistic representation of genuine Pre-Raphaelite painting from its spurious imitators:

> The true work represents all objects exactly as they would appear in nature in the position and at the distances which the arrangement of the picture supposes. The false work represents them with all their details, as if seen through a microscope. Examine closely the ivy on the door in Mr. Hunt's picture, and there will not be found in it a single clear outline. All is the most exquisite mystery of colour; becoming reality at its due distance. In like manner examine the small gems on the robe of the figure. Not one will be made out in form, and yet there is not one of all those minute points of green colour, but it has two or three distinctly varied shades of green in it, giving it mysterious value and lustre. (*Works* 12:331)

Unlike the Pre-Raphaelites, whose work displays an acute sensitivity to and deep awareness of the hues and gradations of color in different kinds of light, the Pre-Raphaelite imitators, Ruskin points out, are impervious to nature's infinite variation, representing instead "the most minute leaves and other objects with sharp outlines, but with no variety of colour, and with none of the concealment, none of the infinity of nature" (ibid. 12:331–32).

Yet Ruskin does not extol Pre-Raphaelite naturalism and realism for its own sake but instead demonstrates its connection to psychological realism. Referring to *Valentine Rescuing Sylvia from Proteus* (1850–1851), for instance, Ruskin declares that he is astonished by "its marvelous truth in detail and splendour in colour." He continues: "[N]or is its general conception less deserving of praise: the action of Valentine, his arm thrown round Sylvia, and his hand clasping hers at the same instant as she falls at his feet, is most faithful and beautiful, nor less so the contending of doubt and distress with awakening hope in the half-shadowed, half-sunlit countenance of Julia" (*Works* 12:324–25). Touching upon the exquisite representation of minute details, a point contemporary reviewers had vehemently denounced, Ruskin demonstrates its significance not only in depicting reality but also in revealing the psychological complexity of the emotions of the figures portrayed. Valentine's and Sylvia's clasping of hands, after her rescue from Proteus, captures an emotionally charged scene; Julia's "half-shadowed, half-sunlit" face in the background depicts her conflicted feelings of "doubt and distress with awakening hope" for Proteus, her wayward lover.

Plate 3. William Holman Hunt, *The Awakening Conscience*, 1853–1854. Oil on canvas, arched top, 30 x 22 in (76.2 x 55.9 cm), Tate Gallery. Reproduced by permission.

In his review of William Holman Hunt's *Awakening Conscience* (1853–1854) (plate 3) Ruskin further elaborates on the Pre-Raphaelites' ability to express psychological realism through visual signifiers. Countering the contemporary critics' objections to the plethora of objects in *The Awakening Conscience*, which they saw as insignificant distractions that call attention away from the two figures in the painting, Ruskin declares the importance of the distinctness and sharpness of each object in capturing the intensity of the emotion the depicted woman experiences at the moment of revelation of her fall from innocence: "Nothing is more notable than the way in which even the most trivial objects force themselves upon the attention of a mind which has been fevered by violent and distressful excitement. They thrust themselves forward with a ghastly and unendurable distinctness, as if they would compel the sufferer to count, or measure, or learn them by heart" (*Works* 12:334). No one would doubt Ruskin's assertion that intense emotion at times of psychological turmoil governs and dictates perception. Thus Ruskin once again, in this case indirectly, links Pre-Raphaelite art to the realist novel, whose fundamental concerns are naturalism and symbolic and psychological realism. On another occasion, in the third volume of *Modern Painters*, when discussing once again the psychological depth and narrative complexity of this painting, he specifically connects *The Awakening Conscience* to the novel, declaring that it takes "its proper position beside literature" (ibid. 5:127).[33]

Recent critics have discussed what Ruskin had early observed in his interpretations of paintings such as *The Awakening Conscience* and *The Light of the World*, that is, the correspondence between the Pre-Raphaelite painters' sharp and minute representation of objects and the intensity of the emotions their subjects, and by extension their viewers, experience. The expression of powerful feelings in Pre-Raphaelite art, Richard Stein asserts, "is not merely a means but an end in itself; the emotional impact of their pictures is part of their meaning and not simply an accidental side-effect. It is precisely this intensity that marks the revolutionary character of Pre-Raphaelite iconography."[34] Carol Christ, on the other hand, points out that the "excessive clarity and brilliance" of the sharp and minute details pervading Pre-Raphaelite art capture "the emotional attitude of most of the subjects" and thus intensify the emotional response of the viewers. These intricate details characteristic of Pre-Raphaelite realism, according to Christ, were arduous attempts to express the "invisible areas of human emotion." In this respect Pre-Raphaelite art is not merely realistic, Christ contends, but expressionistic as well: "The Pre-Raphaelites were seeking expressionistic art to portray strong states of emotion, and by an accident of history they wound up seeking it through naturalism." In the process, they discovered "a new center in the subjective perception of each individual."[35]

Chris Brooks, on the other hand, interprets these details in terms of the new modes of perception through which the Pre-Raphaelites interpreted the world. Arranged without a predetermined structural hierarchy, which would otherwise guide the perception and the interpretation of the viewers, details in the foreground and the background compel viewers to see the world from a completely different perspective, noticing details that were hitherto concealed from established habits of perception. Thus the Pre-Raphaelites, Brooks demonstrates, "challenge our conventions of perceptual organisation and, by extension, the existential and metaphysical structuring we derive from that organisation."[36]

No doubt the Pre-Raphaelites' innovative approaches to realistic representation made them irresistible to Victorian novelists. I have mentioned here but the most significant: the interweaving of scientific accuracy with symbolic realism, the construction of new modes of perception, the expression of "invisible areas of emotion," the depiction of psychological realism through visual signifiers, all primary concerns to the realist as well as to sensationalist novelists. Apart from these innovative techniques for realistic representation, Pre-Raphaelite art offered yet another unique appeal to Victorian novelists: its association with poetry, a genre considered superior to the novel. Vibrant, intense Pre-Raphaelite representations of scenes in Keats's and Tennyson's poetry cannot be separated from their verbal expressions. Hunt's or Waterhouse's life-sized paintings of *The Lady of Shalott*, for instance, will always loom between the lines of Tennyson's eponymous poem, governing the readers' imagination.

From the very beginning, then, the Pre-Raphaelites extended visual and verbal boundaries and became known as poetical painters. In this respect the Victorian novelists' association with them became enticing, for, through evocations of Pre-Raphaelite paintings, they could elevate their genre through its association with poetry. As Kate Flint has recently observed, in the Victorian period "there was an enduring belief that a novel was a lesser form of composition than poetry, and this added to the degree to which, if only by implication, a relatively low aesthetic value was placed on narrative art in 'high' cultural circles. In the eyes of its detractors, particularly in the earlier decades of the Victorian period, the novel was no more than an entertainment, more likely to engage the imagination than the moral or speculative faculties" (*The Victorians and the Visual Imagination* 200).

Ruskin's categorical declaration in "Of Queens' Gardens" is characteristic of the belief in the low status of the novel in the literary hierarchy.

Even the best novel, Ruskin contends, may pose a risk "if, by its excitement, it renders the ordinary course of life uninteresting, and increases the morbid thirst for useless acquaintance with scenes in which we shall never be called upon to act" (*Works* 18:129). In contrast to the novel, poetry was associated with "the most energetic and harmonious activity of all the powers of the human mind," as Matthew Arnold stated in his 1857 inaugural lecture as professor of poetry at Oxford. It is, therefore, "to the poetical literature of an age that we must, in general, look for the most adequate interpretation of that age." Sarah Stickney also voiced the contemporary bias in favor of poetry in her declaration, " 'Art of the highest order is necessarily associated with poetry.' "[37]

The fusion of poetry with painting, the Pre-Raphaelites believed, was one of their highest achievements that distinguished their art from other contemporary painting and elevated it beyond any other. Hunt, for instance, often associates Pre-Raphaelite art with poetry, at times distinguishing it from that of its "dull imitators who were destitute of poetic discrimination." However, Hunt's definition of poetic painting does not merely include their choice of subjects from poetry; instead, he also connects it to the Pre-Raphaelites' ability to capture the beauty of nature in the fleeting moments of the ever-changing light. Unlike most contemporary painters, on one occasion Hunt declares, "we saw that in Nature contours are found, and lost, and what in one point is trenchant, in another melts its form into dazzling light or untraceable gloom; that there is infinite delight to the mind in playing upon the changes between one extreme characteristic and another. . . . Adherents to our reform in the true spirit . . . have proved that poetry in painting is not destroyed by the close pursuit of Nature's beauty" (*Pre-Raphaelitism* 2:400). Thus Hunt, in just one statement, interweaves the principles of Pre-Raphaelite art with those of the realist novel: realism, naturalism, truth, poetical expression, and reform.

On numerous occasions Ruskin also emphasizes the poetic quality of Pre-Raphaelite art. In the third volume of *Modern Painters,* for instance, he distinguishes the Pre-Raphaelites from old masters such as Horace Vernet, Jacques-Louis David, or Domenico Tintoret for their ability to represent " 'noble grounds for noble emotions' " and recognizes them as "poetical painters," not just for seeking inspiration in poetry and for depicting and generating intense emotions, often associated with poetry, but also for "becoming poets in themselves in the entire sense, and inventing the story as they painted it" (*Works* 5:127). The Pre-Raphaelite poetical paintings then offered Victorian novelists multifarious ways through which they could elevate the novel in the cultural and literary hierarchy, endowing it with poetical complexity and sophistication.

As we have seen, the Pre-Raphaelites offered Victorian novelists inno-vative ways to represent perceptual, psychological, and poetical realism. Simultaneously, their intertextual works, most memorably expressed in Rossetti's striking works, offered multifarious ways to translate images into words, the visual into the verbal.[38] In the process of inviting their readers to redraw Pre-Raphaelite paintings they had once seen or often saw, Victorian novelists engaged them not only in contemporary debates on aesthetics but in gender politics as well. Indeed, narrative reconfigura-tions of Pre-Raphaelite visual, gendered boundaries enclosed and dis-closed societal contradictions that revealed alternative constructions of gender. Unlike most contemporary painters, the Pre-Raphaelites often moved beyond the restrictive boundaries of conventional representations, depicting a wider range of gender roles, offering Victorian novelists more choices, subjects, and challenges. The representation of the unconven-tional gender roles depicted in Pre-Raphaelite paintings coincided with legislative movements to ameliorate women's social and legal status and to redress hitherto legalized gender inequities, issues that often became the Victorian novelists' primary topics. An understanding of contemporary resistance to Pre-Raphaelite gender constructs may further illuminate the reasons Victorian novelists chose to reconfigure Pre-Raphaelite represen-tations of gender, especially those of women.

Pre-Raphaelite Gender Constructs

In response to contemporary reviewers' belligerence against the Pre-Raphaelites' purported inclination to represent ugliness, F. G. Stephens points out their allegiance to fourteenth-century Italian painters, who, like the Pre-Raphaelites, captured in their paintings accurate representa-tions of feeling and expression to the exclusion of conventional represen-tations of beauty "from which all life has evaporated."[39] Indeed, Stephens's poignant example of a painting by an unknown Florentine artist, which depicts the Virgin with the Savior in her lap, convincingly illustrates one of the most significant aims of the Pre-Raphaelite artists: their representation of idiosyncratic feeling and expression rather than conventional beauty. What is unique about this painting, Stephens emphasizes, is the fact that the Virgin "is old (a most touching point); lamenting aloud, clutches passionately the heavy-weighted body on her knees; her mouth is open. Altogether it is one of the most powerful appeals possible to be conceived; for there are few but will consider this identification with humanity to be of more effect than any refined . . . treatment of the same subject by later artists" (60). Disregarding nature and truth, later artists, F. G. Stephens points out, continued to represent the Virgin young even though Jesus was an adult.

Most critics, however, disregarded such justifications; instead, they continued to denigrate Pre-Raphaelite representations of gender as violations of established notions of beauty. In reading such reviews we may better understand the means by which Pre-Raphaelite artists undermined conventional gender constructs. John Eagles's "Fine Arts and the Public Taste in 1853" serves as a typical example of reviewers who upbraided Pre-Raphaelites for their transgressions of conventional gender boundaries. Of particular interest is Eagles's review of John Everett Millais's *Order of Release, 1746* (1852–1853) (plate 4) depicting a woman rescuing her husband, a Jacobite imprisoned by the English, when she secures his release. Her ambiguous expression, Malcolm Warner suggests, may indicate that she has "paid the price of her virtue" (Parris, *The Pre-Raphaelites*, 108).

Eagles's objections to *The Order of Release*, as well as those to *The Proscribed Royalist* (1852–1853), disclose the conventional characteristics of traditional femininity and masculinity that the Pre-Raphaelites defied in their own representations of gender. Had he commissioned the artist to paint this subject, Eagles points out, he would have asked him to represent the woman exhibiting all of the conventional feminine qualities. Her face would have been pale, "as if one who had been long watching in weary sadness—let the joy even be tearful in the eye and quivering in the mouth . . . and let her be lovely, tender, and such a one as would make the release to the man a happiness indeed." Unfortunately, the critic notes, Millais transgresses conventional standards of femininity: "Her face, instead of being lovely, is plain to a degree. . . . [F]ar from pale, [it] is blotched with red, and the shadows stippled in with bilious brownish green" (100).

Consequently, the representation of the man, according to Eagles, also violates traditional values of masculinity, for he leans his head on his wife's shoulder (like the baby on her opposite shoulder), seeking protection and solace in a woman. Such reversal of gender constructs, he protests, is repulsive to men abiding by traditional standards of masculinity. One of his friends, Eagles claims, was appalled by such a flagrant violation of gender constructs in the painting to the extent of declaring, "I would rather remain in prison all my life, or even be hanged, than go out of prison to live with that woman" (100). Above all, besides the physical characteristics of the couple and their situations, which defy convention, it becomes apparent that this critic berates Millais for a flagrant reversal of gender roles—a woman rescuing a man.

Precisely for such a reversal, the same critic scoffs at Millais's *Proscribed Royalist, 1651*, representing a woman rescuing a cavalier from persecution

Plate 4. John Everett Millais, *The Order of Release, 1746*, 1852–1853. Oil on canvas, arched top, 40¹/₂ x 29 in (102.9 x 73.7 cm), Tate Gallery. Reproduced by permission.

by hiding him in an oak tree (101). The falsity of the incident, he contends, is apparent in the ignoble representation of gender constructs. Known for their valor, the chief quality of masculinity, cavaliers, he argues, would never have escaped in a tree to eschew danger. "Would you not rather see the great hardiness of a man," he poses the rhetorical question, "that should make him step out with the dignity of a man and say, 'here I am, do your worst,' than the portrayed cowardice of a two-legged vermin in a hole?" (101). Painters of all times, "Raphaelites and pre-Raphaelites," he proclaims, "never forgot that men were men, and should be represented with proper manly actions, and not creeping through fear, like reptiles, into holes" (ibid.). By the same reasoning, following rather than defying traditional representations of men and women, only conventionally beautiful women ought to be subjects of paintings, unlike the woman in the *Proscribed Royalist,* who, according to this critic, "would have been as well if she had used a face-lotion, to have got rid of those yellow and brown little stipples, that some bilious people have in reality, and the pre-Raphaelites love to perpetuate in pictures" (ibid.).

Critics, however, were not unanimous in their disapproval of Pre-Raphaelite gender representations. David Masson of the *British Quarterly Review,* for instance, defends the Pre-Raphaelites' innovations in art by comparing them to those of Wordsworth's in literature, in particular his "truth to nature" and his choice of common people for his subjects. After summarizing the critics' objections to the Pre-Raphaelites' gender representations, he focuses on those characteristics that critics often saw as deviant choices:

> First of all, then, there was universally noted in the earlier works of the Pre-Raphaelites, a kind of contempt for all pre-established ideas of beauty. It even seemed as if, in their resolution to copy literally the forms of Nature, they took pleasure in seeking out such forms as would be called ugly or mean. Thus, instead of giving us figures with those fine conventional heads and regular oval faces and gracefully-formed hands and feet, which we like to see in albums, they appeared to take delight in figures with heads phrenologically clumsy, faces strongly marked and irregular, and very pronounced ankles and knuckles. . . . Are there no beautiful faces, or fingers or feet in Nature, say the fair critics; that clever young men should paint things like those; or have the poor young men been really so unfortunate in their life-series of feminine visions?[40]

In this passage, as well as elsewhere in his long article, Masson justifies the Pre-Raphaelites' disregard for "the conventional ideas of beauty" as a deliberate choice consistent with their goal to accurately represent reality:

"But what we desire specially to note at present is, that this tendency towards forms not conventionally agreeable, which has been found fault with in the Pre-Raphaelites was . . . inevitable on their part; and was, in fact, a necessary consequence of their zeal in carrying out their favourite principle of attention to actual truth" (203–4). Thus, like Ruskin, Masson justifies the Pre-Raphaelites' purported eccentricity in their representations of gender in terms of their desire to represent reality truthfully. The same reviewer observes what hostile critics of Pre-Raphaelite representations of gender had disregarded: "[I]n painting the human figure, their notion was that they should not follow any conventional idea of corporeal beauty, but should take some actual man or woman, and reproduce his or her features with the smallest possible deviation consistent with the purpose of the picture" (200). Thus as early as 1852 critics like Masson had begun to recognize the wider range of gender roles that the Pre-Raphaelites initiated in British culture.

Nevertheless, other critics persisted in abiding by stereotypical representations of femininity and masculinity. In 1856, for instance, when the outrage over the Pre-Raphaelites' unorthodox representation of gender constructs had somewhat subsided, some critics still questioned it. "Why should all the forms be so odd, quaint, and repulsive?" the critic of the *Eclectic Review* rhetorically asks in reference to Hunt's *Claudio and Isabella* (1850–1853). He continues, "Was it needful that Isabella should be commonplace in countenance, and uncouth in general appearance?" And "was it imperatively necessary . . . that Claudio should he high shouldered, wooden in frame and his countenance revoltingly ugly?"[41]

The *Athenaeum* had also focused on the lack of idealization in this painting when it was first exhibited in 1853, attacking Claudio as "a vulgar lout" and arguing that "Isabella . . . never could have inspired the passion of Angelo. If Mr. Hunt will not give us beauty, at least let him refrain from idealizing vulgarity."[42] Such reviews reveal Victorian anxieties over the subversion of traditional gender constructs to the extent that they overlook the psychological complexity, as in this case, of the moral dilemmas the paintings depict. The aforementioned critic, for instance, disregards Isabella's anguish over the decision she must make: She can either compromise her virtue and have her brother released from prison or refuse and thus let him be executed. Instead, he berates Hunt for his antagonism to traditional gender constructs. Once again as in the case of *The Order of Release* or *The Proscribed Royalist*, in this painting a woman must rescue a man, thus reversing conventional gender roles.

Though keenly aware of the male/female, spectator/spectacle, subject/object patriarchal binaries that the hegemonic dynamics of the gaze dictated, the Pre-Raphaelites frequently destabilized the accepted gender binaries of Victorian society, challenging the traditional dynamics of the gaze by dissenting from the dominant tradition. In the process, they compelled their viewers to question established gendered boundaries and consciously or subconsciously collaborate in their extension. In this respect, Pre-Raphaelite paintings anticipate modern theorists' preoccupation with the gendered implications of the gaze. Because the gaze is not simply an act of vision but also an ideological arena that encloses and dramatizes power relations, feminist writers of art history (Berger, Nochlin), film theory (Mulvey, Kaplan), and fiction (Cixous, Bauer, and Newman) have examined its gendered ramifications and implications. Elsewhere I have examined these implications in major Victorian novels. Victorian Eros is inseparable from the politics of the gaze, for encounters between male and female characters unfold through the dynamics of the gaze, regulated by the laws of the dominant tradition. Almost invariably, such dynamics designate the male as a spectator and the female as a spectacle, creating binaries of active/passive and subject/object. Women writers, however, like Elizabeth Gaskell and George Eliot, as we shall see, destabilized in their novels the binaries of patriarchal ideology.

Pre-Raphaelite paintings also represented the destabilization of conventional gender hierarchy registered in the dynamics of the gaze. Often pictorial representations of narratives, such paintings extended not only visual and verbal borders but gender boundaries as well. Hunt's *Claudio and Isabella,* for instance, defuses the traditional dynamics of the gaze as Claudio, imprisoned for fathering a child out of wedlock, shrinks under Isabella's virtuous gaze. Inspired by Shakespeare's *Measure for Measure,* the painting represents Isabella in her brother's prison cell after he has informed her that he will not be executed if she yields to the sexual advances of the ruler of Vienna; she in turn has declared her determination to remain virtuous. The following lines were inscribed in the frame of the painting: "Claudio. Death is a fearful thing. Isabella. And shamed life a hateful." Though the painting seems an explicit illustration of this quotation from the play, Hunt complicates the viewer's interpretation through his symbolic realism, casting Isabella in the sunlight and Claudio in the shadow, the red ribbon on the lute alluding to Claudio's passion, the apple blossom on the floor signifying Isabella's chastity threatened by her brother's willingness to sacrifice it to save his own life.[43] Unlike the stereotypical, self-effacing and self-abnegating Victorian Angel in the House, Isabella asserts her subjectivity by refusing to compromise her own values to save her brother's life. Her gaze is neither stereotypically erotic nor manipulating but reproachful and compassionate. She is Claudio's superior, but she neither gloats nor luxuriates in her superiority; instead she is saddened by their tormenting predicament.

In yet another painting, *The Hireling Shepherd*, Hunt moves beyond the traditional dynamics of the gaze that cast man as the subject and woman as the object of his desire. Though replete with visual biblical signifiers, the painting was mainly criticized for its explicit eroticism and the woman's unabashed sexuality. David Masson, for instance, though he praises the painting for its naturalism as one of the best in the exhibition, "a fine breezy English landscape, on a pleasant summer's day . . . yellow fields in the distance, with rows of trees and swallows . . . flying in the meadows," he regards the truthful representation of the shepherd and the shepherdess as "too harsh for the popular taste," protesting its blatant realism and its lack of subtlety and sophistication: "There is certainly no attempt at poetry here; for a fellow more capable than the shepherd of drinking a great quantity of beer, or a more sunburnt slut than the shepherdess, we never saw in a picture" (216). Representation of gender and class once again becomes the primary focus of his response to the painting.

In spite of the critics' negative comments, Hunt was evidently proud of the realism and naturalism he was able to capture in this painting, as his remarks in a letter reveal: "not Dresden china bergers, but a real shepherd, and a real shepherdess, and a landscape in full sunlight, with all the colour of luscious summer, without the faintest fear of the precedents of any landscape painter who rendered Nature before."[44] What distinguishes this painting from contemporary genre paintings, besides the points Hunt mentions here, is also the untraditional representation of gender: Both parties are represented as equals, intimately enjoying sensuous pleasure. As Prettejohn has already noted, this "scene of rustic lovemaking . . . where the poses, interlocking in a broad triangle across the picture surface, make both partners seem equally active" (214).

Such representation certainly undermined the contemporary double standard, according to which only man could be sexually aggressive and enjoy sexual pleasure.[45] Uninhibited by conventional morality, the woman unabashedly looks at her lover directly; in turn her lover, by no means intimidated, meets her gaze. Considering the double sexual standard of the period, this picture is atypical in registering unconventional sexual equality. Indeed, as Susan Casteras has already convincingly demonstrated, "inappropriate differentiation of the sexes was another subtext of contemporary vituperative responses. The PRB set up their own standards of what was suitable for the depiction of men and women, to some degree turning on its head Walker's of 'minor beauty' for females (all prettiness and delicacy) and 'major beauty' for males (to suggest grandeur, nobility, and power). To the Pre-Raphaelites, both sexes were capable of exemplifying physical hideousness or sublimity."[46]

Although, like the Pre-Raphaelites, art reviewers were disconcerted by prevalent representations of "sentimental prettiness," they were neverthe-less unwilling to accept the Pre-Raphaelite representation of gender con-structs that threatened the eradication of conventional concepts of beauty: "But God forbid that we should thus readily renounce all faith in the truly beautiful," the critic of the *Eclectic Review* protests. "Thus it is ever the pri-mal province and prerogative of art in manifesting to the world a high, pure, and transcendent beauty." This critic is representative of contempo-rary belief that beauty was truth and "truth plus beauty is Art."[47]

Recent critics such as Jan Marsh and Joseph Kestner have contested the belligerent contemporary responses to the Pre-Raphaelites' repre-sentations of gender, claiming that the Pre-Raphaelites inscribed more conventional gender constructs—representing man as "the gallant knight" or "the valiant soldier" and women as "fallen Magdalens," "stunners," or "sorceresses."[48] Other critics, however, such as Susan Casteras and Julie Codell, persuasively explain the Pre-Raphaelites' subversive role.[49] In "Pre-Raphaelite Challenges to Victorian Canons of Beauty," Casteras argues that "Hunt, Millais, and Rossetti all engineered their own self-conscious transformations of conventional norms of beauty, in the process stripping art of what they saw as its pretensions and substituting a new vocabulary of face and figure" (32). If we con-sider that the Pre-Raphaelites deliberately chose to create what con-temporary critics saw as "grotesque" and "ugly" representations of gender constructs in a culture that upheld the belief that "*the most beau-tiful soul must have the most beautiful body,*" we may then realize the extent of their remarkable contribution to the extension of gendered boundaries. A brief overview of some domestic genre paintings, as we shall see, demonstrates the Pre-Raphaelites' deliberate resistance to tra-ditional representations of gender.

As late as 1865, John Ruskin celebrated the notion of the separate spheres, predominant in Victorian culture and society in the by now well-known "Of Queens' Gardens," published in *Sesame and Lilies*:

> We are foolish, and without excuse foolish, in speaking of the 'superior-ity' of one sex to the other, as if they could be compared in similar things. Each has what the other has not: each completes the other, and is com-pleted by the other: they are in nothing alike, and the happiness and per-fection of both depends on each asking and receiving from the other what the other only can give. Now their separate characters are briefly these. The man's power is active, progressive, defensive. He is eminent-ly the doer, the creator, the discoverer, the defender. His intellect is for speculation and invention; his energy for adventure, for war and for con-quest. . . . But woman's power is not for rule, not for battle—and her

intellect is not for invention or creation, but for sweet ordering, arrangement, and decision. . . . Her great function is Praise. . . . This is the true
nature of home—it is the place of Peace: the shelter, not only from all
injury, but from all terror, doubt, and division. (*Works* 18:121–22)

In images of gardens and homes, through positive negations and contradictions Ruskin defines a woman's exclusion from power, unequivocally supporting the separate spheres doctrine. Years earlier, Tennyson had
explicitly confirmed the binary division of masculinity and femininity in
an often-quoted verse in *The Princess* (1847):

> Man for the field and woman for the hearth:
> Man for the sword and for the needle she:
> Man with the head and woman with the heart:
> Man to command and Woman to obey;
> All else confusion. (11.437–41)[50]

These short, terse lines express the binary gender division as unarguably
absolute; the distinction between masculinity and femininity is clear, definite, and sharply differentiated. Years later, when women were steadily gaining social and legal equality through legislative measures such as the Divorce
Act of 1857 and the Married Women's Property Acts of 1870, 1874, and
1882, Tennyson still exalted domesticity and the woman's role in maintaining stability at home and the nation, believing that "upon the sacredness of
home life . . . the stability and greatness of a nation largely depend."[51]

Both Ruskin and Tennyson sought in the evocation of the past the
confirmation of the vanishing ideal of the separate spheres, which advocated and maintained gender roles within rigidly conventional boundaries, by then daily threatened by social movements and legal measures
slowly and gradually promoting gender equality and equity. The distinct
boundaries between femininity and masculinity were also inscribed in
contemporary domestic genre paintings. Images of women enclosed within the walls of domestic bliss proliferated each year in the Royal Academy
exhibits; such images conspicuously resisted slow, contemporary advances
toward gender equality. Even a brief overview of the domestic genre of sentimental paintings reveals that these pictures endorsed the patriarchal
morality of the burgeoning middle classes and the new patrons of art, the
rising industrial magnates, who preferred paintings readily intelligible
upholding their own values, as, for instance, that of the separate spheres
and the sanctity of the domestic sphere.

In *Pre-Raphaelitism* William Holman Hunt gives us a clear view of the
artificiality of pictorial conventions that prevailed in contemporary repre-

sentations of gender in domestic genre paintings, conventions that the Pre-Raphaelite artists detested and attempted to eradicate through their unorthodox representations: "Knights were frowning and staring as none but hired supernumeraries could stare; the pious had virtuous tears on their reverential cheeks; innkeepers were ever round and red-faced; peasants had complexions of dainty pink; shepherdesses were facsimiled from Dresden-china toys; homely couples were ever reading a Family Bible to a circle of most exemplary children; all alike from king to plebeian were arrayed in clothes fresh from the bandbox. With this artificiality, the drawing was often of a pattern that left anatomy and the science of perspective but poorly demonstrated" (1:51). A cursory glance at domestic genre paintings of the period confirms Hunt's remarks and discloses the conventional restrictions imposed upon representations of gender.

Charles Cope's *Life Well Spent* (1862) was perhaps one of the paintings Hunt had in mind when he referred to homely images of parents and exemplary children. The mother in the picture surrounded by immaculately and fashionably dressed children is listening to the lessons of her two boys while she herself remains busy sewing. To her right is a picture of Christ, and on the table the Bible and prayer books consecrate the sanctity of the domestic sphere. Likewise William Nicol's *Quiet* (1860), depicting an affectionate mother reading to her child, who is nestling her head on her shoulder, exalts motherhood and harmonious domesticity.

George Elgar Hicks's triptych *Woman's Mission* (1863) clearly abides by the prevalent sentimentalization of femininity and masculinity, firmly inscribing a woman's role as a caretaker within the boundaries of the domestic sphere. The first picture of the series called *Woman's Mission: Guide to Childhood* shows a young mother leading a child in a wooded path. As Lynda Nead has already pointed out in her extensive interpretation of this triptych, the mother is here depicted as both a physical and spiritual guide to childhood "as she pushes aside the brambles in her son's path (with its Christian connotations of the path of life) and bends over the child, her arms encircling him protectively."[52] The central picture, called *Woman's Mission: Companion of Manhood*, shows the woman in her role as a wife comforting her husband, who is grief stricken after reading a black-edged letter he is holding in his hand. As the woman depicts respectable femininity, so does the husband represent conventionally ideal masculinity, for although exceedingly saddened he shields his face with his hand concealing his tears, thus containing his grief in the presence of his supportive wife. A modern perspective of the picture would probably construe the wife as a burden rather than a support to her grieving husband, for she leans on him, who in turn tilts to the left supporting himself against the wall, seeming rather uncomfortable. In the last picture, titled *Woman's Mission: Comfort of Old Age*, the same woman lovingly offers a glass of water to her ailing aged father. A mother, a wife, and a daughter, the restrictive roles of a Victorian woman's life are visually framed in this popular trilogy.

It is by no means the case that Pre-Raphaelites eschewed representations of domesticity, but their pictures of this subject were consciously and entirely unconventional, devoid of the sentimental overtones of contemporary genre paintings, as Hunt mentions in the earlier statement. Millais's *Mariana* (1850–1851) (plate 5), it could be argued, casts Tennyson's eponymous character in a conventionally feminine predicament, that of the jilted lover who relentlessly awaits her lover, pining his absence and wishing for her death. But the painting captures Mariana in the most original, unprecedented pose, wearily stretching over her embroidery and at the same time unwittingly exhibiting her feminine sexuality, which the tightly fitting, strikingly blue dress and the belt around her hips reveal. The picture conveys a sense of spontaneity and transience, but the meaning or resolution of the scene remains ambiguous and inconclusive.

Most often, Pre-Raphaelites also removed the walls, the physical boundaries of domesticity, setting domestic scenes outdoors in the bright sunlight with figures often surrounded by stunningly beautiful landscapes. Millais's *Spring* (1856–1859) is a startling example of unorthodox domesticity representing young women celebrating springtime by enjoying a meal outdoors, sitting on the luscious grass under an apple tree bursting with blossoms. Each woman is captured in a completely different pose, some of them caught in profile, others awkwardly rather than elegantly posed, overall the picture conveying the aura of arrested motion. The flowers of the apple tree in the background, as well as those on the girl's hair in the foreground, painted in the soft hues of white and pink of apple blossoms in springtime, reveal intense, sensitive, and imaginative realism that appeals to the viewers' senses and draws them into the scene. What seems at first glance a harmoniously idyllic picture is suddenly disrupted by the gaze of the woman on the right who looks directly, yet enigmatically, at the viewer, thus transgressing the boundaries of respectable femininity. Behind her and her basket of flowers a scythe, leaning against a short wall and practically over her, conveys an ominous tone that undermines the idyllic atmosphere of the entire composition and perturbs the viewer's pleasure. Sharply opposing feelings beset the viewer as the eye moves from figure to figure in the picture and attempts to make sense of it. In this painting, as is the case in quite a few other Pre-Raphaelite paintings, domesticity and transgression, polarized and irreconcilable Victorian opposites overlap, eliding the line that differentiates and defines them. In the process of unraveling the ambiguity, unintelligibility, and tension such elision creates,

Plate 5. John Everett Millais, *Mariana,* 1850–1851. Oil on canvas, arched top, 34$^{1}/_{2}$ x 21$^{1}/_{2}$ in (87.6 x 54.6 cm), Makins Collection. Reproduced by permission.

spectators of Pre-Raphaelite paintings willingly or unwittingly do their part of art's labor, their collaboration with the artist, thus entering consciously or unconsciously into what E. H. Gombrich calls "the magic circle of creation."[53]

Ambiguity and indeterminacy govern Millais's later paintings that are devoid of a narrative content, as, for instance, *Autumn Leaves* (1855–1856), which hauntingly evokes the transient, fragile time between light and darkness as the sun sets in the background and illuminates the sky with luscious oranges and reds. In the foreground four young girls burn a pile of orange and yellow and red leaves evoking an evanescent world. Once again Millais depicts a world of soft and fragile femininity but liberates it from domestic boundaries by neither defining it within the domestic sphere nor juxtaposing it with conventional masculinity. An underlying tension also dominates Millais's exquisite *Vale of Rest* (1858–1859), a unique representation of two nuns digging a grave in the late evening. As in *Spring* and *Autumn Leaves*, rather than endorsing the doctrine of separate spheres, Millais here creates a matriarchal world untouched by the Law of the Father. Hard manual work, traditionally associated with masculinity, is undertaken by two women, two nuns, whose unusual task acquires an ominous, inscrutable quality in the mysterious, haunting hues of the twilight.

The direct gaze of the nun on the right engages the reader in the threat of mortality their task conveys. Once again, as in the previous pictures, the viewer may walk away without completely grasping the meaning of this painting, which remains unsettled, indistinct, indeterminate. Thus the demarcation between masculinity and femininity, sharp and distinct in domestic genre paintings, in Pre-Raphaelite paintings often became blurred, unsettling the spectator, raising questions rather than offering answers to life's perplexities.

The Indeterminacy of Pre-Raphaelite Representations of the Fallen

In their attempts to challenge their spectators to new ways of seeing, Pre-Raphaelite artists also involved them in unorthodox ways of considering social issues pertaining to representations of gender constructs. Like their contemporary counterparts, the Pre-Raphaelites also dealt with the highly controversial issue of the "fallen" woman. As several art historians and cultural critics have already noted, the representation of the fallen woman preoccupied artists, novelists, poets, and social critics more so than did her polar opposite, the respectable, middle-class paragon.

Representations of this subject coincided with contemporary studies and investigations of prostitution, which exposed it as an epidemic that should be controlled for moral, social, and health reasons.[54] Various social historians have already explained the fascination with the subject of the fallen woman in terms of the other, the illicit, and the forbidding yet fascinating identification everyone experiences with those who dare transgress entrenched gendered boundaries. Other critics have interpreted the fallen-woman phenomenon as a response to the rising rate of prostitution that threatened the cult of domesticity with its erotic appeal and simultaneous threat of disease.[55]

Through representations of the illegitimate, the illicit, and the unconventional, the Pre-Raphaelites often captured the public fear of the other. As in their depiction of various representations of gender, the Pre-Raphaelite treatment of the motif of the fallen woman differed substantially from its representation in domestic genre paintings. An early, dramatically sentimental example of this motif is evident in the domestic genre painting of Richard Redgrave's *Outcast* (1851), in which an outraged, merciless father forces his daughter, holding a baby in her arms, out of her home into a snowy night, while the other family members, powerless to intercede, beseech him for mercy. Both masculinity and femininity are here represented and asserted in a stereotypical, dramatic fashion. As the legal arbiter of the Law of the Father, the paterfamilias in this scene does not allow emotions to sway his judgment in penalizing his daughter for her transgression of moral boundaries. Only anger at the violation of respectable morality spurs his action, but anger is traditionally acknowledged as a masculine and therefore legitimate emotion. His daughter, on the other hand, hitherto secluded in the domestic sphere, dependent on the socioeconomic privilege of the father for her subsistence, is destined to perish the moment she enters the public sphere, which provides no shelter for her but exposes her to a pernicious existence often leading to death. Most likely that would be the interpretation the Victorian viewer would have reached. Though the painting has been seen as an attempt to encourage change by placing before the viewer a scene of "heart-wrenching cruelty," nevertheless it inscribes the power dynamics entrenched in Victorian society.[56]

As Lynda Nead has already demonstrated, during the 1850s and 1860s the proliferation of visual images and narrative accounts of adultery in Victorian culture coincided with the heated debates over the divorce and the control of contagious diseases legislature in the parliament and in the press. The divorce act initiated in 1854 and passed in 1857 allowed husbands, not wives, to divorce their spouses for adultery. In order to obtain a divorce a woman was required to prove her husband guilty of bigamy, cruelty, desertion, rape, or incest. Lord Chancellor Cranworth, sponsor of the 1857 legislation, unequivocally endorsed the double standard the act legalized: "A wife might, without any loss of caste, and possibly with reference to the interests of her children, or even of her husband, condone an act of adultery on the part of her husband; but a husband could not condone a similar act on the part of a wife. . . . [T]he adultery of the wife might be the means of palming spurious offspring upon the husband, while the adultery of the husband could have no such effect with regard to the wife."[57]

August Egg's *Past and Present*, exhibited at the Royal Academy in 1858, may be seen as a visual response to contemporary debates on adultery, pivoting on the double sexual standard. Initially without a title, the painting was exhibited with the following passage: "August the 4th. Have just heard that B—has been dead more than a fortnight, so his poor children have now lost both parents. I hear she was seen on Friday last near the strand, evidently without a place to lay her head. What a fall hers has been!"[58] Sternly encasing its didactic message in a journalistic style—and therefore a potentially realistic occurrence—this long, descriptive passage, at once a threat and a warning, anchors the painting within the immediate, contemporary social context. The husband, situated in a middle-class home, occupies the focal point of the central picture, where he looks at his prostrate wife repulsively, soon after his sudden arrival from a journey and his interception of a letter to her lover.

The Athenaeum describes the husband's anger in sensational terms and applauds his reaction as a justifiable response to the wife's putatively abhorrent transgression: "He has screamed it forth,—throwing her shame like a dash of burning vitriol full in her spotted face. Poor sinful creature! It has felled her like a blow from a murderer's club." His wife lies on the floor, her clasped hands pointing to the door through which she is destined to depart. In the right panel, the children, now adults, reside in a "poor squalid London room," one of them looking out of the open window at the same moon at which the mother is gazing while the younger sister kneels and prays for her lost mother, "even though the very breath of hell be already hot round her cheek." To the left of the painting was a panel depicting the mother under "the dark gravevault shadow of an Adelphi arch,—last refuge of the homeless sin, vice and beggary of London: the thin, starved legs of a bastard child—perhaps dead at her breast—protrude from her rags. She, too, is looking at the moon, full in its royal brightness."[59] Such relentless, sacrosanct self-righteousness tinged with sensational perversity reveals the moral rigidity of the Law of the Father and the forbidding ideological boundaries of the era.

Unlike Redgrave's and Egg's representations of fallen women castigated as outcasts, those of the Pre-Raphaelites most often undermined the rigid standards of Victorian morality; in fact, rather than providing answers, they raised questions perplexing Victorian and modern art critics alike. Ford Madox Brown's *Take Your Son, Sir!* (1851–1892) is a case in point; its controversial nature partly explains why the painting was never finished or exhibited. A woman in white stands in full length holding a naked baby in front of her as if she had just given birth. The mirror in the background, reflecting the father's figure, appears like a halo over her head. Thus the painting juxtaposes and at the same time deconstructs opposing ideas—Madonna and the fallen woman. At times interpreted as a full-length portrait of Brown's wife, Emma, this painting resists such facile interpretation by its simultaneously triumphant and defiant title. Though in white, the color traditionally associated with virginal figures, the woman in the painting has been construed as a kept woman showing her illegitimate son to her illicit lover. For Nina Auerbach, for instance, the woman "seems to have gained power over size and scale, reducing the cur who impregnated her along with the viewer to a diminutive figure in the mirror" (163).

Such a reading is definite and conclusive, but if we consider Brown's references to his wife, Emma, and his son Arthur in connection with the origin and the development of the painting that remained unfinished, we may surmise that its meaning is ambiguous rather than explicit.[60] As Barringer comments, "Is this, then, an icon of the sacredness of motherhood, or a Hogarthian satire on prostitution and the birth of illegitimate children in Victorian England?" (100). Unlike the prescriptive and didactically conclusive meaning contemporary genre paintings conveyed, Brown's painting, like other Pre-Raphaelite paintings, is characteristically inconclusive and indeterminate, engaging the viewer in the construction of its elusive meaning and in the process implicating the spectator in the woman's condition.

At first glance, Rossetti's unfinished *Found* (1854) (plate 6) seems but an affirmation of traditional gender roles, middle-class values and the rigid morality of the genre paintings representing transgressive women. On January 30, 1855, in a letter to Holman Hunt, Rossetti describes the narrative content of the painting, explaining that he had designed it before Hunt had painted his *Awakening Conscience*.[61] Apparently depicting another theme of rescue, casting the man and the woman in traditional roles, the one as the rescuer, the other as the lost victim, the painting seems to confirm conventional gender roles. Dressed in a white tunic, the drover towers over the fallen woman, who is dressed in a white dress full of roses, emblems of her passion and sexuality. Yet *Found* has been the subject of controversy eliciting numerous contradictory responses. Lynn Nead, for instance, though she highlights the social contradictions the

Plate 6. Dante Gabriel Rossetti, *Found*, 1854. Oil on canvas, 36 x 31³/₄ in (91.4 x 80 cm), Delaware Art Museum. Reproduced by permission.

painting evokes, offers a highly conclusive reading of the picture, seeing it as a sharp juxtaposition of city versus country through visual contrasts: The garish, vulgar appearance of the prostitute is juxtaposed with the simple rustic garb of the country drover.[62] Yet, if we consider *Jenny*, the verbal equivalent of *Found*, Alicia Faxon suggests, we may see that Rossetti "was quite aware that for every fallen woman there must be a fallen man."[63]

Rossetti's identification with the plight of the fallen woman is incisively apparent in an often-quoted statement he made in a letter to Ford Madox Brown in 1873, in which he compares himself to a prostitute: "I have often said that to be an artist is just the same thing as to be a whore, as far as dependence on the whims and fancies of individuals is concerned."[64] F. G. Stephens's reading of the painting reveals yet another facet of its complexity. "The brightening dawn symbolizes," he points out, "peace (with forgiveness) on earth."[65] If we take this point into consideration, we may concede that the meaning of the painting is not conclusive. J. B. Bullen emphasizes the complexity and indeterminacy of *Found*, interpreting it as a representation of "the problematic nature of the relationship between the honourable male and the sexually experienced female . . . concentrated in the entwined hands which fill the center of focus." Unlike the woman in Hunt's *Awakening Conscience*, Bullen points out, the woman in *Found* does not spring to accept the offer of that salvation. . . . In the painting the woman turns away, perhaps in shame, perhaps in rejection, fearing to meet the young man's gaze" (*The Pre-Raphaelite Body* 63).

Millais also blurred the established limits of conventional morality by interweaving transgression and respectability in his representations of fallen women as, for instance, in the watercolor *The Seamstress*, which he painted as an illustration to "The Iceberg," a story by J. Stewart Harrison published in *Once a Week* in October 1860. The narrator recalls tracking down a lost love seduced by an immoral lover. In the watercolor Millais transcribes the text into a visual image of domesticity and respectability, depicting a woman in a clean room dressed in a simple and elegant dress, her hair braided neatly and forming a coronet around her head. Thus Millais, instead of depicting a fallen woman in the conventionally sordid surroundings of a public street, situates her in the domestic sphere.[66] Furthermore, his illustration exposes the plight of the seamstress, a few years earlier depicted in Richard Redgrave's memorable painting *The Sempstress* (1846), an issue debated in contemporary magazines, newspapers, and novels, as for instance, Elizabeth Gaskell's *Ruth*.

Like Millais and Rossetti, Holman Hunt undermined contemporary, melodramatic representations of fallen women, preferring the representation of moments of revelation to moments of degradation often represented by his contemporaries. The perplexing meaning of his much-debated *Awakening Conscience* (1854) has been the subject of controversy among Victorian and modern critics. In *Women, Art, and Power* Linda Nochlin reads this painting as a pendant to Rossetti's *Found;* the two paintings, in her view, represent "opposing visions of a single moral issue: rising versus falling, salvation versus damnation, Christian optimism versus Christian or crypto-Christian despair" (67). However, as we have already seen, *Found* does not necessarily represent "damnation." Depicting an intimate scene between a man and a woman in a parlor, as they are both singing while the man is playing the piano, the woman in *The Awakening Conscience* rises to the revelation of her transgression when the tune her lover is playing triggers a childhood memory. Unlike paintings like *Past and Present* and the *Outcast,* representations of female transgression that were readily interpreted, *The Awakening Conscience* perplexed spectators and critics alike. The *Athenaeum,* for instance, claimed that "innocent and unenlightened spectators suppose it to represent a quarrel between a brother and a Sister."[67] "People gaze at it in a blank wonder, and leave it hopelessly," Ruskin remarks in his letter to the *Times* on May 25, 1854, in which he felt compelled to interpret the painting. At first Ruskin melodramatically draws the viewer's (and reader's) attention to the intense expression in "the countenance of the lost girl, rent from its beauty into sudden horror; the lips half open, indistinct in their purple quivering . . . the eyes filled with the fearful light of futurity, and with tears of ancient days" (*Works* 12:334). He further justifies the plethora of visual signifiers abounding in the painting by relating them to the woman's situation and her inexorable future predicament.[68] Such interpretation, however, was contrary to Hunt's treatment of the subject. In reference to Egg's *Past and Present,* for instance, he had stated, "it is by no means a matter of course that when a woman sins she should die in misery."[69] Recent critics such as Kate Flint and Julie Codell also emphasize the hopeful outcome of the woman's circumstances.[70]

Ascribing a didactic message to this painting, Ruskin overlooks its physical configuration. Though "fallen," the woman towers over her lover, who is apparently unaware of her psychological state. Her inexplicable and unfathomable gaze registers her detachment from her lover and the spectator alike; she is self-contained and inscrutable. In her white dress, as she rises above her lover, she becomes morally superior to him, whose reclining pose in relation to her stance, as well as to her epiphany, registers him as a "fallen man." By contrast the configuration in either Redgrave's *Outcast* or in Egg's *Past and Present* privileges the man who rises above the condemned woman, casting him in the role of the relentless arbiter of her "disgrace" and therefore as her moral superior. Though fallen, the woman in *The Awakening Conscience* is represented in childlike innocence as she reaches a revelation through the memories evoked by the song "Oft in the Stilly Night" her lover plays on the piano. Explaining this epiphanic moment, Hunt states that the woman escapes "from her gilded cage with a startled holy resolve, while her shallow companion still sings on, ignorantly intensifying her repentant purpose" (*Pre-Raphaelitism* 2:430). Moreover, whereas the inexorable fate of the women in the afore-mentioned paintings is a foregone conclusion, that of the woman in *The Awakening Conscience* is open ended and indeterminate. Moral ambiguity rather than rigid morality and psychologically complex individuals rather than the types of domestic genre paintings govern *The Awakening Conscience* as well as numerous other Pre-Raphaelite paintings represent-ing the fallen woman motif.

By reconfiguring Pre-Raphaelite paintings into narrative scenes or por-traits, Victorian novelists created in their novels "an imaginative world where the fictional and the real world came together" (Byerly 121). The Pre-Raphaelites, as we have seen, offered the Victorian novelists new ways of representing realism. Minute details in their paintings convey the intense emotions of their subjects or express "invisible areas of emotion" and by extension compel viewers to experience unique emotions and sympathize with unconventional subjects and situations. The Pre-Raphaelites' "uncompromising egalitarianism" compelled contemporary viewers to see the world from new, unconventional perspectives. Thus Pre-Raphaelite naturalism was interwoven with psychological realism, which promoted the depiction of individuals rather than stereotypes. Furthermore, the Pre-Raphaelites offered Victorian novelists images that flagrantly or subtly defied established class boundaries. That defiance in turn involved and attracted wider audiences including not only people of the upper and middle classes, who frequented art exhibitions, but the lower ones as well. As we have seen, the Pre-Raphaelites often chose ordinary people to represent divine figures, thus dramatizing "the value of the ordinary"—a crucial element of realism. In this respect the Pre-Raphaelites were attuned to contemporary sociopolitical changes moving England from a hierarchical society to a democratic one. Pre-Raphaelite challenges to contemporary ideology were not limited to class but involved gender boundaries as well. Representing unconventional beauty in conventional ugliness, feminine fragility in masculinity, and masculine strength in femininity, the Pre-Raphaelites extended gender roles and offered the Victorian novelists innovative ways of depicting controversial gender issues. In their depictions of the gaze, for instance, the Pre-Raphaelites undermined gender hierarchy and portrayed men and women as equals. Subtly interweaving depictions of prostitution and illegitimacy, two of the most contentious Victorian subjects, with conventional symbols of divinity, the Pre-Raphaelites dared apotheosize the stigmatized and the ostracized, once again offering Victorian novelists implicit yet powerful ways of fighting social inequities and broadening their audiences.

Reconfigurations of Pre-Raphaelite Paintings in the Victorian Novel

In a letter to William Allingham, dated January 23, 1855, Rossetti describes his approach to his illustrations of the Moxon Tennyson, giving us a glimpse into the dynamics of the translation of the pictorial into the verbal: "The other day Moxon called on me, wanting me to do some of the blocks for the new Tennyson. . . . I have not begun even designing for them yet, but fancy I shall try the *Vision of Sin,* and *Palace of Art,* etc.,— those where one can allegorize on one's own hook on the subject of the poem, without killing, for oneself and everyone, a distinct idea of the poet's. This, I fancy, is *always* the upshot of illustrated editions" (Doughty, *Letters* 1:239). Rossetti's own interpretation of Tennyson's "Palace of Art" captured in his illustrations, *St. Cecilia* and *King Arthur and the Weeping Queens,* differed from the poet's to such an extent that Tennyson himself could not see the connection. According to William Michael Rossetti "he had to give up the problem of what it had to do with his verses" (*Dante Gabriel Rossetti* 1:190).

Art historians responding to Rossetti's art and poetry, his "double work of art," have offered different perspectives on the relation between Rossetti's verbal and visual portraits. Ainsworth, for instance, discusses the symbiotic relationship between Rossetti's poetry and painting, pointing out that, through the poems that accompanied his pictures, Rossetti often provided the reader with an opportunity "for active participation in the narrative sequence of the work of art, and facilitated the viewer's entry into the imaginary world of the picture" (4). His verbal portraits, she notes, extend the picture's space beyond its plane by describing past or future events. Quite often in his sonnets to his paintings, he explored the psychological meaning of the subject of a painting. Thus by extending spatial and temporal boundaries, Rossetti guided the viewer's interpretation, engaging the viewer/spectator in a multifaceted rather than a monolithic experience (Ainsworth 3–7).

Like Rossetti, in their reconfigurations of the visual into the verbal, Victorian novelists, when redrawing Pre-Raphaelite paintings in their narratives, delved into the subject's psychology and engaged the reader's imagination in visualizing and identifying with the subject of representation. When choosing to translate a Pre-Raphaelite painting into a verbal portrait, scene, or situation, Victorian novelists did not merely describe the original but, like Rossetti, also chose to "allegorize" on their own hook. In the gaps between the translation of the visual into the verbal, novelists engaged in contemporary debates over representations of gender, subverting conventional gender constructs, extending established boundaries. As they reframed the visual within the textual, in the impalpable and intangible reconfigurations of Pre-Raphaelite paintings into narrative images, Victorian novelists invited their readers' imagination to once again reframe their own interpretations of Pre-Raphaelite art. In this process, like Rossetti, Victorian novelists often extended the limits of the visual and attempted to represent the complexity or multiplicity of experience.

For Ruskin the representation of the multiplicity of experience in narrative involved the evocation of the pictorial and the poetical. "Historical or merely narrative art," he declares in "Of Greatness of Style" in the third volume of *Modern Painters*, "is never great art until the poetical or imaginative power touches it" (*Works* 5:65). In the same section he goes on to offer Hunt's *Light of the World* as an example of a "great poetical picture," which represents the most important traits of greatness, a "high subject," "the love of beauty," "the grasp of truth," and "the poetical power" (ibid. 5:65–66). For Ruskin, what defines greatness in art is "the number of faculties it exercises and addresses" (ibid. 5:66). Even though "high" subjects were not always the choices of Victorian novelists, nevertheless, by redrawing Pre-Raphaelite or poetical art within their novels they could address several of their readers' faculties, including and primarily the imagination. For Ruskin the artist should not merely "address and awaken" but also "guide the imagination; and there is no safe guidance but that of simple concurrence with fact" (ibid. 5:179). As we have already seen, Ruskin lauded Pre-Raphaelite art for its fidelity to nature, which he identified with psychological and poetical realism. By evoking Pre-Raphaelite paintings, Victorian novelists engaged their readers in multifarious experiences, but the stimulation and guidance of their readers' imagination often included ideological issues removed from Ruskin's aesthetics.

In *Body Work: Objects of Desire in Modern Narrative*, Peter Brooks remarks that realism, the "dominant nineteenth-century tradition" "insistently makes the visual the master relation to the world, for the very premise of realism is that one cannot understand human beings outside the context of the things that surround them, and knowing those things is a matter of viewing them, detailing them, and describing the concrete milieux in which men and women enact their destinies. To know, in realism, is to see, and to represent is to describe" (88). More recently, Nancy Armstrong in *Fiction in the Age of Photography: The Legacy of British Realism* also notes that the study of literary realism through the ages has involved the exploration of visual representation (3). Interestingly enough, she sees 1848 (the year when the Pre-Raphaelite Brotherhood was formed) as the year "when realism was just coming into its own" (5). Referring to critics such as Ian Watt, Harry Levin, George Levine, Elizabeth Ermarth, D. A. Miller, Naomi Schor, and Michael Fried, she notes their agreement on the realist "novel's use of painterly technique, perspective, detail, spectacle, or simply an abundance of visual description served to create, enlarge, revise, or update the reality shared by Victorian readers. Indeed, today many of us would hold the very kind of description we associate with realism at least partly responsible for changing the terms in which readers imagined their relation to the real" (6). Through evocations of Pre-Raphaelite paintings, Victorian novelists shaped their readers' "relation to the real" by challenging their conventional notions of class and gender.

By redrawing Pre-Raphaelite paintings in their novels, Victorian novelists enabled their readers to see not just figuratively but literally as well. Even if their readers could not visit art exhibits, they could see widely circulated engravings of Pre-Raphaelite paintings either as separately sold copies or in illustrated papers such as the *London Illustrated News*, the *Athenaeum*, and even *Punch*. Reconfigurations of Pre-Raphaelite paintings in the realist novel integrated the visual with the verbal; thus the fictional concretely partook of the visual world the readers could see in their quotidian lives. The reader then could more readily enter the fictional world and accept its premises. Certainly, it could be argued, the interweaving of the visual with the verbal in the novel could be accomplished through the evocation of the visual arts, not just the Pre-Raphaelites. Nevertheless, the Pre-Raphaelites, as we have seen, offered the novelists new ways of perceiving, feeling, and representing reality. Most importantly, some of the fervid controversies that Pre-Raphaelite paintings generated involved new representations of gender. Taking such Pre-Raphaelite representations as their point of departure, Victorian novelists such as Elizabeth Gaskell and George Eliot extended Pre-Raphaelite gendered boundaries even further, as we shall see in the following chapters.

In these impalpable and intangible reconfigurations of Pre-Raphaelite paintings into narrative texts, as Victorian novelists reframed the visual within the verbal, they engaged their readers' perception and imagination, often compelling them to question their own interpretations of representations of gender in Pre-Raphaelite art. Thus the reconfigurations of Pre-

Raphaelite paintings into narrative scenes and portraits in the Victorian novel were most often governed by the laws of gender rather than those of genre.[71] Victorian novelists were not merely interested in extending the fictional boundaries of their narratives but were also involved in delivering Pre-Raphaelite pictorial subjects from silence. In his discussion of ekphrasis, Hefferman reminds us of its root meaning, "speaking out" or "telling in full." The meaning of ekphrasis, he suggests, is bound to its function, for "besides representational friction and the turning of fixed forms into narrative, ekphrasis entails prosopopeia, or the rhetorical technique of envoicing a silent object. Ekphrasis speaks not only *about* works of art but also *to* and *for* them. In so doing, it stages—within the theater of language itself—a revolution of the image against the word."[72] Narrative reconfigurations of paintings, according to Hefferman, mobilize static visual representations and animate them by breaking their inherent silence. Hefferman's assertion is relevant to the Victorian novel. Through subtle and implicit ekphrasis, Victorian novelists did not merely speak about Pre-Raphaelite paintings but also gave voice to the subjects of these paintings.

George Eliot speaks about ekphrasis indirectly in *Middlemarch*, privileging the verbal over the visual for its power to represent a subject more accurately and more truthfully and, somewhat paradoxically, for enabling us to hear a person's voice. To Naumann's insistence to paint Dorothea's portrait, Will Ladislaw protests by pointing out the limitations of painting in accurately representing an exceptional woman like Dorothea: "And what is a portrait of a woman? Your painting and Plastik are poor stuff after all. They perturb and dull conceptions instead of raising them. Language is a finer medium." But Naumann rightly undercuts Will's objection with the remark, "Yes, for those who can't paint." Yet Ladislaw persists in his defense of language over painting as a superior mode of representation: "Language gives a fuller image, which is all the better for being vague. After all, the true seeing is within; and painting stares at you with an insistent imperfection . . . As if a woman were a mere coloured superficies! You must wait for movement and tone. There is a difference in their very breathing: they change from moment to moment.—This woman whom you have just seen, for example, how would you paint her voice, pray? But her voice is much diviner than anything you have seen of her."[73] Rather than maintaining the boundaries between the verbal and the visual, Eliot conflates them here in Will's claim that "language gives you a fuller image." She further complicates matters by contrasting imagination with perception and presenting the former as a superior way of seeing: "[T]he true seeing is within; and painting stares at you with insistent imperfection." For Eliot language, not painting, is the most realistic representation, for unlike painting, which is static, language in her view is dynamic and multidimensional. As Will contends, language represents an individual more fully, for it can express her voice. Though Eliot does not address the Pre-Raphaelites specifically, this exchange between two artists, appropriately so, a painter, Naumann, and a poet, Will, may be seen as a description of the dynamics involved in the transformation of Pre-Raphaelite paintings in the Victorian novel.

Like George Eliot, Elizabeth Gaskell, Wilkie Collins, and Thomas Hardy, through their narrative reconfigurations of Pre-Raphaelite subjects, often empowered them by endowing them with a voice that their visual representations had denied to them. That voice in turn invariably involved contemporary debates over representations of gender, constantly evolving and transformed by social movements and legal measures. By evoking Pre-Raphaelite paintings, these novelists, as we shall see, grounded their novels intertextually and contextually in reality.

CHAPTER TWO

Elizabeth Gaskell's Resistance to Pre-Raphaelite Gendered Silence

E lizabeth Gaskell has charmed yet puzzled Victorian and modern critics, for her complex and multifarious literary art can be neither contained nor easily classified within distinct literary categories. At the very beginning of her impressive biography, Jennifer Uglow encapsulates the bewilderment critics have experienced when dealing with this versatile writer: "I had always admired Gaskell's fiction and the vigour and humour of her letters. I liked the way she stood at odds with orthodoxies and eluded pigeon-holes. Conservatives and radicals, Christians and skeptics, Marxists and feminists, all acclaimed different aspects of her work, but all in the end seemed to tap their pens in frustration: she somehow did not 'fit.' "[1] It is precisely in the fluidity and elusiveness of Gaskell's literary art that, Deidre d'Albertis suggests, we may discover a better understanding and deeper appreciation of her work: "Gaskell's life and writing become legible once we accept the failure of fixed or stable identity categories to describe them accurately." Throughout most of her works, D'Albertis points out, we encounter "multiple subject positions and overlapping ideological discourses," some of which include "textual practices as a non-conformist Unitarian (theological), reformer (liberal/political), philanthropist (social), bourgeoisie (economic), and writer of novels (professional/literary)."[2] Uglow and D'Albertis bring attention to the multiplicity and complexity of Gaskell's literary discourse and her appeal to diverse audiences. I wish to discuss here yet another unexplored facet of Gaskell's literary art, her reconfigurations of famous and popular Pre-Raphaelite paintings in her controversial novel *Ruth* (1853). By redrawing Pre-Raphaelite paintings in her narrative, Elizabeth Gaskell seeks to further participate in contemporary debates on gender inequities; simultaneously, she explores the role of Pre-Raphaelite visual art in the endorsement or subversion of gender stereotypes.

Elizabeth Gaskell and the Pre-Raphaelites

In 1851, when the memory of the hostile reception of *Mary Barton* was still painful, Elizabeth Gaskell undertook the task of composing *Ruth*, an "immensely courageous book," in which she chose as her heroine a social outcast, a subject suppressed in Victorian society and art: a teenage woman with an illegitimate child. Like the Pre-Raphaelites, who challenged preestablished notions about worthy subjects of representation, Gaskell takes up an unlikely candidate for a subject of representation, contrary to stereotypical heroines. And like the Pre-Raphaelites, who in their early paintings often represented individuals rather than types in order to depict unique experiences, Gaskell chose for this novel a unique person she herself encountered, as we shall see, in an actual incident.

As we have already seen in chapter 1, the Pre-Raphaelites experimented with portrayals of women in unconventional roles. David Masson, in his extensive and laudatory "Pre-Raphaelitism in Art and Literature" in 1852, found the Pre-Raphaelites' subversion of traditional gender constructs consistent with their goal to accurately represent reality (200). Most of the famous, or notorious, paintings of these early years were unorthodox representations of traditional subjects drawn from the Bible, such as Hunt's *A Converted British Family Sheltering a Christian Missionary from the Persecution of the Druids* (1849–1850), *The Hireling Shepherd* (1851), Rossetti's *Girlhood of Mary Virgin* (1848–1849) and *Ecce Ancilla Domini!* (1849–1850), Millais's *Christ in the House of His Parents,* or from literature, primarily Tennyson, Shakespeare, and Keats, such as Millais's *Mariana* (1850–1851) and *Ophelia* (1851–1852) and Hunt's *Valentine Rescuing Sylvia from Proteus* (1850–1851) and *Claudio and Isabella* (1850–1853). Whether biblical or literary, these paintings blended the unconventional with the conventional, quite often redefining gender constructs within conventional situations.

It is precisely this convergence of the unconventional with the conventional that Gaskell explores in her redrawings of popular Pre-Raphaelite paintings in her contentious novel *Ruth*, thus raising questions not only about established gender constructs but also about Pre-Raphaelite gendered boundaries. Like the Pre-Raphaelites, who called into question normative and stereotypical understandings of women in these early paintings, Gaskell also questioned normative distinctions by portraying an outcast and a virtuous person in one, blending and challenging the contemporary conventional binaries of the fallen woman and the Virgin Mary. The uniqueness of Gaskell's blending of attributes, however, lies in their interdependence, for, as she demonstrates, Ruth's virtuous qualities are partly the cause of her fall; she is a victim precisely because she displays stereotypical, feminine qualities.

Through reconfigurations of Pre-Raphaelite paintings Gaskell launches a critique not merely of the prevalent norms (unfair stereotypes) but also of a society that extols the very feminine qualities and attributes that make women candidates for exploitation and victimization. Gaskell endows Ruth with stereotypical beauty, typical fragility, and meekness most likely in order to show the inevitably disastrous consequences women quite often face when conforming to paradigms of idealized femininity. For this purpose she borrows from Pre-Raphaelite paintings some idealized versions of feminine beauty, but in her reconfigurations of these paintings she demonstrates that idealized versions of women quite often sustain and nourish conditions of victimization.

Gaskell's concern with the social conditions of victimization may also explain her reconfiguration of a notable Pre-Raphaelite painting such as *Ophelia* (1851–1852) (plate 7), which displays the tragedy of an innocent victim, blending youthful features and vibrant female beauty with the finality of a tragically premature death. Gaskell seeks a similar effect, as we shall see, but for a different purpose. Her own portrayal of the relationship between innocence and victimization focuses not on some inevitable tragic fate but on social conditions that are concrete and situational and, as such, ought to be changed if further victimization is to be avoided. Gaskell's vision of the social realm is that of a sphere lacking permanence, a sphere subject to change. For this reason her representation of Ruth involves a fallen woman who, unlike the stereotypical representations of the period, is able to overcome the stigma of her condition and to suspend her grief and become an agent of social change, rejecting gestures of respectability and acceptance (through marriage). Gaskell enables Ruth to emerge out of the social norms that have victimized her.

Subtly embedded within the subtext of the novel, Gaskell's narrative reconfigurations of Pre-Raphaelite paintings in *Ruth* are not merely echoes of these paintings but rather attempts to further extend Pre-Raphaelite gendered boundaries and reveal the constraints imposed on women even in seemingly liberal or untraditional Pre-Raphaelite representations. Gaskell's transformations of Pre-Raphaelite images into narrative scenes simultaneously reveal her engagement with contemporary debates on gender issues and disclose her efforts to empower women by redrawing Pre-Raphaelite representations that, even those seemingly unconventional, often perpetuated traditional gender roles.

Though recent critics have focused on Gaskell's unorthodox treatment of the subject of the fallen woman, few have pursued what could have led them to recognize the Pre-Raphaelite presence in the novel.[3] Some, however, have touched upon a few Pre-Raphaelite elements; referring to *Ruth*, Jennifer Uglow, for instance, remarks, "Gaskell's novel is erotic in the

Plate 7. John Everett Millais, *Ophelia*, 1851–1852. Oil on canvas, 30 x 44 in (76.2 x 111.8 cm), Tate Gallery. Reproduced by permission.

manner of Pre-Raphaelite paintings whose women gaze out with pale enigmatic faces, while their bodies, drapery and surroundings flow with life" (329). Furthermore, Hilary Schor contends that the Pre-Raphaelites' representation of female beauty transforms woman into an aesthetic object of the male gaze. By presenting Ruth's beauty as the cause of her exploitation, Gaskell, according to Schor, exposes a woman's precarious existence in a culture that worships feminine beauty: "[F]or Rossetti and the Pre-Raphaelites, a woman's only story is her beauty made into narrative, that is, when she is seen by a man. . . . Gaskell, on the other hand, refuses to ignore the possibility that a woman's beauty is a fact not in an abstract moral or aesthetic situation, but in a very real context in a socially determined world."[4]

Ruth can be further understood as the site of the intersection of narrative and painting, a woman writer's attempt to revise stereotypical representations of women, engrained in contemporary culture not only by literary works but also by paintings widely circulated in engravings, prints, and illustrations of poems or novels. By reconfiguring Pre-Raphaelite pictorial, static representations of women into narrative, dynamic, images in *Ruth*, Elizabeth Gaskell breaks the silence of stereotypical, passive female figures, giving them, and by extension her readers, the voice to resist the dominant tradition. In *Ruth*, then, the intersection between painting and narrative is primarily ideological, governed not so much by the laws of genre as by the laws of gender.

Gaskell's familiarity with the three founders of the Pre-Raphaelite brotherhood, Dante Gabriel Rossetti, William Holman Hunt, and John Everett Millais, is attested in her numerous references to these artists and their paintings in her letters. In a letter to Charles Norton about her experiences in London in the autumn of 1859, for instance, she describes, as we have already seen, her emotionally charged response to Rossetti's and Hunt's paintings: "And then we saw Holman Hunt's picture, and Holman Hunt's self. I am not going to define & shape my feelings & thoughts at seeing either Rossetti's or Hunt's pictures into words; because I *did* feel them deeply, and after all words are coarse things."[5] She goes on to recount in a humorous tone her encounter with Rossetti:

> Let me think what we did worthy of record—I think we got to know Rossetti pretty well. I went three times to his studio, and met him at two evening parties—where I had a good deal of talk with him, always excepting the times when ladies with beautiful hair came in when he was like the cat turned into a lady, who jumped out of bed and ran after a mouse. It did not signify what we were talking about or how agreeable I was; if a particular kind of reddish brown, crepe wavy hair came in, he

was away in a moment struggling for an introduction to the owner of said
head of hair. He is not as mad as a March hare, but hair-mad. (*Letters* 580)

Rossetti in turn regarded Elizabeth Gaskell as a friend. In a letter to
William Michael Rossetti, for instance, he remarks, "I have some idea
(with Christina's approval) of sending the *Goblins* to Mrs. Gaskell, who is
good natured and appreciative, and might get it into the *Cornhill* or elsewhere."[6]

Though we have no direct evidence that Gaskell met the three leaders of the Pre-Raphaelite movement before the publication of *Ruth*, it is
entirely possible that she had seen their early paintings during her frequent travels to London. Even before meeting Millais, for instance, in
April 1853, she had seen *The Order of Release* and *The Proscribed Royalist*
(*Letters* 231). In 1849 she visited the Royal Academy; she also spent con-
siderable time in London in 1850 and 1851, when she could have seen
Rossetti's early paintings (Uglow 225, 254, 273). From 1850 on Dickens
became her chief publisher. More than two-thirds of her stories and arti-
cles between 1850 and her death were published in *Household Words* and
All the Year Around (ibid., 254–55). In fact she had published "Lizzie
Leigh" (whose theme she expanded in *Ruth*) in *Household Words* on
April 30, 1850 (Chapple, *Further Letters* 72). It would have been impos-
sible then for her not to have read Dickens's notorious article on the Pre-
Raphaelites, published in *Household Words* on June 15, 1850. Like other
Victorian novelists, Gaskell had direct access to *The Times*, which pub-
lished reviews of Pre-Raphaelite paintings and Ruskin's letters defending
Pre-Raphaelite art, as well as to journals embroiled in the Pre-Raphaelite
controversy, some of which, like *London Illustrated News*, reproduced
Pre-Raphaelite paintings. Her earliest reference in her letters to *The
Times* occurs in a letter to Catherine Winkworth on November 21, 1848
(*Letters* 60–61).

Gaskell was also an avid reader of *Athenaeum*; her earliest reference
occurs on October 29, 1848, in a letter to Barbara Fergusson, in which she
informs her of a positive review of *Mary Barton* in that journal (Chapple,
Further Letters 40). Gaskell published two reviews in the *Athenaeum* issue
for December 13, 1851, the first the lead review, of Longfellow's *Golden
Legend*, and the second a review of *Spiritual Alchemy*.[7] The second review
is especially noteworthy for Gaskell's views on the art of the novel, which
reveal her knowledge of visual arts and her interest in adopting Pre-
Raphaelite techniques in her novels. In this review she objects to the
handling of the perspective in *Spiritual Alchemy*, noting that it "reminds
us of the old willow-pattern plates, where the man in the boat away at sea
is just as large and prominent as the three men on the bridge close at

hand." A good novelist, like Jane Austen, for instance, Gaskell asserts, describes scenes accurately and truthfully so that we can "unconsciously picture" them. Although she does not mention the Pre-Raphaelites, she refers to some of their early principles, such as the importance of "simplification and truth," which can be acquired by "much conscientious observation of life,—and of a severe training in the art of describing correctly what is correctly observed." Furthermore, like Ruskin, who in his defense of the Pre-Raphaelites in his letters to *The Times* on May 13 and 25 of that year, underscored the connection between the Pre-Raphaelite truth to nature and morality, Gaskell points out, "the cause of religion and morality will be better served by faithfully depicting, to their homeliest details, the sorrowful consequences inevitably resulting from wrongdoing than by personifying "Death," "Foul Injustice," "Spirits sacred and beloved" (832). Indeed her letters, containing references to contemporary newspapers and journals that reviewed Pre-Raphaelite art, are too numerous to mention here. Undoubtedly, by 1853, when *Ruth* was published, Gaskell had read reviews of Pre-Raphaelite art, was familiar with their aesthetic principles, and must have eagerly sought their paintings in art exhibits, prints, or engravings. Her interest in the Pre-Raphaelites, as her letters attest, continued to the end of her career.

The Genesis of Ruth

Gaskell's emotional investment in *Ruth* is revealed in her various comments in several letters. In a letter to R. Monckton Milnes, for instance, she says, "I am so glad you liked 'Ruth.' I was so anxious about her, and took so much pains over writing it, that I lost my own power of judging, and could not tell whether I had done it well or ill" (*Letters* 225). The hostile reviews the novel received, conjoined with her friends' alienation, made Elizabeth Gaskell physically ill, at one point suffering from "Ruth fever" as she playfully states in a letter to Eliza Fox: "I think I must be an improper woman without knowing it, I do so manage to shock people," she remarks. "Now *should* you have burnt the 1st vol of Ruth as so *very* bad? even if you had been a very anxious father of a family? Yet *two* men have; and a third has forbidden his wife to read it; they sit next to us in Chapel and you can't think how 'improper' I feel under their eyes" (*Letters* 222–23).[8]

Feminist writers such as Margaret Homans, Mary Jacobus, and Mary Poovey, to mention but a few, discuss nineteenth-century women writers' attempts to revise "the cultural myth of language's process and structure that situates them as the silent and absent objects of representation."[9] I wish to extend this argument by taking into consideration women's silencing in Pre-Raphaelite paintings, in this case Rossetti's and Millais's. By redrawing such paintings in her narrative, Gaskell simultaneously attempts to revise literary history. Her narrative breaks the silence of stereotypical passive, submissive women and engages her readers in questions regarding those women's individual experiences. In this respect her quest to represent individuals rather than types parallels the Pre-Raphaelite commitment to idiosyncratic representation (Prettejohn 256).

Even at its inception, *Ruth* was connected to the story of a woman's silence, representative of numerous other victimized women who had no legal recourse to sexual exploitation. In a letter to Charles Dickens in 1850, in which Gaskell asks for his advice to assist a young woman named Pasley to emigrate to Australia, she describes an incident that served as the genesis of *Ruth:* "I am just now very much interested in a young girl, who is in our New Bayley prison. She is the daughter of an Irish clergyman who died when she was two years old; but even before that her mother had shown most complete indifference to her; and soon after the husband's death, she married again, keeping her child out at nurse. The girl's uncle had her placed at 6 years old in the Dublin school for orphan daughters of the clergy; and when she was about 14, she was apprenticed to an Irish dress-maker, here, of great reputation for fashion" (*Letters* 98).[10] She goes on to describe how the dressmaker eventually lost her business and the girl was placed with an acquaintance who "connived at the girl's seduction by a surgeon in the neighbourhood who was called in when the poor creature was ill." She recounts the girl's desperate situation as she attempts to reach her mother:

> Then she was in despair, & wrote to her mother, (*who had never corresponded with her all the time she was at school and an apprentice;*) and while awaiting the answer went into the penitentiary; she wrote 3 times but no answer came, and in desperation she listened to a woman, who had obtained admittance . . . solely as it turned out to decoy girls into her mode of life, and left with her; & for four months she has led the most miserable life! in the hopes, as she tells me, of killing herself, for "no one had ever cared for her in this world,"—she drank, "wishing it might be poison," pawned every article of clothing—and at last stole. (ibid., 98)

She continues with her first meeting of the girl: "I have been to see her in prison at Mr Wright's request, and she looks quite a young child (she is but 16,) with a wild wistful look in her eyes, as if searching for the kindness she has never known,—and she pines to redeem herself" (ibid., 99). In her description of Pasley, Gaskell focuses on her inarticulate "wild wistful look." The inarticulate anguish that look conveyed must have left an indelible mark on Gaskell's memory and imagination, for she relates it to Ruth on numerous occasions. When Benson, for instance, discovers Ruth contemplating suicide by the pond where Bellingham had adorned her hair with water lilies, we see her "crouched up like some hunted creature, with a wild, scared look of despair, which almost made her lovely face fierce."[11] On another occasion, when Bellingham suddenly reappears on the beach at Abermouth, we are told that Ruth's young pupils notice her face in the "low, watery twilight," when she encounters her erstwhile lover: "So pale, so haggard, so wild and wandering a look, the girls had never seen on human countenance before" (chapter XXIII). Wild inarticulate looks, silence stifling overwhelming emotions, and dreams offering a liberating space for utterances otherwise forbidden are all expressions of what Julia Kristeva describes as the nonverbal essence of the semiotic. In *Speaking the Unspeakable* Anne-Marie Smith interprets Kristeva's semiotic as "an articulation of unconscious processes which fracture the common idealization of those images and signs which secure the status quo, and guarantee the establishment. It is a constant subversive threat to the symbolic order of things, which itself, Kristeva stresses, is no monolithic structure, but an illusion of stability"(16). In the impalpable and intangible transformation of the Pre-Raphaelite paintings into narrative images, reframing the visual in the textual and inviting the readers' imagination to once again reframe their own interpretations of Pre-Raphaelite art, Gaskell must have sought the means by which she could transgress ideological boundaries in order to redefine female subjectivity. By these means in *Ruth* Gaskell undertakes the great challenge of offering the unauthorized an opportunity to speak and to become social agents of change.

Reconfigurations of Pre-Raphaelite Paintings in Ruth

At the onset of the story Ruth underscores women's difficulty of breaking silence or articulating resistance to the dominant tradition. We first encounter Ruth at two o'clock in the morning, her silent face framed by "a window (through which the moonlight fell on her with a glory of many colours)" (chapter I). Like the Lady of Shalott, Mariana, and countless other silenced literary and painterly figures, Ruth longs for the liberating escape the public sphere seductively offers as she presses "her hot forehead against the cold glass" and strains "her aching eyes in gazing out on the lovely sky of a winter's night" (chapter I). Soon after this description, we follow Ruth to a corner of the house where she is busy sewing a beautiful evening gown destined for the wealthy class from which she is excluded:[12]

Ruth's place was the coldest and the darkest in the room, although she
liked it the best; she had instinctively chosen it for the sake of the wall
opposite to her, on which was a remnant of the beauty of the old draw-
ing-room. . . . It was divided into panels of pale sea-green, picked out with
white and gold; and on these panels were painted . . . the most lovely
wreaths of flowers, profuse and luxuriant beyond description . . . the
branches of purple and white lilac—the floating golden-tressed labur-
num boughs. Besides these, there were stately white lilies, sacred to the
Virgin. . . . At the bottom of the panel lay a holly-branch, whose stiff
straightness was ornamented by a twining drapery of English ivy . . . and,
crowning all, came gorgeous summer and the sweet musk-roses. (ibid.)

Drawn in the manner of the Pre-Raphaelite "egalitarian methodology"
(Prettejohn 172), including as much attention to the surrounding objects
as to the central figure, Ruth's first full-figure portrait evokes Dante
Gabriel Rossetti's *Girlhood of Mary Virgin* (1849) (plate 8), a painting representing the Virgin Mary as a docile, diligent maiden whose face, like that
of Ruth's, is absorbed by her embroidery. Printed in the catalog of the Free
Exhibition, where the painting was first exhibited, was Rossetti's sonnet
that extols the Virgin's virtues, thus guiding the reader's interpretation of
the painting:

This is that blessed Mary, pre-elect
God's Virgin. . . .
Her kin she cherished with devout respect:
Her gifts were simpleness of intellect
And supreme patience. From her mother's knee
Faithful and hopeful; wise in charity
Strong in grave peace; in duty circumspect.
So held she through her girlhood; as it were
An angel-watered lily, that near God
Grows and is quiet.[13]

Explicating Rossetti's sonnet, Alicia Faxon underscores the symbolism
of the colors chosen even for the books stacked on the side, bound, as she
explains, in colors "traditionally associated with certain virtues: white for
Temperance, red for Fortitude, blue for Faith, green for Hope, and gold for
Charity. . . . The dove represents the presence of the Holy Spirit, the red
robe beneath the cruciform trellis foretells Christ's passion, the rose and
the lily are symbols of the Madonna, and the palms and thorny branch in
the foreground refer to Christ's martyrdom" (53–54). Barringer further
notes the ivy on the trellis and points out that the lily represents the puri-

Plate 8. Dante Gabriel Rossetti, *The Girlhood of Mary Virgin*, 1848–1849. Oil on canvas, 32³/₄ x 25³/₄ in (83.2 x 65.4 cm), Tate Gallery. Reproduced by permission.

ty of the Virgin Mary (8). A careful observation of the panels Ruth sees, as she, like the Virgin Mary, diligently sews, reveals that Gaskell in her redrawing of Rossetti's painting has included all the colors and the flowers of that painting, and, throughout the novel she ascribes to young Ruth Mary's aforementioned virtues.

A few pages later, Gaskell evokes Rossetti's *Ecce Ancilla Domini!* (Behold the Servant of the Lord!) (1849–1850) (plate 9), which, as Tim Barringer observes, "continues the narrative of *The Girlhood of the Virgin Mary*" (42). The scene represented in the painting is described in Rossetti's early sonnet "Mary's Girlhood":

> Till one dawn, at home,
> She woke in her white bed, and had no fear
> At all,—yet wept till sunshine, and felt awed;
> Because the fulness of the time was come. (11–14)

When Ruth first encounters Mr. Bellingham at the ball where she mends his partner's, Miss Duncombe's, dress, he offers her a white camellia in an attempt to attenuate the impact of her sharp impertinence to Ruth. Ruth returns home enraptured by the "exquisite beauty" of the "perfect" and "pure" flower and talks to her friend Jenny about it till she falls asleep (chapter II). In the early morning, Jenny observes Ruth's happy face as she dreams smiling: " 'She is dreaming of last night,' thought Jenny. It was true she was; but one figure flitted more than all the rest through her visions. He presented flower after flower to her in that baseless morning dream, which was all too quickly ended" (ibid.). As in the scene of the Annunciation, represented in Rossetti's painting, Ruth's dream takes place in the early morning. Like the Archangel Gabriel, who offers the Virgin Mary a white lily announcing her conception of Christ, Bellingham offers Ruth a white flower that initiates her relationship with him and that results in Leonard's conception.[14]

Yet another dream earlier in the novel also resembles Rossetti's *Ecce Ancilla Domini!* in setting and style. After isolating herself from the other seamstresses and gazing at the falling snow through a window, Ruth expresses a desire to run outdoors and enjoy the purity of the landscape. Thus Ruth is identified with the white purity of the outdoors that evokes the whiteness of Rossetti's painting. That same night she goes to bed exhausted, but soon Jenny decides to waken her since "she was crying in her sleep as if her heart would break" (chapter I). The startled Ruth, "sitting up in bed, and pushing back the masses of hair," recounts her dream: " 'I thought I saw mamma by the side of the bed, coming, as she used to do, to see if I were asleep and comfortable; and when I tried to take hold

Plate 9. Dante Gabriel Rossetti, *Ecce Ancilla Domini!* 1849–1850. Oil on canvas, 28 7/8 x 16 1/2 in (72.6 x 41.9 cm), Tate Gallery. Reproduced by permission.

of her she went away and left me alone—I don't know where; so strange!' "
(ibid.). Ruth's startled gaze, as she sits in her bed and recounts her dream,
recalls the awkward posture of the Virgin Mary with the astonished glance
in Rossetti's painting. In the sonnet accompanying the painting Rossetti
describes her crying "till sunshine" and feeling "awed." Ruth is represented in a similar situation, bewildered by her mother's mysterious appearance
and disappearance, which in turn resembles the sudden appearance of the
Archangel Gabriel standing by the Virgin Mary's bed.

These are not the only two occasions on which Gaskell redraws
Rossetti's painting. Throughout the novel, her description of Ruth quite
often strikingly resembles Rossetti's representation of the Virgin Mary in
his *Ecce Ancilla Domini!* When, for instance, Ruth keeps vigil during
Bellingham's sickness, hiding behind his closed door all night, she is
startled by the splendid light of a sunrise replete with the colors of the
religious symbolism in Rossetti's painting: "Just above the horizon, too,
the mist became a silvery grey cloud hanging on the edge of the world;
presently it turned shimmering white; and then in an instant, it flushed
into rose, and the mountain tops sprang into heaven, and bathed in the
presence of the shadow of God. With a bound the sun of a molten fiery
red came above the horizon" (chapter VII). Against this splendid background of dazzling whites and reds, the awkwardness of Ruth's pose is
even more prominent: "She sat curled up upon the floor, with her head
thrown back against the wall, and her hands clasped round her knees."
To Mrs. Bellingham, who suddenly opens the door of her sick son's
room, Ruth in her white dress against the wall appears like a "white
apparition" (ibid.). Here Ruth's gawky posture seems yet another transformation of the shrinking posture of Rossetti's Virgin, startled by the
archangel at sunrise. Later in the novel, when Sally decides to cut her
hair so that Ruth will appear more like the purported widow to the community, Sally walks into Ruth's room to find "the beautiful, astonished
Ruth, where she stood in her long, soft, white dressing gown, with all
her luxuriant brown hair hanging disheveled down her figure" (chapter
XIII). In these scenes, whether it be Ruth's awkward poses or her astonished, vulnerable gaze, her "auburn hair with a fair complexion" (chapter I), her disheveled hair hanging down her face, or her white gown,
these details all correspond strikingly to Christina Rossetti's appearance
as the Virgin Mary in *Ecce Ancilla Domini!* By associating Ruth with the
Virgin Mary, Gaskell defies, subverts, and elides the conventional distinction between the polarized Victorian gender oppositions: the Virgin
and the fallen woman.

Her reconfiguration of Rossetti's *Girlhood of the Virgin Mary* also serves
as an occasion for implicit and subtle criticism of conventional represen-

tations of femininity. No doubt this painting celebrates the Madonna as the supreme paradigm of the Angel in the House, an angel whose silence is so extensive that she could be compared to an inanimate lily "that near God/Grows and is quiet" (10–11). This sonnet, originally printed in the catalog of the Free Exhibition for this painting, highlights the Victorian paradigm of the domestic woman who suppresses her voice and ornaments her home with her beauty—"an angel-watered lily." Indeed the sonnet underscores the patriarchal qualifications of femininity, a long list of virtues all defining female passivity, beginning with "respect," which often involves the suppression of one's own voice, followed by "simpleness of intellect," both qualities at the very top of the list. Yet the narrator in *Ruth* takes pains to demonstrate that it is precisely this "simpleness of intellect," often associated in contemporary culture with feminine morality, that is the cause of Ruth's demise. In fact the qualities Bellingham first notices in Ruth and readily decides to exploit echo those that Rossetti's sonnet on the Virgin Mary exalts and Victorian culture sustains: "There was, perhaps, something bewitching in the union of the grace and loveliness of woman-hood with the *naiveté*, simplicity, and innocence of an intelligent child. There was a spell in the shyness, which made her avoid and shun all admiring approaches to acquaintance" (chapter III). Later on, when Bellingham convinces her to go to London with him, after Mrs. Mason has unjustly and summarily dismissed her from her service, Ruth's virtues make her a vulnerable victim. When Ruth proposes that she could live with old friends instead, Bellingham promptly rejects the idea and takes her to London. Ruth, however, does not protest or resist, for, we are told, "she was little accustomed to oppose the wishes of any one—obedient and docile by nature, and unsuspicious and innocent of any harmful consequences" (chapter IV). Thus Gaskell demonstrates the contradictory nature of social demands imposed on women in an androcentric culture: selfless devotion and blind obedience are quite frequently tantamount to women's victimization. In this structure, as Ranita Chatterjee points out, "women are never allowed to grow up; they are permanently infantilized in the service of the Father's Law both literally, in their exclusion from power, and symbolically, in their relations with men" (132).

In a letter to Anne Robson, Elizabeth Gaskell admits that she herself would hesitate to read a book about the seduction of a fifteen-year-old girl, but even the anticipation of hostile criticism would not deter her from articulating a subject often silenced in proper Victorian circles: " 'An unfit subject for fiction' is *the* thing to say about it; I knew all this before; but *I determined notwithstanding to speak my mind out about it*; only how I shrink with more pain than I can tell you from what people are saying though I wd [sic] do every jot of it over again to-morrow. . . . In short the only comparison I can find for myself is to St. Sebastian tied to a tree to be shot with arrows" (*Letters* 220–21, my emphasis). In the same letter she reiterates her conviction in the importance of protesting inequities silenced by Victorian ideology. "I have spoken out my mind in the best way I can, and I have no doubt that what was meant so earnestly *must* do some good, though perhaps not all the good, or not the *very* good I meant" (ibid., 221).

Gaskell's choice of Pre-Raphaelite paintings suggests her determination to undermine the feminine passivity and silence endorsed by literature and art. Her novel includes notable examples such as *Ophelia* and *Mariana*. On a walk in the woods during their stay in Wales, Bellingham and Ruth come across a "circular pool overshadowed by the trees" (chapter VI). Although flowers bloom by the pond, they are barely seen in the dark shadows the trees cast, but the water lilies catch Ruth's and Bellingham's attention, and Bellingham gathers a few and proceeds to create his own painting: "[H]e took off her bonnet, without speaking, and began to place his flowers in her hair. . . . Her beauty was all that Mr. Bellingham cared for, and it was supreme. It was all he recognized of her, and he was proud of it. She stood in her white dress against the trees which grew around; her face was flushed into a brilliancy of colour which resembled that of a rose in June; the great heavy white flowers drooped on either side of her beautiful head, and if her brown hair was a little disordered, the very disorder only seemed to add a grace" (ibid.).

Bellingham's "painting" transforming Ruth into a spectacle, the object of his gaze, seems an amalgamation of John Everett Millais's *Ophelia* (1850–1852) and Arthur Hughes's painting of the same title. Representative of the iconography of madness, as Showalter points out, Hughes's painting depicts Ophelia before her suicide: "In the Royal Academy show of 1852, Arthur Hughes's entry shows a tiny waif-like creature—a sort of Tinker Bell Ophelia—in a filmy white gown, perched on a tree trunk by the stream. The overall effect is softened, sexless, and hazy; although the straw in her hair resembles a crown of thorns. Hughes's juxtaposition of childlike femininity and Christian martyrdom was overpowered, however, by John Everett Millais's great painting of Ophelia in the same show."[15] Gaskell chooses water lilies instead of straw, but the effect is the same. Turning from the earlier evocation of *The Girlhood of Mary Virgin*, wherein Gaskell associates Ruth with the lily of the Virgin Mary, here in her redrawing of *Ophelia*, she, like Hughes, through her choice of the crown of flowers, foreshadows her martyrdom, underlined by Ruth's constant sighs to Bellingham's utter irritation.

Simultaneously, though, the details of the scene in the novel also evoke Millais's *Ophelia*. Her disordered hair resembles Ophelia's disheveled hair in the stream. A contemporary review of the painting by *The Athenaeum* in 1852 lauded the beauty of the painting, attributing it partly to the depiction of Ophelia's passivity and silence: "The expression aimed at is that of an incapability of estimating 'her own distress.' The open mouth is somewhat gaping and gabyish,—the expression is in no way suggestive of her past tale. There is no pathos, no melancholy, no one brightening up, no last lucid interval. If she dies swan-like with a song, there is no sound or melody, no poetry in this strain."[16] The reviewer's description of Ophelia is based primarily on negation: no sound, no melody, no voice—the denial of subjectivity. In spite of the luxuriantly detailed and seductively vibrant landscape, the reviewer focuses on absence and silence. Ophelia's stifled voice, the swan song that is vanquished by silence, is his primary concern, at once underscoring the stereotype of victimized, passive, silent femininity.

Like Millais's *Ophelia,* Ruth is surrounded by flowers; in particular, Gaskell evokes the rose floating by Millais's *Ophelia* when she describes Ruth's face "flushed into a brilliancy of colour which resembled that of a rose in June" (chapter VI). Furthermore, Gaskell's pond closely resembles that of Millais's rather than Hughes's, which, according to Millais, is inaccurately represented:[17] "The speed-well grew in the shallowest water of the pool, and all around its margin, but the flowers were hardly seen at first, so deep was the green shadow cast by the trees. In the very middle of the pond the sky was mirrored clear and dark, a blue which looked as if a black void lay behind" (ibid.). Showalter's interpretation of Millais's *Ophelia* as "a sensuous siren and a victim" (63) would be an apt description of Gaskell's representation of Ruth as Ophelia.

Yet by evoking Shakespeare's Ophelia, a literary stereotype engrained in contemporary culture by popular paintings and engravings, Gaskell attempts to rewrite literary history by giving a voice to a hitherto silent figure of passive femininity. Shortly after Bellingham abandons Ruth, she returns to the pond to commit suicide, but when she hears Benson's cry of pain as he falls over a sharp, projecting rock, she runs to his rescue and abandons her plan. Thus Ruth, unlike Ophelia, does not yield to despair, a typically feminine gesture; instead, she undertakes a traditionally masculine role in becoming someone's rescuer. In this case the setting and the motif anticipate those in *The Proscribed Royalist.* Later on when she jeopardizes her own health to rescue Bellingham by nursing him back to health, Bellingham in his delirium sees her as the beautiful, passive spectacle he had once created but no longer possesses since Ruth has already rejected his marriage proposal. Towering over him, Ruth no longer lowers her gaze: "[H]er looks were riveted on his softly-unclosing eyes, which met hers as they opened languidly. . . . She was held fast by that gaze of his, in which a faint recognition dawned, and grew to strength. He murmured some words . . . 'Where are the water-lilies? Where are the lilies in her hair?' " (chapter XXXV). Later on her deathbed, Ruth's image once again evokes Ophelia when her "unconscious eyes" tell of "a sweet, childlike insanity within." Like Ophelia, Ruth dies singing: "[S]he was happy and at peace. They had never heard her sing; indeed the simple art which her mother had taught her, had died, with her early joyousness, at that dear mother's death. But now she sang continually, very soft and low. She went from one childish ditty to another without let or pause" (ibid.). Unlike Ophelia though, Ruth does not die as a victim but as a rescuer and a redeemer. Her final moments allude to her initial image as a Madonna figure deified through her magnanimous altruism: " 'I see the Light coming,' " said she. " 'The Light is coming,' " she said.

As in Ophelia's case, Gaskell reconstructs the literary Mariana and reframes the pictorial one. When we first meet Ruth, she bemoans her fate as Mrs. Mason's apprentice: "Oh! how shall I get through five years of these terrible nights! in that close room! and in that oppressive stillness! which lets every sound of the thread be heard as it goes eternally backwards and forwards" (chapter I). The intertextual connections here multiply, for Tennyson, through his epigraph to "Mariana," "Mariana in the moated grange," a quotation from Shakespeare's *Measure for Measure*, alludes to the eponymous heroine who for five years has been living a lonely life in a moated grange after being rejected by her fiancé, Angelo, after her marriage dowry is lost in a shipwreck. Unlike Tennyson's other poems, which are replete with vibrant visual images, "Mariana" concentrates on auditory images that underscore and intensify her inconsolable loneliness. She can hear "the flitting of the bats" (17), "the nightfowl crow" (26), "the shrill winds" (50), "the slow clock ticking" (73), and even the mouse "behind the moldering wainscot" shrieking (64). Ruth, like Mariana, is intensely aware of the oppressive silence to the extent that she can hear even the sound of the thread. Moreover, like Mariana, Ruth, throughout the novel, longingly looks through a window, most often feeling incarcerated within the domestic sphere. John Everett Millais's *Mariana* (1850–1851), inspired by Tennyson's poem, portrays Tennyson's character standing in front of a window wearily stretching over her embroidery. When this painting was first exhibited in 1851, the following lines from Tennyson's poem were printed in the catalog:

> She only said, "My life is dreary,
> He cometh not," she said:
> She said, "I am aweary, aweary,
> I would that I were dead!" (9–12)

Millais's painting encapsulates a traditionally feminine predicament, the forlorn woman who pines for her lover and would rather die than experience life on her own. Simultaneously, though, Millais adds his own unconventional touches by displaying Mariana's sexuality in her tightly fitting, vibrant blue dress and her unorthodox pose. Several critics have commented on the erotic quality of the painting. Pearce, for instance, observes, "Mariana is presenting her body for inspection, while she gazes desirously into the eyes of the Archangel Gabriel represented in the stained glass" (66).

Elizabeth Prettejohn notes not only the unconventionally sensuous quality of Mariana but also the modernity of the painting: "Thus the stretching pose seems to express sexual tension as well as the woman's weariness with the embroidery. . . . This is not the awakening of adolescent sexuality but the longing or fantasy of mature woman. . . . Female sexuality seems important to this picture, but not in a predictable way. The spectator is neither enticed by a *femme fatale* nor titillated by a virginal girl. Indeed the picture acknowledges the sexuality of a mature woman in a way that is difficult to reconcile with our conventional preconceptions about the Victorians" (12). As we contemplate the picture, Prettejohn notes, we may interpret it in several ways. It is precisely the indeterminacy of the meaning of the painting, even with the contextualization of Tennyson's poem or Shakespeare's play, that reveals the avant-garde nature of Pre-Raphaelite art—its modernity: "The picture's interpretative implications cannot be simply decoded, any more than its visual intricacy can be mastered without prolonged close looking. *Mariana* thus has the complexity that we expect to find in significant works of modern art" (13).

It is interesting to note that Millais, in his interpretation of Tennyson's "Mariana," adds his own touches. Instead of Tennyson's dreary landscape, Millais opts for the vibrant colors of a stained-glass window depicting the Annunciation. According to Malcolm Warner, "the fulfillment the archangel brings the Virgin Mary emphasizes by contrast Mariana's deep frustration" (Parris, *The Pre-Raphaelites* 89). To the right of that window we perceive the motto *"in coelo quies,"* "in Heaven there is rest," with a snowdrop, signifying consolation in the language of flowers, painted underneath it. Death, then, the painting implies, is Mariana's only viable alternative.

It is very likely that Ruth's death wish, shortly after she rejects Bellingham's marriage proposal on the beach at Abermouth, is an explicit allusion to Tennyson's and Millais's Mariana: " 'I am so weary! I am so weary!' she moans aloud at last. 'I wonder if I might stop here, and just die away' " (chapter XXIV). But here the similarities between the literary and the pictorial Mariana end, for, unlike them, instead of subordinating her subjectivity to male authority, Ruth asserts it when Bellingham finally returns and offers to marry her. Unlike Tennyson's Mariana, who, we are led to assume, would have rejoiced at the reunion, Ruth rejects Bellingham in an articulate, eloquent voice hitherto stifled and repressed to silence: " 'I do not love you. I did once. Don't say I did not love you then; but I do not now. . . . We are very far apart. The time that has pressed down my life like brands of hot iron, and scarred me for ever, has been nothing to you. You talked of it with no sound of moaning in your voice—no shadow over the brightness of your face; it has left no sense of sin on your conscience, while me it haunts and haunts. . . . You shall have nothing to do with my boy, by my consent, much less by my agency. I would rather see him working on the roadside than leading such a life— being such a one as you are' " (ibid.).

Ruth's fiery eloquence is indeed a surprising repudiation of the meek self-effacement of Tennyson's and Millais's Marianas. As Shirley Foster remarks, Gaskell defies convention "in her overt admiration for sturdy female reliance"; her rejection of Bellingham is "a denial of convention-al morality."[18] By alluding to both the literary and the pictorial Mariana, Gaskell vividly underscores their differences and articulates the alterna-tives that even fallen women may have in a culture that suppresses their voice.

Unlike Tennyson's Mariana, who, engulfed in sorrow, is insensible to nature's beauty, Ruth is perfectly attuned to natural rhythms, often seek-ing comfort and peace in them. Such intense affinity with nature reach-es its culmination when her Mariana-like wailing, following her rejection of Bellingham, is suddenly disrupted by the piercing beauty of the sunset framed by her window: "Ruth forgot herself in looking at the gorgeous sight. She sat up gazing and, as she gazed, the tears dried on her cheeks; and, somehow, all human care and sorrow were swallowed up in the unconscious sense of God's infinity. The sunset calmed her more than any words, however wise and tender, could have done. It even seemed to give her strength and courage" (chapter XXIV).

Reminiscent of the Romantic poets' solitary meditations over natural phenomena that often lead to revelations or epiphanies, captured in notable poems such as Wordsworth's *Tintern Abbey* or Coleridge's *This Lime Tree-Bower My Prison*, Ruth's meditative seclusion also fuels spiritu-al regeneration and empowerment. Through a fusion of the external with the internal, Gaskell's portrayal of Ruth in this particular scene sur-mounts the divisive boundaries of the public and private spheres that both Tennyson's poem and Millais's painting uphold. Unlike Millais's and Tennyson's self-preoccupied heroine, Ruth here, as on various occasions in the novel, extricates herself from the restrictive boundaries of dependence and self-pity and identifies with nature. In this respect, Gaskell's representation of Ruth as Mariana in a way anticipates Marie Spartali Stillman's *Mariana* (1867–1869), whose open window offers the liberation and spiritual expansion that Millais's and Rossetti's Marianas, both enclosed within the domestic sphere, are denied. Like Gaskell's version of Mariana, Stillman's is depicted in a moment of meditative reverie, her gaze averted from both the indoors and the outdoors, thus signaling self-containment rather than expectation.

A close observation of the words Gaskell chooses in her textual reconfigurations of Millais's painting further reveals her attempt to align her narrative with the famous painting while simultaneously undermining its motif. Ruth's room in Benson's home, for instance, reflects some of the qualities of the stained glass in Millais's painting: "[T]he white dimity bed, and the walls, stained green, had something of the colouring and purity of effect of a snowdrop, while the floor . . . suggested the idea of the garden-mould out of which the snowdrop grows" (chapter XIII). In this context, by no means is the allusion to the snowdrop accidental. Later in the novel, when Leonard is born, Miss Benson gives her a bouquet of snowdrops: " 'Look Ruth! . . . my brother sends these. They are the first snowdrops in the garden.' And she put them on the pillow by Ruth; the baby lay on the opposite side" (chapter XV). Unlike Millais's Mariana, who contemplates consolation in death, signified by the snowdrop under the motto, *"in coelo quies,"* Ruth finds consolation in her love for her newborn child.

Even after the disclosure of the secret of her "fall," when Bradshaw ruthlessly turns her out of his house and she loses her job as governess, Ruth does not wallow in despair or spiritually disintegrate by becoming a prostitute, the stereotypical predicament of a fallen woman, but channels her energy into her work as a nurse in the local hospital. Thus Elizabeth Gaskell enables Ruth to become a social agent of change whose work is finally recognized by the citizens at Eccleston. One evening, walking by the hospital, her son Leonard, hitherto stigmatized and traumatized by his mother's transgression, overhears an old man's words celebrating Ruth's work: "Such a one as her has never been a great sinner; nor does she do her work as a penance, but for the love of God, and of the blessed Jesus. She will be in the light of God's countenance when you and I will be standing afar off" (chapter XXXIII). Thus Ruth, as this scene and her death scene indicate, becomes the light of the Eccleston world, possibly an implicit allusion to Hunt's celebrated *Light of the World.*

In a letter to Gaskell in April 1852, Charlotte Brontë protested the ending of the novel: "Why should she die? Why are we to shut the book weeping?"[19] Since its publication several critics have also objected to the anticlimactic ending. Deidre D'Albertis's objection is representative: "Gaskell dispatched her heroine through martyrdom in much the same way that both male and female middle-class reformers expatriated 'fallen' working-class recipients of Victorian charitable 'rescue' to another, better world beyond the shores of England" (13). After her defiant stance against traditional gender boundaries, Ruth dies, effecting no apparent social change. Literary, gender, and ideological conflicts seem unresolved as the narrative closes.[20] In *Bearing the Word,* Margaret Homans defines the context within which Gaskell seemed bound: "[F]or nineteenth-century women writers, the collision between the urgent need to represent female experience and women's silencing within language and literary history remained a collision articulated but not resolved" (xiii).

The Voice of the Silenced

Throughout her fiction Elizabeth Gaskell records a multiplicity of voices traditionally silenced by dominant ideologies and monolithic histories. In "The Crooked Branch," "Lizzie Leigh," and "Clopton Hall," *Sylvia's Lovers* and *Wives and Daughters* women are denied their voice and their identity. Her works voice resistance to monological ideology and recognize the importance of sociopolitical change in offering the unauthorized an opportunity to speak and to become social agents. In her preface to *Mary Barton,* Gaskell recounts her reason for writing it as the desire to give voice to the oppressed, whose misery was unheeded by their oppressors: "The more I reflected on this unhappy state of things between those so bound to each other by common interests, as the employers and the employed must ever be, the more anxious I became to *give some utterance to the agony which, from time to time, convulses this dumb people*" (lxxx, my emphasis). Prescient of terrorism, Gaskell warns that oppression ultimately affects everyone, even those who are responsible for it and tend to dismiss its threat and danger:

> If it be an error that the woes, which come with ever returning tide-like flood to overwhelm the workmen in our manufacturing towns, pass unregarded by all but the sufferers, it is at any rate an error so bitter in its consequences to all parties, that whatever public effort can do in the way of merciful deeds . . . should be done, and that speedily, to disabuse the work-people of so miserable a misapprehension. At present they seem to me to be left in a state, wherein lamentations and tears are thrown aside as useless, but in which the lips are compressed for curses, and the hands

clenched and ready to smite. I know nothing of Political Economy, or the theories of trade. I have tried to write truthfully; and if my accounts agree or clash with any system, the agreement or disagreement is unintentional. (Preface to *Mary Barton*, lxxx)

Carlyle apprehended Gaskell's message as his letter to her, shortly after receiving a copy of the novel, attests: "I gratefully accept it as a real contribution (about the first real one) towards developing a huge subject, *which has lain dumb too long, and really ought to speak for itself, and tell us its meaning a little, if there is a voice in it at all*" (my emphasis).[21] Following the belligerent reception of *Ruth*, Gaskell felt vindicated by the power of her utterance. In a letter to Lady Kay-Shuttleworth she begins by relating the adverse and extreme reaction to the novel, but she continues self-assured about her achievement: "[I]t [*Ruth*] has made them talk and think a little on a subject which is so painful that it requires all one's bravery not to hide one's head like an ostrich and try by doing so to forget that the evil exists" (*Letters* 227).

Gaskell knew the power of one woman's dissenting voice to break the silence of the unauthorized and give them the power of representation and social activism. Margaret in *North and South* (1854), overcoming women's conventional reticence, does not hesitate to criticize Thornton's treatment of his employees and protests against the abuse of power. Moreover, when she and Frederick discuss the possibility of his being exonerated from his involvement in mutiny, Margaret passionately defends his defiance of authority: "You disobeyed authority—that was bad; but to have stood by, without word or act, while the authority was brutally used, would have been infinitely worse" (chapter XXXI). Margaret's social activism, which is not limited to philanthropy, the domain within which the middle-class women's involvement was restricted, extends to the sociopolitical sphere of the workers' rights and the industrialists' responsibilities for the welfare of their employees. Indeed, Margaret is responsible for Thornton's implementation of more humane working conditions in his mills and later on for his conviction and willingness to interact with his workers and to respect their opinions. In turn, Thornton convinces Mr. Colhurts, a member of parliament, that legislative measures protecting workers' rights may avert future strikes.

At the end of the novel the conventional theme of the wealthy bachelor's rescue of the woman in distress is reversed when Margaret rescues Thornton from his financial straits, thus becoming his business partner and his equal. When Thornton dismisses Mr. Lennox's offer to rescue him from his financial misfortunes, Margaret takes a traditionally masculine, assertive role and offers him her business proposal:

"You are unjust," said Margaret, gently. "Mr. Lennox has only spoken of
the great probability which he believes there to be of your redeeming—
your more than redeeming of what you have lost—don't speak till I have
ended—pray don't!" And collecting herself once more, she went on
rapidly turning over some law papers, and statements of accounts in a
trembling hurried manner. "Oh! here it is! and—he drew me out a proposal . . . showing that if you would take some money of mine, eighteen
thousand and fifty-seven pounds lying just at this moment unused in the
bank, and bringing me in only two and a half per cent, you could pay me
much better interest, and might go on working Malborough Mills."
(chapter LII)

More like a postmodern heroine, keenly aware of her own self-worth, protecting her own assets in the process of becoming involved with a potential lover and husband, just about signing a "prenuptial agreement,"
Margaret in no way resembles the Angel in the House confined within the
domestic sphere, condemned, like the Lady of Shalott, to the loss of identity once she asserts her own will or desire and ventures into the public
sphere. The scene simultaneously evokes Millais's *Order of Release* and
The Proscribed Royalist, both pictures in which women rescue persecuted
men and paintings that Gaskell highly admired. In a letter to John Foster
in late April 1853, a year before the publication of *North and South,* when
Millais was exhibiting these two paintings, she asks, "is not Millais's picture this year very beautiful?" (*Letters* 231).

Earlier in the novel Margaret is also instrumental not only in saving
Thornton's life but also in averting a violent riot. When his workers go
on strike and furiously demonstrate, threatening him by his own home,
"She only thought how she could save him. She threw her arms around
him; she made her body into a shield from the fierce people beyond"
(chapter XXII). The subject and the configuration of the scene evoke
Millais's immensely popular painting to critics and the public alike, *A
Huguenot, on St. Bartholomew's Day, Refusing to Shield Himself from Danger
by Wearing the Roman Catholic Badge* (1851–1852). Like the Huguenot,
who does not allow his lover to bind a white cloth around his arm identifying him as Catholic and thus enabling him to escape the massacre,
Thornton rejects Margaret's "shield": "Still, with his arms folded, he
shook her off" (ibid.), but later when she is wounded by a sharp pebble
thrown by one of the demonstrators, he "unfolded his arms, and held her
encircled in one for an instant." The Huguenot's arms also encircle his
lover as he tries with one to gently untie the white cloth she is binding
around it. However, whereas Millais's painting inscribes the conventional masculine and feminine roles by having the woman motivated by pas-

sion and the man by duty, Gaskell's redrawing of the painting reverses traditional roles by having the woman, Margaret, address the crowd and appeal to their reason: " 'For God's sake! do not damage your cause by this violence. You do not know what you are doing.' " By contrast, the outraged Thornton resorts to conventional gender boundaries to sway the mob's anger: " 'You do well,' said he. 'You come to oust the innocent stranger. You fall—you hundreds—on one man; and when a woman comes before you, to ask you for your sake to be reasonable creatures, your cowardly wrath falls upon her!' " (ibid.) Later on, once again guided by traditional gender roles (in the chapter titled "Mistakes Cleared Up"), Thornton proposes to Margaret, assuming that her action was motivated by feminine passion, a mistake that a shocked Margaret quickly clears up, to Thornton's distress and dismay. " 'Yes! . . . I do feel offended; and I think, justly. You seem to fancy that my conduct of yesterday . . . was a personal act between you and me; and that you come and thank me for it, instead of perceiving, as a gentleman would . . . *that any woman . . . would come forward to shield . . . a man in danger from the violence of numbers*' " (chapter XXIV, my emphasis). Once again Margaret asserts her subjectivity in defiance of conventional gender boundaries.

If a woman is to play an active role in the public sphere, as Gaskell through Margaret's positive contribution to the industrial North indicates, she must be educated in order to have a voice that will make a difference; furthermore, she must be respected as a man's equal and be treated as such. Although not a political figure, Margaret is quick to teach Thornton that wealthy industrialists are the new leaders of the Victorian world and as such need to exercise their authority, power, and wealth for the benefit of the people who work for them and for society at large. In Gaskell's view, sociopolitical reform must expand conventional boundaries and grant privileges to those whom hegemonic figures overlook. Female characters such as Mary, Ruth, Margaret, Sylvia, and Molly become representative of the multiple voices that traditional historiography has silenced. In their exchanges with male characters, we witness the disintegration of the boundaries between the public (or masculine) and the domestic (or feminine) spheres in times of sociopolitical change. Though traditionally relegated to the domestic sphere, women like Ruth and Margaret have the political vision that male characters like Bellingham and Thornton lack. The traditional dichotomy between the public and the domestic, Gaskell shows, collapses in times of change. Although the women in her novels and stories have no political rights, they become active social agents. Sociopolitical reform, Gaskell demonstrates, is too important to be left entirely to the prerogative of the already franchised; to be meaningful, social activism must begin within every person's domain of experience and must be carried out by the force of personal commitment.

Such characters are fictional representations of actual women like Harriet Taylor and Florence Nightingale, who at that time voiced the exigent need for women's social and legal rights. Through their social activism they broke the long-held silence that patriarchal ideology had imposed on women. Their hitherto suppressed voices were widely uttered through liberal journals like *The Westminster Review* and the novels of the period, like *Ruth* or *North and South*, which reached even larger audiences. Pre-Raphaelite paintings such as *Mariana* and *Ophelia*, however, were most likely seen by women writers like Elizabeth Gaskell as attempts to sabotage and silence emergent feminist voices and to confirm existing stereotypes of feminine passivity and vulnerability, endorsed by canonical writers such as Shakespeare and Tennyson. Yet they could also have been interpreted as visual representations of the patriarchal victimization of women and by extension as appeals for legislative measures that could avert further victimization and protect women from culturally endorsed inequities.

The collision between silence and articulation, poignantly expressed in *Ruth*, remained a problem in Gaskell's own private life as her letters, particularly those responding to hostile reviewers, attest. Yet Gaskell's simultaneously reticent and multifarious rhetoric invites us to explore more diligently the nuances and subtleties of her literary discourse. In *Ruth*, as well as in her other novels, that discourse takes on pictorial nuances as scenes in the novel reveal feminist reconfigurations of Pre-Raphaelite paintings, at times paradigmatic of her culture's representations of women and at other times subversive of conventional gender constructs. If we are to appreciate and recognize Gaskell's alternative possibilities for gendered subjectivity, we must also take into consideration the pictorial dimension of her narratives, for, as *Ruth* and *North and South* disclose, Gaskell's challenge to gender ideology is often embedded within subtle Pre-Raphaelite iconography.

CHAPTER THREE

Wilkie Collins's Reconfigurations of Pre-Raphaelite Gendered Shadows

C ollins's intimate and lasting friendship with John Everett Millais and William Holman Hunt, founders of the Pre-Raphaelite Brotherhood, is recorded in numerous letters to them as well as to friends and relatives.[1] Shortly after the formation of the Pre-Raphaelite Brotherhood, we find his support of their art in a letter to his publisher, Richard Bentley, where he suggests that Millais, Hunt, and his brother Charley (also a Pre-Raphaelite artist) draw the illustrations for his Christmas story, *The Mask of Shakespeare*. This letter reveals his conviction in the greatness of Pre-Raphaelite art at a time when denunciatory reviews raged in the press:

> I should propose that the three illustrations should be done by three young gentlemen who have lately been making an immense stir in the world of Art, and earned the distinction of being attacked by the Times (any notice *there* is a distinction)—and defended in a special pamphlet by Ruskin—the redoubtable *Pre-Raphael-Brotherhood!!*
>
> One of these "Brothers" happens to be *my* brother as well—the other two Millais and Hunt are intimate friends. For *my* sake as well as their own they would work their best—and do something striking, no matter on how small a scale. (*Letters* 1:73; October 23, 1851)

Certainly Collins could see that in spite of adverse criticism the Pre-Raphaelites would succeed once Ruskin became their fervent advocate. But even earlier that year, in a long, laudatory review of the 1851 Royal Academy Summer Exhibition, he had praised the fundamental Pre-Raphaelite principles: their "earnestness of purpose, their originality of thought, their close and reverent study of nature."[2]

71

Collins's admiration of Pre-Raphaelite painting and his conviction in
its superiority to contemporary Victorian art remained constant through
the years as attested in a letter he wrote to Hunt late in the century in
response to the exhibit of his paintings in 1886. Curiously enough, his
effusive comments are not dedicated to recent paintings but to a very
early one, *A Converted British Family Sheltering a Christian Missionary from
the Persecution of the Druids* (1849–1850), the subject of critical denigration when it was first exhibited. His remarks are worth quoting at length,
for they also reveal some of Collins's techniques in his own narrative art:

> My first impression, on entering the room, was of such a feast of magnif-
> icent colour as I had not seen since I was last at Venice. My next plea-
> sure was to study the pictures in detail. You know so well how incapable
> I am of flattering anybody—least of all, a dear old friend—that I shall say
> freely what is in my mind. As a painter of human expression, the most
> difficult of all achievements in your Art, there is no man among your liv-
> ing English Colleagues (and not more than two or three among the
> dead) who is fit to be mentioned in the same breath with you. To my
> mind, you are a great teacher as well as a great painter.
>
> With obstacles and discouragements which I lament, you are never-
> theless steadily doing good in teaching the people to see for themselves
> the difference between true art and false. Such a reform as this in the pop-
> ular Taste works, as we both know, insensibly on the popular mind, and
> clears its way slowly through the thousand modern obstructions of con-
> ventionality and claptrap. But the reform does go on. I saw some people
> silently wondering before the picture of the Christian priest, saved from
> the Druids. They consulted in whispers, and went on to the next picture.
> But the Priest had got them. They came back—and had another long
> look—and consulted again. Slowly and surely that fine work was plead-
> ing the good cause with people ignorant of the subtle beauty of it; but
> insensibly discovering its appeal to their sense of nature and truth. I am
> absolutely certain that the next Royal Academy Exhibition will not suc-
> ceed as well as usual in imposing on those innocent strangers. (*Letters*
> 2:521–22; July 24, 1886)

In this letter, written at the latter part of the century, when the Pre-
Raphaelites had finally gained the public's and the critics' recognition
and approbation, Collins emphasizes the principles that served as the
foundation of the Pre-Raphaelite Brotherhood: naturalism, unconventional subjects, emphasis on expression rather than beauty, the primary
principles that represented their resistance to the canonized aesthetics of
the Royal Academy. Hunt of course was the only founding member of the

Pre-Raphaelite Brotherhood to uphold these values to the end of his career, and Collins, as his close friend, was keenly aware of the essence of his art. In the process of appraising Hunt's art, however, Collins might also have been indirectly referring to those Pre-Raphaelite concepts that he himself pursued in his own narrative art, particularly in his later novels. Here I wish to discuss Collins's reconfigurations of Pre-Raphaelite modes of perception in his popular *Woman in White*, the novel Collins considered as his masterpiece, memorably encapsulated in his unique request to have its title inscribed on his tombstone: "Author of *The Woman in White* and other works of fiction" (Symons 7).

Like the realist novelists, putatively representing life accurately, Collins, though the founder of the sensation novel that capitalized on the mysterious, the macabre, and the sensational aspects of life, insisted on declaring his dedication to realism. In the "Preamble" of *The Woman in White*, for instance, he underscores the importance of his innovative approach to the novel in representing realism, accuracy, and "truth": "[T]he story here presented will be told by more than one pen, as the story of an offence against the laws is told in Court by more than one witness—with the same object, in both cases, *to present the truth always in its most direct and most intelligible aspect*" (5, my emphasis). Some critics have already commented upon Collins's emulation of Pre-Raphaelite realism, particularly his attention to minute details in his drawing of landscapes. Patricia Frick, for instance, observes that his interest in the Pre-Raphaelites' "strict adherence to the truth as it is in Nature, provided Collins with a sense of landscape, which enabled him in his later writings to establish his scenes with vivid effect."[3] Here I wish to explore Collins's new modes of perception developed in *The Woman in White*, originally represented in Pre-Raphaelite art, not merely in connection to landscapes but also in regard to identity formation and the extension of conventional gender boundaries.

No doubt Collins, like the other novelists discussed in this book, was keenly aware of the reviewers' demand for "visual" narratives. A contemporary reviewer's comments on *The Woman in White* are representative of the prevalent tendency to interpret novels in pictorial rather than narrative terms; in this case the reviewer points out what was to become for years a representative perspective on Collins's work: his convoluted plot construction at the expense of realistic and psychologically complex characters. "He does not attempt to paint character or passion," the reviewer contends; his characters "are not staring at the spectators, or, if they are, they are staring listlessly and vacantly . . . their eyes bent in one direction . . . half-painted, sketchy figures."[4] Undoubtedly Collins considered such critical expectations when he interwove in *The Woman in White*, as well as in his other narratives, contemporary artistic techniques and subjects.

Pre-Raphaelite Subjects in The Woman in White

The Woman in White, one of the most popular novels in Victorian England (published in four editions within the first month of its publication), was preceded by several Pre-Raphaelite women in white, depicting Victorian oppositions and contradictions: the virgin and the fallen woman.[5] Charley Collins's *Convent Thoughts* (1852), for instance, the painting Ruskin described as "Mr. Collins' lady in white" (*Works* 12:320–21), and the vulnerable, divine figure in Rossetti's *Ecce Ancilla Domini!* represent idealist conceptions of the Victorian woman as a virginal, pure, unattainable figure. Yet, women in white such as in Ford Madox Brown's *Take Your Son, Sir!* (1856–1857) or William Holman Hunt's *Awakening Conscience* (1854), as we have seen, disclose cultural anxieties about the other, in this case the fallen woman, the outcast.[6]

Besides these figures with whom Collins's woman in white shares affinities, several other Pre-Raphaelite subjects are also redrawn in his novel. Even a cursory look, for instance, at Rossetti's "haunting and somewhat bizarre drawing" *How They Met Themselves* (1850–1860), which depicts a couple in medieval costume meeting their doubles in a dark wood (Faxon 140–41), seems but an illustration of Collins's rendering of the doppelgänger theme in *The Woman in White.* Laura's reaction to Anne Catherick, when the two first meet in the boat house, is reminiscent of the facial expression of the fainting woman in *How They Met Themselves* when she meets her double. Like the meeting of the two figures, which takes place in the shadows of a forest at night, Laura's and Anne's encounter is also drawn in the darkness. Recounting that meeting to Marian, Laura describes her shock at the discovery of her resemblance to Anne: "While I was looking at her, while she was very close to me, it came over my mind suddenly that we were like each other! Her face was pale and thin and weary—but the sight of it startled me, as if it had been the sight of my own face in the glass after a long illness. The discovery— I don't know why—gave me such a shock, that I was perfectly incapable of speaking to her, for the moment."[7] And, as in the legend of doppelgänger, Anne dies after her encounter with her double, while Laura is presumed dead.[8] By transposing the illegitimate Anne Catherick with her respectable half-sister Laura Fairlie-Glyde, the outcast with the privileged, Collins undermines contemporary concepts of femininity, demonstrating that women, as long as they are kept uninformed, run the same risks whether they be outcasts or honored members of the upper classes.

On the other hand, John Everett Millais's drawing *Retribution* (1854), which, as Susan Casteras points out, depicts the ironic reversal of roles of the fallen woman, portrayed as a regal figure, and the respectable wife as a pitiful suppliant in a society ruled by a sexual double standard (*Images* 30–31), can also be seen as an illustration of the ironic reversals in *The Woman in White*. Certainly the pivotal situation in the novel seems to duplicate this tableau. Whereas Laura Fairlie, the upper-middle-class woman, is imprisoned in her own house by her husband, Sir Percival Glyde (who later on commits her to an asylum, where she is deprived of her own identity and property), Mrs. Catherick, "the fallen woman," mother of Laura's half-sister, enjoys respectability. Furthermore, because of Mr. Fairlie's infidelity, Anne Catherick and Laura Fairlie never know that they are sisters. Besides, Walter Hartright's passionate commitment to "unknown Retribution" (278), his pursuit of Sir Percival, which his love for Laura engenders, is a theme that unifies the various narratives of the novel.

Pre-Raphaelite Light and Shade

In addition to themes for the novel, Pre-Raphaelite paintings also provided Collins with ideas for his primary narrative technique in this novel, namely his treatment of light and shade. Early reviews of Pre-Raphaelite exhibitions reveal the Pre-Raphaelites' departure from traditional modes of perspective and treatments of light and shade. In 1849, for instance, a reviewer of the *Athenaeum*, responding to John Everett Millais's *Isabella* (1849) and William Holman Hunt's *Rienzi* (1849), proclaims that "the faults of the two pictures under consideration are the results of the partial views which have led their authors to the practice of a time when knowledge of light and shade and of the means of imparting due relief by the systematic conduct of aerial perspective had not obtained" and concludes "that hard monotony of contour" in *Isabella* is due to the "absence of shadow."[9] Two years later, an outraged reviewer in the *Times* of May 7, 1851, responding to an exhibition of Millais's *Mariana*, Collins's *Convent Thoughts*, and William Holman Hunt's *Valentine Rescuing Sylvia from Proteus*, censures the painters' eccentric techniques, particularly their disregard for the established rules of light and shade:

> Their faith seems to consist in *an absolute contempt for perspective and the known laws of light and shade*, an aversion to beauty in every shape, and a singular devotion to the minute accidents of their subjects, or rather seeking out, every excess of sharpness and deformity. . . . That morbid infatuation which sacrifices truth, beauty, and genuine feeling to mere eccentricity deserves no quarter at the hands of the public, and though the patronage of art is sometimes lavished on oddity as profusely as on higher qualities, these monkish follies have no more real claim to figure

in any decent collection of English paintings than the aberrations of intellect which are exhibited under the name of Mr. Ward.[10] (my emphasis)

This reviewer connects the Pre-Raphaelites' defiance of the established laws of light and shade with their unconventional representations of gender—"an aversion to beauty in every shape." Thus, as was often the case, this reviewer interweaves aesthetics with gender ideology. Though the reviewer notes that the Pre-Raphaelites' unorthodox treatment of perspective reveals hitherto concealed excesses of "sharpness and deformity," he fails to recognize the possibilities for new modes of perception that such an eccentric perspective may entail.

The extent of the reviewers' preoccupation with the violation of traditional renderings of light and shade, which continued through the 1850s, is also evidenced in the *Morning Chronicle* on April 29, 1854, in which a reviewer of Hunt's *Light of the World, The Awakening Conscience*, and Collins's *Thought of Bethlehem* focused on the shadow in the background of *The Awakening Conscience*, a relatively minor detail in such a heavily cluttered painting: "The complicated compound shadow in the mirror is also a mere piece of intricacy without any good or valuable effort" (cited by Hunt, *Pre-Raphaelitism* 1:406). Here the reviewer disregards the realistic effect of the woman's shadow reflected in the mirror, for the established laws of aesthetics of the time did not aim at naturalistic effects. Two years later the *Athenaeum*, reviewing Millais's *Autumn Leaves*, pointed out that Millais's style was no longer as finished as in his earlier paintings (even though such finish was the target of critical censure): "Though true to texture, his drawing is now frequently coarse and careless—his colour treacly and harsh, and his *shadows are heavy and disturbed*"[11] (my emphasis).

The lack of the conventional perspective in Pre-Raphaelite paintings, which had hitherto balanced and harmonized interplays of light and shadow, agitated contemporary reviewers for several reasons. To begin with, the interplay of light and shade in highly acclaimed paintings endorsed by the Royal Academy governed perspective by placing secondary figures and objects in the background, partially concealed by shadows and therefore less finished than the figures or objects in the foreground. Such configurations were artificially arranged, disregarding naturalistic effects. This artificial arrangement simultaneously established a hierarchical order within the painting that confirmed the spectators' own preconceived notions of hierarchical social structures, thus assisting them in their interpretations. Such guidelines, however, did not exist in Pre-Raphaelite paintings, which, instead of following the established laws of light and shade, depicted reality with scientific accuracy and treated subsidiary areas of the painting with the same meticulous care as that lavished on the primary figures. Thus the Pre-Raphaelite egalitarian and naturalistic, rather than hierarchical and artificial, representation of life made new demands on the spectators, compelling them to see hitherto overlooked details, further disturbing them by subverting their hierarchical modes of perception. Alone and unassisted, the viewer's glance moved from object to object, large and small, in the foreground and in the background without any recognized guidelines. Lacking a hierarchical order between primary and secondary figures, Pre-Raphaelite paintings compelled spectators to make decisions about meaning and interpretation alone, without any directive from the artist.

Aware of the Pre-Raphaelites' egalitarian treatment of their subjects, Collins in *The Woman in White* associated the Pre-Raphaelite technique of the innovative treatments of shade and light with new ways of seeing. To him, the Pre-Raphaelites were engaged with the project of initiating novel modes of perception; in effect, they were teaching their viewers to engage themselves with new ways of knowing and thus understanding the world and those around them. As we have already seen in his letter to Hunt regarding his early painting, *A Coverted British Family Sheltering a Christian Missionary from the Persecution of the Druids*, Collins extolled Hunt's talent as both a great teacher and a great painter and attributed to him the ability to teach "people to see for themselves the difference between true art and false." In the same letter, what Collins calls Hunt's "reform in popular taste" was essentially true of the collective Pre-Raphaelite project that complicated the simplistic and stark contrasts of conventional thought and subverted or conflated the prevailing binary gender oppositions of Victorian culture. In portraying women uncharacteristically and unexpectedly, Collins followed the general spirit of the Pre-Raphaelites. As with other Pre-Raphaelite women in white, Collins's woman represents attributes of both the virgin and the fallen. Similarly, the plotline of the novel seems to be built around role reversals so crucial in Pre-Raphaelite paintings. Assigning women stereotypical roles, the illegitimate and the privileged, the fallen and the respectable, the narrative progresses by withdrawing the roles it established and then reversing them, as is the case with Anne Catherick and Laura Fairlie. In this sense, the narrative underscores the arbitrary character of the standards around which social conventions shape people's understanding of each other.

Recent critics such as Balee, Bernstein, Elam, Langbauer, and Williams have focused on Wilkie Collins's subversion of Victorian stereotypes in *The Woman in White* but have overlooked the Pre-Raphaelites' effect on Wilkie Collins's representation of gender constructs.[12] Like the Pre-

Raphaelites who used light and shade to create new perspectives and to oblige their viewers to see things differently, Collins situates his characters in scenes that distort ordinary contents of perception and engender new ways of perceiving the external world. Unlike the Pre-Raphaelites, who used brushstrokes of light and shadow to give light to objects in the background and to enable viewers to see what ordinarily is partially concealed or lost in the background, Collins uses brushstrokes of light and shade to obscure objects in the foreground as well, thus concealing what normally appears in full view and distorting what usually stands in center stage and commands all the attention. Most often Collins positions his characters in scenes partially lit and partially darkened, surrounded by objects that viewers can hardly detect. His landscapes often evoke states of consciousness between waking and dreaming and forms of knowledge between the real and the imaginative.[13] Collins's reputation as the founder of the sensation novel may largely be attributed to the ways he adapted the Pre-Raphaelite techniques of representing scenes and characters to his narrative purposes. The Pre-Raphaelite influence on *The Woman in White* did not go unnoticed by contemporary critics. The *Critic*, for instance, noted "that there is an inclination of over-minuteness we cannot deny, but pre-Raffaelitism is in the ascendant."[14]

Pre-Raphaelite Modes of Perception

Even before the woman in white appears to Walter Hartright at the opening of the novel, we are aware of a landscape suffused with light and shade. As a teacher of drawing, Walter is naturally sensitive and receptive to his surroundings, describing them in Pre-Raphaelite interplays of light and shadow: "[T]he long hot summer was drawing to a close; and we, the weary pilgrims of the London pavement, were beginning to think of the cloud-shadows on the corn-fields, and the autumn breezes on the sea-shore" (6). Oppressed by the humidity, he decides to "stroll home in the purer air . . . to follow the white winding paths across the lonely heath" in the "mysterious light" of the moon. Hartright in a moonlit landscape—a half-lit, mysterious, and eerie setting, the scene before the appearance of the woman in white—is representative of Collins's ability to interweave the sensational with the realistic to the extent that one cannot be extricated from the other. As Hartright enjoys "the divine stillness of the scene," admiring "the soft alternations of light and shade . . . over the broken ground," he is startled by the sudden appearance of the solitary figure of Anne Catherick, the woman in white: "[T]here, as if it had that moment sprung out of the earth or dropped from the heaven—stood the figure of a solitary Woman, dressed from head to foot in white garments, her face bent in grave inquiry on mine, her hand pointing to the dark cloud over London, as I faced her" (19–20). Adapting the Pre-Raphaelite technique of light and shade to his own literary landscapes, Collins creates a scene where the sight of a person registers not as a human being but as a ghostly figure, a shadow—"an extraordinary apparition"—that partakes of the substantial and the ethereal, the conscious and the unconscious, the real and the possible (20). Anyone familiar with William Holman Hunt's popular painting *Light of the World*, "the most famous of all Victorian religious images,"[15] would have no difficulty seeing that Collins's woman in white, a ghostly figure silhouetted in the moonlight, her hand raised, pointing toward London, evokes Hunt's most famous painting.

In this painting Christ, his hand raised, knocking on a sinner's door, is captured in the moonlight, the moon in the background serving as his halo. It is entirely possible that Wilkie Collins had this painting in mind when he drew its literary transformation in *The Woman in White*. After all, he had observed Hunt working on this painting when he spent time with his brother Charley, John Everett Millais, and William Holman Hunt at Rectory Farm in Ewell in 1851 (Hunt, *Pre-Raphaelitism* 1:302). Collins must have been struck by the extraordinary circumstances of Hunt's work on the painting. True to the Pre-Raphaelite principle of representing nature accurately, Hunt worked from 9 PM to 5 AM, when the moon was full, in the light of a lantern suspended from a tree (Judith Bronkhurst in Parris, *The Pre-Raphaelites*, 119). Collins must have also known that "the character of the head was a composite taken from several male sitters . . . while Lizzie Siddal and Christina Rossetti sat for its colouring" (ibid.). In the hands of a Pre-Raphaelite artist, then, the creation of the image of the ultimate patriarchal figure became possible through the fusion of opposite genders.[16] It is not surprising that Collins would transform this representation of Christ into the image of a destitute woman—the other. Moreover, Collins's readers, who saw the woman in white as the narrative redrawing of *The Light of the World*, would also have been aware of Collins's subtle allusion to *The Awakening Conscience*, a painting that Hunt conceived as the "material interpretation of the idea in 'The Light of the World.' " "My desire," Hunt states, "was to show how the still small voice speaks to a human soul in the turmoil of life" (Hunt, *Pre-Raphaelitism* 1:347). Like *The Light of the World*, *The Awakening Conscience* represents a figure in white fraught with cultural contradictions and ambivalent messages, as we have already seen. Thus Collins, like his Pre-Raphaelite friends, further complicates the concept of the other by interweaving it with projections of cultural anxieties and contradictions.

In an attempt to master his bewilderment, Hartright responds to Anne's call for help by resorting to Victorian standards of respectability and conventional gender roles: "All I could discern distinctly by the moonlight, was a colourless, youthful face, meagre and sharp to look at, about the cheeks and chin; large, grave, wistfully-attentive eyes; nervous, uncertain lips; and light hair of a pale, brownish-yellow hue. There was nothing wild, nothing immodest in her manner: it was quiet and self-controlled . . . not exactly the manner of a lady, and, at the same time, not the manner of a woman in the humblest rank of life" (20–21). Indeed the details relating to Anne Catherick's appearance, "colorless, youthful face . . . large, grave, wistfully-attentive eyes," could very well be those describing Christ's face in *The Light of the World*. It is interesting to note that Ruskin's interpretation of the painting, in his May 5, 1854, letter to the *Times*, contains details Collins relates to Anne's appearance and role in the novel: "The legend beneath it is the beautiful verse,—'behold, I stand at the door and knock. . . .' On the left-hand side of the picture is seen this door of the human soul. . . . Christ approaches it in the night-time. . . . It is fast barred. . . . He wears the white robe, representing the power of the Spirit upon him. . . . Now, when Christ enters any human heart, he bears with him a twofold light: first the light of conscience . . . and afterwards the light of peace, the hope of salvation" (*Works* 12:328). From her first appearance till the end of the novel, Anne becomes a Christ figure, an integral part of Hartright's identity formation (his conscience, "the still small voice") and later a potent force in Sir Percival's and Count Fosco's lives.

Yet Collins takes the situation of the initial shock produced by the perception of a person eluding conventional categories to a greater extent than Hunt. For unlike Hunt, who is obliged to focus on the object of perception, Collins can as a novelist explore the full range of the effects that the object of perception can produce on the observer. Moreover, these effects, as we have seen in Collins's own response to Hunt's painting of the missionaries sheltering a priest from the druids, are not confined merely to the pleasure of seeing something new and atypical, but also, more importantly, to the capacity of seeing things in new and atypical ways, without "the obstructions of conventionality." The shock of Hartright's intriguing encounter with the woman in white initiates an identity crisis that is not resolved until the end of the novel. "Was I Walter Hartright?" he asks himself; "had I really left, little more than an hour since, the quiet, decent, conventionally-domestic atmosphere of my mother's cottage?" (23). His bewilderment may be partly explained by Anne Catherick's transgression of conventional gender and class boundaries. When, for instance, he consents to help her, he is astonished by her defiance of conventional feminine behavior: " 'You are very kind.' . . . The first touch of womanly tenderness that I had heard from her, trembled in her voice as she said the words; but no tears glistened in those large, wistfully-attentive eyes of hers, which were fixed on me" (22). In this case Anne does not meet Walter's preconceived notions of femininity; she is neither frail nor conventionally timid. Furthermore, Anne undermines the traditional dynamics of the gaze that dictate the male/female, spectator/spectacle, subject/object, hierarchical gaze relations.

Equally disturbing to Hartright is his inability to act out his own conventional role. Whereas the meeting creates a conventional situation, a woman in distress, a man coming to her rescue, Collins, like his Pre-Raphaelite friends, opts for the unconventional, depriving Hartright of the opportunity to affirm his masculinity by acting out the traditional role of the rescuer. Thus Collins intimates that Hartright's identity crisis is bound to the suspension of gender constructs during his extraordinary meeting with the woman in white. As the novel progresses, several incidents involving destabilizations of gender constructs constitute the most important phases of Hartright's journey toward identity formation.

Collins's representation of Walter's encounter with the woman in white revolves primarily around the effect that it produces on Walter. The scene, whose depiction follows the Pre-Raphaelite techniques of light and shade, sets the conditions that undermine the certainty associated with ordinary sense perception. Thus Walter, and the reader vicariously, is beset by unsettling questions: Is he seeing or imagining things? Is it the figure of a woman or a ghost that stands before him? Yet the limits Collins imposes on ordinary perception turn out to be the very conditions for seeing things differently. Precisely because Walter is caught between the dark and the light, the real and the imagined, the narrator intimates, he has an opportunity to see something new, to perceive reality without "the obstructions of conventionality." But because he does not yet trust what he sees, he lets convention and habit form the content of his perception; that is, he translates what he sees in terms of ready-made attributes and conventionally established roles. Thus from his perspective, Anne Catherick must be a lady or a servant, a woman in trouble or one in some kind of mischief. Restricted within conventional modes of perception, he does not realize that Anne may partake of both roles or of neither.

The full effect of the encounter culminates in Walter's bewilderment over his own role in this situation. Once again he resorts to traditional roles: He is either to rescue her and escort her to London or to report her to the authorities. Uncomfortable with the two conflicting notions that self-understanding evokes, Walter attempts to settle the conflict and step out of the gray area that has opened up before him, acting out one of his possible roles: He decides to see himself as a rescuer and proceeds to offer her his help. Partly accepting and partly rejecting it, Anne disappears, leaving Walter further overwhelmed. After Walter assists the woman in white to find a cab and get away, he is uneasy about his decision and confesses that he "was perplexed and distressed by an uneasy sense of having done wrong, which yet left me confusedly ignorant of how I could have done right" (27). Hartright's perplexity and bewilderment turn into torment when he realizes, after he sees her pursuers, that she has escaped from an asylum: "What had I done? Assisted the victim of the most horrible of all false imprisonments to escape; or cast loose on the wide world of London an unfortunate creature, whose actions it was my duty, and every man's duty, mercifully to control?" (28–29). Through these questions the narrator engages the readers' involvement in this extraordinary situation that may not be comprehended or resolved through conventional standards of conduct.

The initial encounter between Walter and Anne, then, turns out to be a mis-meeting, a failure on his part to come to terms with the ambiguity of perception or, more precisely, to turn an ambiguous perception into a resource for a new self-understanding. Realizing his failure, Walter experiences an identity crisis over a woman who will continue to haunt him until he learns to open his eyes and his thinking to the ambiguities in life. Through this sensational encounter and its impact on Walter, Collins may have attempted to dramatize the disorienting and somewhat bewildering effect the Pre-Raphaelites' unorthodox treatment of perspective or egalitarian distribution of light and shade often produced on their viewers. In addition, like the Pre-Raphaelites, Collins connects the effect of a sensational scene drawn in interplays of light and shadow to the very identity of the observer. For it is this event that sets off the process of identity formation that Walter will undergo throughout the rest of the novel. In order to understand who he is, Walter must learn to trust what he perceives (however unorthodox) and to shape his identity according to what he comes to know firsthand.

His first encounter with Marian at Limmeridge is yet another test of his conventional modes of perception, once again masterfully interwoven with his traditional gender notions. Like his initial mysterious and bewildering meeting with the woman in white, his first encounter with Marian is yet another failure and another mis-meeting. Here too Walter's perception is guided by stereotypical lenses that afford him ways of dealing with a person who does not fit preestablished molds and ready-made frames of knowledge. As Marian is standing by a window gazing outside with her back turned on Hartright, he is unable to see her, yet he indulges in the stereotypical male/female, spectator/spectacle, masculine/feminine, superior/inferior, subject/object gender binaries. From a distance, before he even meets her, her figure half concealed in shadows, Hartright's gaze objectifies, fragments, and appropriates Marian's body: "The instant my eyes rested on her, I was struck by the rare beauty of her form, and by the unaffected grace of her attitude. Her figure was tall, yet not too tall; comely and well-developed, yet not fat; her head set on her shoulders with an easy, pliant firmness; her waist, perfection in the eyes of a man for it occupied its natural place, it filled out its natural circle, it was visibly and delightfully undeformed by stays" (31). Gradually Walter's gaze turns Marian into an object of male desire. In the process Walter defines femininity within the conventional boundaries of masculinity: "The easy elegance of every movement of her limbs and body as soon as she began to advance from the far end of the room, set me in a flutter of expectation to see her face clearly." However, his anticipation is thwarted as she moves closer, for Marian's face transgresses conventional standards of feminine beauty, and thus Collins defuses the hierarchical dynamics of the gaze that cast Hartright as the subject and Marian as the object of desire: "She left the window—and I said to myself, The lady is dark. She moved forward a few steps—and I said to myself, The lady is young. She approached nearer—and I said to myself (with a sense of surprise which words fail me to express), The lady is ugly!" (31). Hartright's response echoes that of contemporary reviewers' who, as we have seen, often berated the Pre-Raphaelites' predilection for ugliness and disfigurement.

In this case his conventional expectation of conventional femininity is unsettled by the disjunction of femininity with masculinity. As such Collins's somewhat androgynous portrait is consciously Pre-Raphaelite: "The lady's complexion was almost swarthy, and the dark down on her upper lip was almost a moustache. She had a large, firm, masculine mouth and jaw; prominent, piercing, resolute brown eyes; and thick, coal-black hair, growing unusually low down on her forehead" (32). Indeed, Marian becomes a composite Pre-Raphaelite figure resembling Rossetti's "dark Venuses" with an "Amazonian body (often with enlarged hands)" and Hunt's "exotic, 'swarthy' models," which were the targets of the reviewers' racial slurs in the 1850s (Casteras, "Pre-Raphaelite Challenges," 29, 31). As Susan Balee has already pointed out, through the representation of the androgynous and strong-minded old maid, Marian Halcombe, Collins contributed to an existing sociopolitical demand for "a new ideal of womanhood" in place of the outdated Angel in the House.[17]

When Walter first meets Marian, however, he may perceive her only within the constrictive parameters of conventional gender boundaries. From a distance Marian is the stereotypical object of desire, a desirable form of femininity; from up close she is the typical "ugly" woman since her characteristics are stereotypically masculine. Oscillating from one type to the other, Walter cannot see between them or through them; thus he is unable at the time to recognize that Marian is neither conventionally feminine nor traditionally masculine, but her face and figure partake of both characteristics. Yet even on this occasion Hartright is struck by Marian's expression. As we have already seen, the early Pre-Raphaelites opted for the representation of unique modes of expression rather than conventional beauty. Her expression, Hartright remarks, "bright, frank, and intelligent—appeared, while she was silent, to be altogether wanting in those feminine attractions of gentleness and pliability, without which the beauty of the handsomest woman alive is beauty incomplete" (32). In Hartright's conventional perspective, Marian's feminine figure and "masculine form" are disconcerting incongruities akin to "the anomalies and contradictions of a dream" (ibid.). Relying on the Pre-Raphaelites' by then well-known transgressions of conventional femininity and masculinity, Collins produces a new type of ideal woman, a convergence of femininity and masculinity.

Marian gazing outside a window is reminiscent of John Everett Millais's popular *Mariana*, also standing in front of a window, anxiously waiting for her lover, who never returns. The choice of the name itself, Marian, seems a deliberate allusion to that painting. But unlike Mariana, who pines away for her lover and remains imprisoned, Marian's fierce independence from any romantic attachment enables her to become both Laura's and Hartright's rescuer. Initially unable to see beyond gender boundaries, Hartright eventually recognizes Marian's beauty beyond the boundaries of conventional constructs. When he decides to leave Limmeridge after he realizes the futility of his love for Laura, who is already engaged to Percival, he goes to bid Marian farewell and is struck by her warm sympathy: "She caught me by both hands—she pressed them with the strong, steady grasp of a man—her dark eyes glittered—her brown complexion flushed deep—*the force and energy of her face glowed and grew beautiful with the pure inner light of her generosity and her pity*" (125, my emphasis). Even though he still notices the masculine grasp of her hands, he now focuses on the beauty of her expression, thus, even if momentarily, perceiving her beauty, which his own restrictive gender boundaries initially concealed. At the end of the novel, though he sees himself instrumental in reinstating Laura's identity, he nevertheless realizes that his accomplishment would not have been possible without Marian's (conventionally masculine) rescue of Laura from the asylum and her protection from Sir Percival's and Count Fosco's schemes: "I was indebted to Marian's courage and Marian's love," (557) he admits when, after a few days' absence in search of clues for Percival's secret, he returns home, where Hartright, Marian, and Laura are hiding.[18] As Susan Balee has already demonstrated, "the first line in *The Woman in White* . . . presages what the novel is really about: the subversion of sexual stereotypes. Because this is the story of what a man with *a woman's patience* can endure, and what a woman *with the resolution of a man* can achieve" (211).

Initially attempting to extricate himself from the anxiety the woman in white entails, Hartright unwittingly becomes once again engaged in her predicament as her image becomes imperceptibly fused with that of Laura's when Walter first meets Laura in the summerhouse at Limmeridge. It is important to note that on this occasion, when Walter narrates his first meeting with Laura, he does not dwell on her physical appearance as he recalls her, but instead he describes his own watercolor which he has drawn in an attempt to capture his first impression of her. When we first meet Laura, then, it is not herself, but rather Walter's Pygmalion-like recreation of her. In its detail and the seemingly arbitrary placement of the shadow of her hat, with the emphasis Walter places upon it, this drawing very closely resembles a Pre-Raphaelite watercolor, as, for instance, Rossetti's *Meeting of Dante and Beatrice in Paradise* (1852), which depicts Beatrice in a lush landscape with the minute details of the blades of grass in the foreground and the leaves of the trees in the background. Beatrice faces Dante as she raises her headdress, the shadow of her right hand reflected in its lining. In a Pre-Raphaelite sensitivity to light and shadow, Walter draws our attention to the seemingly insignificant shadows in Laura's portrait, thus unconsciously fusing her image with that of Anne's.

> I look at it, and there dawns upon me brightly, from the dark greenish-brown background of the summer-house, a light, youthful figure, clothed in a simple muslin dress, the pattern of it formed by broad alternate stripes of delicate blue and white. A scarf of the same material sits crisply and closely round her shoulders, and a little straw hat of the natural colour, plainly and sparingly trimmed with ribbon to match the gown, covers her head, and throws its soft pearly shadow over the upper part of her face. Her hair is of so faint and pale a brown—not flaxen, and yet almost as light; not golden, and yet almost as glossy—that it nearly melts, here and there, into the shadow of the hat. (48–49)

Laura's features melting in the shadow of her hat, thus unconventionally casting a shadow on the focal point of his watercolor, evoke the seemingly arbitrary choice of Pre-Raphaelite interplays of light and shade.

Like the Pre-Raphaelites, who were often berated for the unabashed inclusion of blemishes in their representations of masculinity or femininity, Walter represents, somewhat apologetically, Laura's flaws: "It is hard to see

that the lower part of the face is too delicately refined away towards the chin
to be in full and fair proportion with the upper part; that the nose, in escap-
ing the aquiline bend (always hard and cruel in a woman, no matter how
abstractedly perfect it may be), has erred a little in the other extreme, and
has missed the ideal straightness of line" (49). Yet even though consciously Pre-Raphaelite, Walter's watercolor portrait of Laura at this point
involves Reynoldsian touches of idealism, thus revealing Walter's tendency
to allow his preconceptions to supersede his actual perceptions. Thus,
though he paints her portrait with the details requisite of Pre-Raphaelite art,
he encases Laura in the conventionally Victorian paradigm of the angel of
ideal feminine beauty, "the woman who first gives life, light, and form to
our shadowy conceptions of beauty, fills a void in our spiritual nature that
has remained unknown to us till she appeared" (50).

In this respect Walter's reading of his own portrait of Laura closely
resembles that of mainstream reviewers hostile to Pre-Raphaelites, who,
opposing Pre-Raphaelite unorthodox subjects, firmly upheld conventional standards of beauty, insisting that "the most beautiful soul must have the
most beautiful body" (Wornum 271). Considering Laura's conventional
role in the novel as the Angel in the House, we can see why Hartright's
Reynolds-like portrait here is appropriate: "and the eyes are of that soft,
limpid, turquoise blue, so often sung by the poets. . . . Lovely eyes in colour,
lovely eyes in form—large and tender and quietly thoughtful—but beautiful above all things in the clear truthfulness of look that dwells in their
inmost depths, and shines through all their changes of expression with the
light of a purer and better world" (49). Such idealization lacking in
Hartright's response to Anne Catherick's sister, who strikingly resembles
her, underscores Collins's awareness that gender is a relational construct
determined by socioeconomic conditions. Seeing her in the luxurious surroundings of the aristocratic Limmeridge House, Hartright defines Laura as
the ideal woman. By contrast, Anne Catherick, Laura's double, alone in the
street in the dark, lacks conventional beauty. Yet their figures become
interchangeable by the machinations of her husband, Sir Percival, and his
ally, Count Fosco. By transposing the illegitimate Anne Catherick with her
respectable half-sister Laura Fairlie-Glyde, the outcast with the privileged,
Collins further undermines conventional femininity, demonstrating that
women, as long as they are deprived of social and legal rights, run the same
risks whether they be outcasts or honored members of the upper classes.

As the novel progresses, Collins demonstrates that Laura Fairlie is representative of an outdated ideal of femininity—a fair lie—vulnerable to
abuse and exploitation. This is why Collins chooses Reynolds's principle
of ideal beauty when drawing Laura's portrait. Such a construct of femininity, Collins implies, is a vanishing, outdated, pernicious ideal, a rem-

nant of the past. Furthermore, Laura herself is certainly victimized by the past since her fate has been sealed through her promise to her dying father to marry Sir Percival Glyde, representative of corrupt and degenerate aristocracy. It is precisely truthfulness, honesty, innocence, and trust, the qualities Victorian society upholds as paramount to ideal womanhood, that Percival thoroughly exploits, incarcerating Laura in an asylum as Anne Catherick and depriving her of her identity in order to inherit her property.[19]

Walter's initial encounter with Laura, drawn in Pre-Raphaelite interplays of light and shadow, represents another mis-meeting fraught with contradictions and governed by preconceived stereotypes that determine and control perception. It is interesting to note that on this occasion, as Walter sets aside his Pre-Raphaelite perception in preference for the Reynolds-like idealization, he also unconsciously interweaves the ideal with the profane in the description of his irresistible attraction to Laura: "Lulled by the Syren-song that my own heart sung to me, with eyes shut to all sight, and ears closed to all sound of danger, I drifted nearer and nearer to the fatal rocks" (65). The juxtaposition of the angel with the siren is especially curious if we consider that at the time prostitutes were often compared to sirens. In a study of prostitutes in Liverpool, for instance, William Bevan warns young tradesmen of the danger of prostitution: "He lounges in lassitude about the neighborhood. He is allured by a syren voice that charms but to destroy. . . . He yields and is undone."[20] Once again Collins discloses the sociopolitical contradictions inherent in contemporary views of women; simultaneously the contrasting images reveal Collins's insight into human psychology—the other within the self.

A few hours after his first meeting of Laura, on the evening of the same day, while he and Marian try to fathom the mystery of the connection of the woman in white to Laura's mother, Walter is stunned to see Laura dressed in white, walking on the terrace, bathed in moonlight—a Pre-Raphaelite figure enveloped in light and shadow: "A thrill of the same feeling which ran through me when the touch was laid upon my shoulder on the lonely high-road chilled me again. There stood Miss Fairlie, a white figure, alone in the moonlight; in her attitude, in the turn of her head, in her complexion, in the shape of her face, the living image . . . of the woman in white! The doubt which had troubled my mind for hours and hours past flashed into conviction in an instant. That 'something wanting' was my own recognition of the ominous likeness between the fugitive from the asylum and my pupil at Limmeridge House" (60–61).

Stunned by Laura's extraordinary appearance in the moonlight, Walter refuses to trust what he perceives, consciously disregards Laura's striking resemblance to the woman in white, and tenaciously holds on to his earlier, stereotypical way of perceiving her as an ideal angel. Immediately he regrets his recognition of a resemblance between Anne and Laura, for, he thinks, "to associate that forlorn, friendless, lost woman, even by accidental likeness only, with Miss Fairlie, seems like casting a shadow on the future of the bright creature" (61). Yet Walter's endeavor to extricate himself from the social responsibility to the "forlorn figure" is futile the moment Laura's and Anne's images are interchanged.

Together these initial encounters, Walter's first meetings with Anne, Marian, and Laura, cast in Pre-Raphaelite interplays of light and shadow, or, in the case of Marian, representative of a much–resisted, Pre-Raphaelite representation of femininity more closely aligned with androgyny, deeply unsettle and disturb Walter's conventional notions of femininity and masculinity. Walter, much like the viewers of early Pre-Raphaelite paintings, at first resists new ways of perceiving the world but gradually realizes that in the process he also misses opportunities of understanding the self and the other or the other within the self. Walter's initial encounters with these women could then be considered as mis-meetings that frame the entire novel, underscoring both the enormous difficulty involved in perceiving the world the way it presents itself and the extraordinary courage required of people to rely on their own unmediated perception when the latter defies ready-made categories.

Indeed, secondary characters in the novel demonstrate how far people are willing to abide by conventional ways of experiencing the world. Gilmore, for instance, whose profession requires him to bracket preconceptions in the face of evidence, is far more comfortable with the safety that comes with conventional interpretation than with the risks involved in pursuing justice that might unsettle convention and habit. Justifying his conduct as "practical" by juxtaposing it with Walter's "romantic" view, Mr. Gilmore, Laura's lawyer, resists any doubts he himself experiences about Sir Percival's defense against Anne Catherick. When he is made uneasy by Marian's suspicions, Mr. Gilmore muses complacently, "in my youth, I should have chafed and fretted under the irritation of my own unreasonable state of mind. In my age, I knew better, and went out philosophically to walk it off" (137). Like Laura's uncle, who refuses to participate in drawing a marriage settlement that would protect her from Sir Percival's abuse and who later on prefers her dead lest a legal action to establish her identity disturb his "fragile nerves," Mr. Gilmore prefers his peace of mind to the pursuit of justice, the solipsist cocoon of individual complacency to social responsibility. In this respect he prefigures his successor, Mr. Kyle, who, though he believes that Laura has been the victim of a gross deception (imprisoned in an asylum as Anne Catherick and, after Anne Catherick's death, declared dead and deprived of all her legal rights), tells

Walter that he does not have "the shadow of a case" (450).

Undermining the contemporary social and gender hierarchy, Collins seems to enjoy playing with a series of contrasts and ironic situations, thus destabilizing traditional class and gender constructs. A destitute, vulnerable, seemingly outcast figure, Anne Catherick could be easily perceived as the guilty party. Wealthy, respectable, "a really irresistible man—courteous, considerate, delightfully free from pride—a gentleman, every inch of him" (147), Sir Percival Glyde, on the other hand, is beyond suspicion. Tradition becomes valorized and convention upheld even when all evidence points elsewhere. Hence Collins carries to the point of ridicule the successful claims to tradition by Percival and Fairlie.

Through his representations of Sir Percival and Fairlie, Collins also criticizes the contemporary corrupt and decadent manifestations of traditional constructs of masculinity. Indeed, Sir Percival's name evokes the Arthurian eponymous knight, distinguished for his innocence and chivalry, glorified by Tennyson. The cynical aspect of the allusion is underscored in a scene in the novel that takes place in Rome, when Laura and Sir Percival visit the tomb of Cecilia Metella, a memorial of her husband's love. "Would you build such a tomb for *me*, Percival?" Laura asks. "If I do build you a tomb," Percival sarcastically responds, "it will be done with your own money" (262). This scene with husband and wife leaning over a woman's tomb evokes "one of Rossetti's finest medieval watercolours," *How Sir Galahad, Sir Bors and Sir Percival Were Fed with the Sanc Grael; but Sir Percival's Sister Died by the Way*, whose design was based on the mural *The Attainment of the Sanc Grael*, painted for the library of the Oxford Union in 1857 (Wood, *The Pre-Raphaelites* 29). Here the three knights, bowing reverentially, receive the Grail from an angel at an altar; in this pose they seem to simultaneously pray for Percival's dead sister, who lies beneath them on the ground before her burial. In a letter to Charles Eliot Norton, Rossetti discussed his intention to have this mural as a companion to *Sir Launcelot's Vision of the Sanc Grail*. Unlike his father, Sir Launcelot, whose sin prevents him from attaining the Holy Grail, Rossetti explains, Galahad, his son, is allowed to reach it: "As a companion to this [*Sir Launcelot's Vision of the Sanc Grail*] I shall paint a design, which I have made for the purpose, of the attainment of the Sanc Grail by Launcelot's son Galahad, together with Bors and Percival (*Letters* 1: 337). As Poulson explains, the mural with Sir Galahad is a composite of two stories from *Morte d'Arthur*, that of Galahad and Percival's sister, who, "Christ-like, she gives her life to heal a lady who can be saved only by the blood of a virgin who is also a king's daughter" (85–86).

The narrative reconfiguration of Rossetti's watercolor adumbrates Laura's subsequent victimization and plotting for her death; at the same time it underscores the narrator's cynicism over idealized constructs of masculinity sanctioned by the aristocratic tradition. Collins further draws the ironic connection between King Arthur's knight and Sir Percival in his novel when the villagers, gathered around the burning church in which Percival perishes while attempting forgery, question his identity: " 'Who was he? A lord, they say.' 'No, not a lord. *Sir* Something; Sir means Knight' " (531). Thus Collins evokes a chivalric construct of masculinity only to cynically deconstruct it, in the process underscoring its obsoleteness in a highly materialist age.

Like Percival, Mr. Fairlie also represents the decadent, effete, and self-centered members of the aristocracy abiding by tradition and convention. Unlike Hartright, who jeopardizes his own life in his determination to restore Laura's identity, Mr. Fairlie, "nothing but a bundle of nerves dressed up to look like a man," completely detaches himself from her predicament as long as his own tranquility is preserved (356). It is not accidental that he is identified with the artists sanctioned by the Royal Academy, Raphael and Rembrandt. In fact, the first time Hartright meets him in the Limmeridge house, he instantly becomes aware of "a picture of the Virgin and Child, protected by glass, and bearing Raphael's name on the gilt tablet at the bottom of the frame" (39). By underscoring Fairlie's effeminate nature, perceived at the time as a deviation from masculinity, Collins once again associates tradition with decadence.

Unlike Percival, Fairlie, or Mr. Gilmore, Walter engages the doubts that come with the disjuncture between new perceptions and conventional forms of knowledge. The formation of his identity depends on his ability to undertake an honest self-examination in view of this disjuncture, a reorganization of his life in view of forms of knowledge that defy customary ways of thinking. Signs that he is beginning to extricate himself from the boundaries of preconceived notions appear in his second meeting with Anne at the cemetery. This scene evokes Pre-Raphaelite representations of rescue, yet it is destabilized by Anne's relative freedom from gender constraints that her unique situation has entailed.

When Hartright meets her in the cemetery, where she is cleaning the cross on Mrs. Fairlie's tomb, he is keenly aware of her resemblance to Laura, seeing her for the first time as Laura's double: "I had seen Anne Catherick's likeness in Miss Fairlie. I now saw Miss Fairlie's likeness in Anne Catherick. . . . Although I hated myself even for thinking such a thing, still, while I looked at the woman before me, the idea would force itself into my mind that one sad change, in the future, was all that was wanting to make the likeness complete. . . . If ever sorrow and suffering set their profaning marks on the youth and beauty of Miss Fairlie's face, then and then only, Anne Catherick and she would be the twin sisters of chance resemblance, the living reflexions of one another" (96–97). In this scene the narrator emphasizes Anne Catherick's posture, her kneeling by the cross, several times. When Hartright tries to speak to her, we are told, "she turned from me, and knelt down before the inscription once more" (97). At this point, in an attempt to garner information against Sir Percival, Hartright presents himself as Anne's rescuer: " 'You remember me?' I said. 'We met very late, and I helped you to find the way to London' " (95). When she refuses to cooperate, Hartright informs her that he knows she is the author of the anonymous letter she sent Laura, incriminating Sir Percival.

Anne's shocked reaction could very well describe details in Rossetti's painting *Found*: "She had been down on her knees for some little time past. . . . The first sentence of the words I had just addressed to her made her pause in her occupation, and turn slowly without rising from her knees, so as to face me. The second sentence literally petrified her. . . . [H]er lips fell apart—all the little colour that there was naturally in her face left it in an instant" (103). Anne here strikingly resembles the kneeling figure with the petrified, ashen face in *Found* who has turned her head toward the wall as her former fiancé tries to reclaim her. Even the response of the fallen woman in the painting, "Leave me—I do not know you—go away" echoes Anne Catherick's reaction to Hartright's intrusion (Faxon 64). Turning to the cross over Mrs. Fairlie's tomb, she murmurs, " 'Oh, if I could die, and be hidden and at rest with *you!*' " (103). However, unlike the fiancé in *Found*, who, leaning over the kneeling woman, attempts to rescue his former sweetheart, Hartright, instead of a rescuer, unwittingly becomes a pursuer, for Anne springs to her feet and disappears from his sight. Thus Collins once again undermines a stereotypical representation of masculinity by defusing the power that traditional gender relations ascribe to men. At the same time, however, he connects Hartright's identity with the woman in white. As in her first sensational appearance in the light and shadows of the moonlight, here Anne Catherick disappears in the lengthening shadows of twilight: "I looked after Anne Catherick as she disappeared, till all trace of her had faded in the twilight—looked as anxiously and sorrowfully as if that was the last I was to see in this weary world of the woman in white" (107).

Catherick's mystery haunts Hartright during his adventure in Central America, where he escapes after confessing to Marian his love for Laura and discovers that she is already engaged to Percival. The arduous journey, the distance and time, he believes, may efface his feelings for Laura. At that time, Marian's prophetic dream depicts Walter's struggle with Eros and Thanatos, prefiguring his eventual rebirth; simultaneously, the dream conveys a fusion of the real and the imaginative or possible. In this exotic dream Walter appears in a landscape drawn in Pre-Raphaelite touches of light and shade cast by immense tropical trees that "shut out the sky, and threw a *dismal shadow* over the forlorn band of men on the steps. *White exhalations* twisted and curled up stealthily from the ground" (278). Later on, in the same dream Walter appears "kneeling by a tomb of *white* marble, and the *shadow* of a veiled woman rose out of the grave beneath, and waited by his side" (279, my emphasis). Thus, once again, the Pre-Raphaelite "soft alternations of light and shade," against which Walter's meeting of the woman in white first occurred, highlight this important episode that prefigures Sir Percival's deception, the burial of Anne Catherick as Lady Glyde.

When Walter resumes the narrative after his return from Central America, he seems to celebrate his higher state of consciousness signaled by his symbolic death in Marian's dream. Through his social involvement, his determination to vindicate Laura and thus become fully involved in exposing the deplorable inefficiency of the legal system, Walter emerges as a reborn figure, a self-reliant, self-assured individual, seemingly disengaged from tradition, believing that "in the stern school of extremity and danger my will had learnt to be strong, my heart resolute, my mind to rely on itself" (415).

After this recognition, the following scene in the cemetery, where he believes Laura is buried, is yet another transformation of his initial encounter with the woman in white; in fact, his reaction to Laura's touch is almost identical to that of the mysterious shadow: "[T]he springs of my life fell low, and the shuddering of an unutterable dread crept over me from head to foot" (419). In this case, however, Walter does not resist the call, does not attempt to extricate himself from social responsibility, but undertakes the seemingly impossible task of vindicating Laura, which he realizes may be possible only through his subversion of tradition and convention: "through all risks and all sacrifices—through the hopeless struggle against Rank and Power, through the long fight with armed deceit and fortified Success, through the waste of my reputation, through the loss of any friends, through the hazard of my life" (422). When, following her imprisonment and escape from the asylum, Laura strikingly resembles Anne, Hartright no longer resists his perception but sorrowfully accepts the similarity:

> The outward changes wrought by the suffering and the terror of the past had fearfully, almost hopelessly, strengthened the fatal resemblance between Anne Catherick and herself. In my narrative of events at the time of my residence in Limmeridge House, I have recorded, from my own observation of the two, how the likeness, striking as it was when viewed generally, failed in many important points of similarity when

tested in detail. . . . The sorrow and suffering which I had once blamed myself for associating even by a passing thought with the future of Laura Fairlie, *had* set their profaning marks on the youth and beauty of her face; and the fatal resemblance which I had once seen and shuddered at see-ing, in idea only, was now a real and living resemblance which asserted itself before my own eyes. (442–43)

Thus Hartright at this point reconciles the hitherto tormenting disparity between his conventional ways of knowing and his new perceptions and recognizes the necessity of thinking beyond conventional class and gen-der boundaries. Finally he stands determined to risk all of the safety that convention provides in order to vindicate Laura's identity.

His journey toward identity formation concludes with the most impor-tant event in Hartright's struggle for Laura's vindication, an event that coincides with his ability to rely on his own perception. In the nightmar-ish scene of the church vestry fire, where Sir Percival (the secret of his illegitimacy having been discovered) tries to surreptitiously add the names of his parents to the church marriage register but accidentally starts a fire with his lantern, Hartright responds instinctively to an unforeseen situation by renouncing his passionate commitment to retri-bution—a traditional construct remnant of the chivalric age. Like the sudden appearance of the woman in white, the sudden fire represents another call, another temptation to gratify the ego by letting Sir Percival burn to death. Nevertheless, unlike the first occasion, when Walter relies on convention by seeking to ascertain Anne Catherick's respectability before he offers help, this time Walter immediately responds to his per-ception of danger and tries to rescue Sir Percival: "I rushed to the door. The one absorbing purpose that had filled all my thoughts, that had con-trolled all my actions, for weeks and weeks past, vanished in an instant from my mind. All remembrance of the heartless injury the man's crimes had inflicted; of the love, the innocence, the happiness he had pitilessly laid waste; of the oath I had sworn in my own heart to summon him to the terrible reckoning that he deserved—passed from my memory like a dream. I remembered nothing but the horror of his situation. I felt noth-ing but the natural impulse to save him from a frightful death" (527).

The description of the scene of Hartright's attempted rescue evokes yet another Pre-Raphaelite painting, Millais's *Rescue* (1855), which depicts a fireman rescuing two children from a fire and delivering them to their anguished mother, a scene illuminated by the intermittent light and shadow cast by the fire in the background. The red glare of the fire permeates the entire painting, illuminating the faces of the subjects. Millais worked fever-ishly on this painting to meet the deadline for the exhibition, and with the help of Wilkie Collins's brother, Charley, who painted the water hose, he was able to complete it in time (Malcolm Warner in Parris, *The Pre-Raphaelites*, 132).

Unlike Millais's painting, which celebrates heroic masculinity and iconographically delineates gender power relations by casting the fireman, carrying the two children, as the rescuer, towering above the distraught mother, who longingly reaches out for her children, Collins's narrative redrawing of a similar scene defuses masculine power by emphasizing Hartright's helplessness and powerlessness at rescuing Percival, who dies in the fire. In an interplay of light and shadow and the mysterious atmosphere it evokes, Collins reconfigures a conventional scene representing traditional gender relations into an unconventional situation, a man attempting a heroic feat but ultimately defeated by forces beyond his control. At the same time, however, Hartright at this point trusts his own perception, refusing to submit to conventional notions of retribution. It is not accidental that a sense of renewal permeates the last part of the novel.

Rebirth follows death as the novel closes in the springtime and Walter traces the full circle of his journey: "From their long slumber, on her side and on mine, those imperishable memories of our past life in Cumberland now awoke, which were one and all alike, the memories of our love" (570). Yet Hartright's marriage to Laura, who exhibits no mental or psychological growth by the end of the novel and still remains representative of conventional femininity in spite of the ordeals she has suffered, is somewhat of an anticlimax, casting doubts on any conjectures about Hartright's new level of consciousness. Disappointment with the ending of the story, particularly with its return to a conventional order after the subversion of tradition and the suspension of conventional gender relations, has been expressed by several critics, most notably by Nina Auerbach, who appropriately calls Laura "the nebulous, incompetent heroine" (135). Carl Jung's explanation of a man's love choice may explain Hartright's marriage to Laura: "[M]an, in his love-choice, is strongly tempted to win the woman who best corresponds to his own unconscious femininity—a woman, in short, who can unhesitatingly receive the projection of his soul. Although such a choice is often regarded and felt as altogether ideal, it may turn out that the man has manifestly married his own worst weakness."[21] Few readers would dispute that Laura represents Hartright's worst weakness—lack of individualism. This is perhaps one of the reasons that Collins chooses the strong-minded and independent Marian, holding Laura's and Hartright's child, as the focal point of the closing scene narrated by Hartright: "So she spoke. In writing those last words, I have written all. The pen falters in my hand; the long, happy labour of many months is over! Marian was the good angel of our lives—

let Marian end our Story" (643). Yet the traditional Victorian closure of the novel, the marriage of Hartright to Laura, discloses Collins's keen sensitivity to the forces of the marketplace, simultaneously revealing his exquisite ability to gratify his middle-class readers while severely criticizing them. Once again, however, at the end of the novel, Collins displays his Pre-Raphaelite ability to interweave the conventional with the unconventional. Though the ending does not culminate in a complete rejection of gender stereotypes toward which the novel moves, nevertheless it is representative of a new symbolic order, as Diane Elam has already observed, for the marriage of Hartright, the impoverished, self-reliant, and defiant drawing master, to an heiress "effects a change from an old to a new social order, legitimizes a new genealogical order in preference to the impotent tradition Sir Percival represents" (54).

Wilkie Collins often attempted to gain recognition as a literary artist, the founder of the sensation novel that moved beyond the limits of the realistic without violating realism. As Jenny Bourne Taylor states, Collins has been recognized as a novelist who "breaks down stable boundaries between wildness and domesticity, self and other, masculinity and femininity, 'black' and 'white.' Moreover, his stories involve not only complex explorations of forms of perception, of consciousness and cognition, but also of the shaping of social identity" (1). The new ways of seeing initiated by the Pre-Raphaelites, Collins demonstrates, are essential to an understanding of the self and the other, crucial to identity formation. In the liberating dream space of the sensation novel, Collins successfully undermines Victorian society, which displaces women by either apotheosizing them as angels or condemning them as outcasts—in either case confining them within conventional gender boundaries. Through his emphasis on Walter's mysterious entanglement in someone else's fate—an outcast, the illegitimate daughter of a fallen woman—Collins, like his Pre-Raphaelite friends, fuses the shadow of the other with the self, exploring psychological anxieties generated by the incongruities inherent in conventional gender constructs. Drawing like his Pre-Raphaelite friends' landscapes and portraits in hitherto Pre-Raphaelite unconventional alternations of light and shade, Collins underscored the significance of new perceptions beyond the constrictive boundaries of tradition.

Through the Pre-Raphaelite paintings Collins evokes and redraws in *The Woman in White*, he compelled his "audiences to reconsider what was decorous or 'correct' in art as well as private life" (Casteras, "Pre-Raphaelite Challenges" 32). In a letter addressed to a friend on November 26, 1887, he explained that the central idea of *The Woman in White* was the destruction and the recovery of a woman's identity (*Letters* 2: 545). The question of a woman's identity seemed to have gradually evolved to the subject of gender identity, Collins's central preoccupation in *The Woman in White*, particularly gender defined beyond the stereotypical Victorian boundaries. As Susan Balee argues, *The Woman in White* subverts "Victorian sexual stereotypes (the angel in the house, the manly man) in order to promote new icons. *The Woman in White* actively works to dismantle old myths of sexuality in order to construct new ones that would be of greater use to an economically-altered society" (201–202). Some of these new icons were represented in Pre-Raphaelite paintings of the period, but Collins further revised these representations by redrawing them in his novel and thus demonstrating that even the seemingly unorthodox Pre-Raphaelite representations of gender were at times framed within restrictive gendered boundaries. Wilkie Collins's narrative reconfigurations of these paintings give us insights into not only his novel but also literary history and nineteenth-century gender conflicts. If we are to fully appreciate Collins's disguised criticism of his culture's conventional gender constructs, then we must take into consideration the Pre-Raphaelite dimension of his narratives. Indeed, *The Woman in White* seems to orient us toward a new perspective on Collins's challenge to gender constructs inextricably bound with modes of perception, some of which his Pre-Raphaelite friends initiated.

CHAPTER FOUR

George Eliot's Pre-Raphaelite Gendered Imperialism

George Eliot's expressed interest in the Pre-Raphaelites dates since the early years of the Brotherhood, in 1851, when she visited the Royal Academy Exhibition. In 1852, as we have seen, she wrote to John Chapman that she was envious of an article appearing in the *British Quarterly* in praise of the Pre-Raphaelites (Haight 1968, 107). In 1854 she reviewed John Ruskin's *Lectures on Architecture and Painting* in the *Leader*. The fourth of these lectures, according to Eliot, expressed Ruskin's "latest 'mission' . . . the interpretation of the Pre-Raphaelite principles" and exalted the Pre-Raphaelites for their naturalistic and realistic details in their paintings (545). By 1856, she had internalized the Pre-Raphaelites' perspective on landscapes, as she records in her Ilfracombe journal: "I have talked of the Ilfracombe lanes without describing them, for to describe them one ought to know the names of all the lovely wild flowers that cluster on their banks. Almost every yard of these banks is a 'Hunt' picture—a delicious crowding of mosses and delicate trefoil, and wild strawberries, and ferns great and small" (Harris and Johnston 272).

The various Pre-Raphaelite paintings Eliot used to guide her own portrayals of her fictive characters, especially in her work from 1856 to 1871, are briefly documented in recent scholarship. Joseph Nicholes, for instance, identifies John Everett Millais's *Mariana* with images of Dorothea in *Middlemarch*; Andrew Leng notes the transformation of *The Awakening Conscience* in *Middlemarch*. Several other scholars have briefly noted the Pre-Raphaelite qualities in her novels. According to Gillian Beer, for example, Dorothea's first portrait in *Middlemarch* is that of "a genuinely pre-Raphaelite Madonna" (102). Will's thought of a "world apart, where the sunshine fell on tall white lilies," is considered by Gordon Haight to be an allusion to Pre-Raphaelite poems and paintings

(1973, 33). Hugh Witemeyer traces the Pre-Raphaelite influence in Eliot's novels more extensively, yet, like other critics, overlooks its presence in *Daniel Deronda*.

As Leonée Ormond has already remarked, George Eliot's interest in the Pre-Raphaelites was both ongoing and developing: "George Eliot's statements on the work of the Pre-Raphaelite group are entirely appropriate to the history of the movement. She began by writing of them as part of an exciting new trend, and by concentrating on the work of Hunt, arguably the member who most closely obeyed the rules of the brotherhood. Very shortly, however, she began to think of the painters separately, and to judge Pre-Raphaelite works on an individual basis. Her response to the work of Burne-Jones suggests that she had, at least by 1873, become less concerned with realism and more open to concepts of symbolism and mood creation" (2000, 313).

In this chapter I extend the scope of the Pre-Raphaelite presence in George Eliot's fiction by demonstrating that her fascination with Pre-Raphaelite paintings continues in her last novel, *Daniel Deronda*, where images of Gwendolen may be perceived as narrative reconfigurations of paintings of women by Dante Gabriel Rossetti and Edward Burne-Jones. In addition, I also argue that the Pre-Raphaelites' impact on Eliot's *Daniel Deronda* is significantly different from that on her earlier novels.

Part of this difference may be accounted for by the fact that Eliot met Edward Burne-Jones and Rossetti and became seriously interested in their work fairly late in her career. Indeed, it was only four years before beginning *Daniel Deronda* that Eliot first met Rossetti, when Burne-Jones brought him to the Priory in January 1870 (*Letters* 5:78). A mere four days after this meeting, she went to see Rossetti's paintings, including *Pandora*, *Beatrice*, *Cassandra*, and *Mrs. Morris* (ibid.). The Jane Morris paintings were *Mariana* (1868–1870) and *La Pia dé Tolomei* (1868–1880) (Nicholes 104). Eventually, these paintings, which reflect Rossetti's ongoing preoccupation with heroines from myth and literature, found their way into *Daniel Deronda*. Additionally, these paintings also represent a new direction in Rossetti's art toward classical revival, espoused by other Pre-Raphaelites and most importantly by Burne-Jones. Eliot's changed relation to Pre-Raphaelite art, then, may have resulted from her recent exposure to new individual paintings as well as to the group's changing trends.

Indeed, Eliot's shifting attitude and developing understanding of Pre-Raphaelite art is suggested by the renewed excitement she expressed toward Burne-Jones's work, with which she had been familiar for a number of years through her frequent visits to his studio. Georgiana Burne-Jones records the intimate friendship that she and her husband enjoyed with Eliot, noting her husband's admiration for Eliot's work and for her intellectual power. Burne-Jones himself confirmed this admiration when he wrote in reference to her that "there is no one living better to talk to . . . for she speaks carefully, so that nothing has to be taken back or qualified in any way. Her knowledge is really deep, and her heart one of the most sympathetic to me I ever knew" (Georgiana Burne-Jones 2:4). In turn, Eliot lavishly expressed her appreciation of Burne-Jones's work on several occasions. However, after her 1873 visit to his studio (a year before she began to write *Daniel Deronda*) her enthusiasm toward him took a new turn. In a letter occasioned by that visit, she attempts to express the new understanding that she was forming toward his work:

> It would be narrowness to suppose that an artist can only care for the impressions of those who know the methods of his art as well as feel its effects. Art works for all whom it can touch. And I want in gratitude to tell you that your work makes life larger and more beautiful to me—I mean that historical life of all the world in which our little personal share often seems a mere standing room from which we can look all round, and chiefly backward. Perhaps the work has a strain of special sadness in it—perhaps a deeper sense of the tremendous outer forces which urge us than of the inner impulse towards heroic struggle and achievement: but the sadness is so inwrought with pure elevating sensibility to all that is sweet and beautiful in the story of man and in the face of the earth, that it can no more be found fault with than the sadness of midday when Pan is touchy—like the rest of us.
>
> I cannot help telling you a sign that my delight must have taken a little bit the same curve as yours. Looking, *a propos* of your picture, into Iphigenia in Aulis to read the chorus you know of, I found my blue pencil marks made seven years ago . . . against the dance-loving Kithara, and the footsteps of the Muses and the Nereids dancing on the shining sands. I was pleased to see that my mind had been touched in a dumb way by what has touched yours to fine utterance. (ibid. 2:31)

What occasioned this letter and sparked her enthusiasm is the quality of drama Eliot perceived in Burne-Jones's work. She considers his work classic enough to capture human drama in its most basic form and popular enough to speak to all human beings open to its effect, not just to technical experts. Eliot locates the particular appeal of Burne-Jones's art in his ability to position viewers in a vantage point from which it becomes possible to witness the larger forces of history colliding with individual struggles. From such a vantage point—which she associates with the "special sadness" of tragic knowledge—viewers "can look all around, and chiefly backward," gain "a deeper sense of the tremendous outer forces," and presumably reach an understanding as to why a particular conflict ended up in disaster, as well as what one could have done to avoid being crushed by the larger forces of history. The relation between great drama and historical understanding that Eliot assigns to Burne-Jones's work is also hinted at by her reference to *Iphigenia in Aulis*, her use of his "picture" as an angle to read this drama, and her discovery that this dramatic work has deeply touched them both. All this leads us to presume that Eliot sees Burne-Jones following in the footsteps of the great dramatist Euripides. Perhaps she considers both to be creating the kind of drama that exposes their subjects' illusions and, in the process, paves the way for an audience to gain the historical understanding that their protagonists lacked. Perhaps she sees the tragedy of Agamemnon, humanized by the pen of Euripides, as a case of misreading history—a great king sacrificing his daughter under the illusion that political bonds in his society have a far greater significance than familial bonds.

If this reading of Eliot's letter is tenable, then we may assume that Eliot emphasizes an understanding of Pre-Raphaelite art that extends her previous interest in forging a link between literature and painting in the direction of history. At this point she underscores the significant role historical knowledge plays in dramatic representations whether literary or visual. Evidently she regards as great those artists who depict human conflicts in ways that expose the control of mythical and magical forces on their subjects' imagination, thereby clearing the way for people to understand how their own "inner impulses" can be aligned in congruence with the "outer forces" of history. Indeed, as I argue, Edward Burne-Jones represents some of the key concepts that Eliot develops in her last novel; specifically, his painting *The Wheel of Fortune* (1875–1883) (plate 10) is the locus of the Pre-Raphaelite effect on *Daniel Deronda*. I also contend that, more than Burne-Jones, Eliot is interested in the potential that historical understanding carries as a social corrective. Her mild criticism of his work as having "a strain of special sadness in it," because it places a greater weight "on the tremendous outer forces" than on "the inner impulse toward heroic struggle," is telling of her own view that historical understanding need not necessarily lead to tragic knowledge. Her own preference, she implies, is to approach historical understanding as a corrective to societal illusions and as a resource for averting tragedy. Her disagreement with Burne-Jones, then, is over the question of human agency. As we will see, she prefers to depict "the inner impulse toward heroic struggle and accomplishment" as having the potential to materialize, provided people are guided by historical self-understanding.

To be sure, this new role the Pre-Raphaelites play in her fiction does

Plate 10. Edward Burne-Jones, *The Wheel of Fortune*, 1875–1883. Oil on canvas, 78 ³/₈ x 39 ³/₈ in (199 x 100cm), London Borough of Hammersmith and Fulham, Archives and Local History Centre. Reproduced by permission.

not represent a complete break from their earlier one. As with her previous novels, so with *Daniel Deronda,* Eliot looks to Pre-Raphaelite painting techniques as sources for her narrative strategies and to their subjects
as inspiration for her literary portraits. What is new about this stage in her
writing is the level of complexity she introduces to her already successful
ways of merging literature and painting. Furthermore, that complexity, as
the narrator of *Daniel Deronda* indicates, is inevitable when history is
added to the amalgamation. Indeed, the connection between storytelling
and portrait painting is vividly illustrated in the novel when the narrator,
having drawn a splendid image of Gwendolen in her archery dress, comments on that image as appropriate subject matter for a great painter.

Casting images of fictive characters as possible portraits by famous
painters is, by the time of *Daniel Deronda,* a commonplace gesture in the
novels of the period. What is atypical in this case is the narrator's invoca-
tion of history as a necessary constituent of the link between storytelling and
painting: "[I]t was the fashion to dance in the archery dress, throwing off
the jacket; and the simplicity of her white cashmere with its border of pale
green set off her form to the utmost. A thin line of gold round her neck, and
the gold star on her breast were her only ornaments. Her smooth soft hair
piled up into a grand crown made a clear line about her brow. Sir Joshua
would have been glad to take her portrait; and he would have had an easi-
er task than the historian at least in this, that he would not have had to represent the truth in change—only to give stability to one beautiful
moment."[1]

Why does the narrator, who invites readers to imagine the image of
Gwendolen they have just read next to a painter's portrait of Gwendolen,
feel compelled to address a historian's handling of this same image?
Clearly the narrator thinks that a painter alone cannot do justice to what
the narrative has been conveying about Gwendolen and that the two of
them, painter and historian, must put their quite different talents together if they are to capture the kind of storytelling the narrator is aiming at.

As the narrator indicates, capturing the image of Gwendolen and of
the artistic ends assigned to that image by the narrative would also
require the talents of a historian and the much more difficult task of representing "the truth in change"—one of the major achievements of Pre-
Raphaelite art. In other words, it would take a historical sensibility to
show how this particular image has been aligned vis-à-vis the "outer
forces" of history at that particular moment, given that the ever-shifting
rhythm of history subjects such an alignment to the changes of time. In
obvious tension with the stability that a traditional painter would give to
Gwendolen's image, then, the narrator is also calling for a representation
of the true value of that image, a truth that can be understood only as

fleeting, time bound as well as context bound, a "truth in change." In Eliot's view it is one thing to have a Pre-Raphaelite painter capture Gwendolen's beauty at that moment, a beauty that radiates the confidence of a winner-to-be and the assurance of a beautiful woman about to make the two conquests she prizes the most—the championship of the archery contest and the heart of Grandcourt. It is quite another to contextualize Gwendolen's beauty as the only resource available to her in a world that valorizes women on that basis alone or to align Gwendolen's "inner impulse" for power with the "outer forces" of history that are compelling people in her world to grow and prosper at the expense of one another. Only a painter with an eye for history could contextualize Gwendolen's beauty in such a way as to position viewers in a vantage point from which they could see that the same illusions (and misreadings of history) that sustain their own society's struggles for power and prosperity along the lines of imperial conquest also support Gwendolen's struggle for power and conquest. In a word, it would take Burne-Jones, not Sir Joshua, to capture Gwendolen's beauty and to present this image as "truth in change."

Joining Rossetti and Burne-Jones in their turn toward classical revival, Eliot depicts her protagonist's thirst for power along the lines of legendary and literary heroines who provided classic examples of women obsessed with power. At the same time, she seeks to contextualize the representations of her heroine by casting Gwendolen's thirst for power as the inevitable outcome of the forces controlling the world she lives in. As a result, Eliot's aesthetic representations of women become socially pertinent to the readers of her novel who, at a time of an expanding British Empire, may reach an understanding of women as colonized others. Drawing on the aesthetic strength of Rossetti and the dramaturgic energy of Burne-Jones, Eliot transforms stereotypes of women into people who are shaped by the historical necessity that propels the underprivileged and unauthorized to acquire and wield power.

Eliot's Narrative Theory and the Pre-Raphaelite Germ

Before examining Eliot's representations of women, it is worthwhile noting that Eliot's emphasis on a socially oriented aesthetic in her representations of characters in her last novel has been partly shaped by her ongoing and shifting relation to Pre-Raphaelite aesthetics. As I have already suggested, the Pre-Raphaelites' impact on her work does not really lend itself to a clear-cut division between an early and a late one. The developing nature of a Pre-Raphaelite effect on her narrative theory becomes most apparent in her steady efforts to build her narrative techniques around the Pre-Raphaelite notion of "the germ." One of the most notable aspects of Pre-Raphaelite aesthetics, "the germ," captured their commitment to an art that would seek above all else to convey the expression of intense emotions. As we have already seen, the short-lived, Pre-Raphaelite publication, *The Germ* (a title chosen out of sixty-five proposed names),[2] originally subtitled *Thoughts Towards Nature in Poetry, Literature and Art* (only to be renamed *Art and Poetry, Being Thoughts Towards Nature, Conducted Principally by Artists*), extended the relevance of the germ to other arts, such as poetry and narrative fiction, in addition to painting. In effect, this publication promulgated a way of attaining the intersection between literature and painting through its focus on the representation of intense emotions. While Eliot seems to be more interested initially in developing the Pre-Raphaelite notion of the germ into an aesthetic theory of narration, she gradually extended her understanding of the germ and developed it into an aesthetic that integrated narrative technique with historical understanding and social critique.

Scattered throughout her letters and essays, a number of statements appear on Eliot's understanding of the germ, some of which relate it directly to the Pre-Raphaelite publication, *Germ*. As with the Pre-Raphaelites, so with Eliot, the germ signified a locus of powerful emotions, an intense feeling originating in the artist's encounter with the world and in turn shaping the artist's work. Her early essay "Liszt, Wagner, and Weimar" (1855) connects the germ to the origins of a given work and defines this origin in terms of a "prevision" to the rest. An opera, she remarks, should not be "a mosaic, of melodies stuck together" but an "organic whole, which grows like a palm, its earliest portion containing the germ and prevision of all the rest" (102). Like the Pre-Raphaelites, she construes the germ in terms not only of the feeling that inspires the composition of a work but also of the emotion a work produces in the reader: "What one's soul thirsts for is the word which is the reflec[tion] of one's aim and delight in writing—the word which shows that what one meant has been perfectly seized, that the emotion which stirred one in writing is repeated in the mind of the reader" (*Letters* 5:374). In her essay "Notes on Form in Art," she suggests that the most effective way of expressing these powerful emotions is by means of visual rather than verbal terms, that is, through an image: "Poetry begins when passion weds thought by finding expression in an image" (*Essays* 435). To experience the feeling that "stirred her in writing," a reader would have to witness the germ of inspiration, note the image that functioned as the origin or visual "preview" of the entire novel, and follow this condensed version of an intense emotion as it unfolds fully throughout the novel.

Throughout her career, Eliot adjusted her notion of the germ by making it pertain to the effect an artist sought to produce in the audience. Thus, in her "Notes on Form in Art," she points out that "the choice and sequence of images . . . are more or less not determined by emotion but intended to express it" (*Essays* 434–35). This audience-oriented conception of the germ might have preoccupied her as early as 1855, when she described the germ in her "Liszt, Wagner, and Weimar" essay in dramatic rather than static terms, embodying a collision of oppositional forces. Putting herself in the position of an audience, she witnessed in Wagner's operas "a gradual unfolding and elaboration of that fundamental contrast of emotions, that collision of forces, which is the germ of the tragedy; just as the leaf of the plant is successively elaborated into branching stem and compact bud and radiant corolla" (Essays 104). Years later, in her "Notes on the Spanish Gypsy and Tragedy in General," she explicitly comments on the types of collisions embodied in the artistic germ of *The Spanish Gypsy*, mentioning oppositions such as "an adjustment of our individual needs to the dire necessities of our lot" and the "irreparable collision between the individual and the general" (Cross 31–32 n. 4,). In this respect Eliot suggests a conception of the germ already advanced by the Pre-Raphaelites, whose paintings focus on moral and psychological collisions, as in Hunt's *Claudio and Isabella* and *Valentine Rescuing Sylvia from Proteus* and Millais's *Huguenot* and *The Order of Release*, to mention but a few.

Eliot's habit of discussing the genesis of her novels in her letters and journals provides a challenge for scholars to identify the germ of each of her novels in terms of a key image and to explore how this image unfolds through the narrative to encompass the entire novel.[3] Two letters she wrote, one to John Blackwood and the other to Mrs. Cross in 1872 (four years before the publication of *Daniel Deronda*), recount an incident she witnessed as well as its profound effect on her. While in Homburg, she writes, she had come across a gambling establishment and had seen a young woman gambling amid a crowd of elderly people. Eliot was especially struck with the young woman's face—that "young, fresh face among the hags and brutally stupid men around her" (*Letters* 5:314). The frequent occurrences of this scene and its transformations throughout the novel make the incident in Homburg a likely candidate for the artistic germ of *Daniel Deronda*.[4] Prior to the writing of *Daniel Deronda*, Eliot's favorite procedure had been to record moments of her artistic inspiration by infusing ordinary phenomena of everyday life with the extraordinary emotions they generated in the heart of an astute, passionate observer.

The incident in Homburg, with its focus on an ordinary face in the crowd, along with the accompanying powerful emotions it generated in her, seems to follow Eliot's characteristic procedure. But there is something new here. Far from assuming the position of a detached observer, Eliot describes this incident by situating herself in the double position of an observer and a social critic. At once describing and denouncing what she sees, she characterizes the participants as "completely in the grasp of this mean, money-making demon." Perhaps aware that she is departing from her customary habit of observing rather than judging, she remarks, "I am not fond of denouncing my fellow-sinners, but gambling being a vice I have no mind to, it stirs my disgust even more than my pity. The sight of the dull faces bending round the gambling tables, the raking-up of the money, and the flinging of the coins towards the winners by the hard-faced croupiers . . . all this seems to me the most abject presentation of mortals. Burglary is heroic compared with it" (*Letters* 5:312). Already in its inception, the artistic germ of *Daniel Deronda* assumes the burden of delivering a social critique.

Gwendolen: The Goddess of Luck

Indeed Gwendolen's youthful face concentrating on the movements of the spinning roulette at the onset of the novel seems but an isomorphic transformation of the young woman at Homburg. Transported into the novel, the event Eliot recorded in Germany turns into a timeless story of gains and losses.[5] The timelessness of the theme is ensured by the overtones of luck and superstition that, as critics have noted, dominate the gambling scene.[6] Like Fortune's wheel, the spinning roulette blindly distributes gains and losses to the participants. Indeed, the roulette on which Gwendolen's fortune depends seems to be but a transformation of Fortune's wheel, magnificently represented in Burne-Jones's *Wheel of Fortune*, a painting whose meaning, as we shall see, becomes the center on which the entire novel pivots.

Certainly, the gambling scene offers us a look at a world controlled by chance and happenstance, a world whose participants have surrendered their agency to the fortuitous turns of events. The narrator is quick to point out what happens when contingency becomes the governing law of human affairs: "[S]uch a drama takes no long while to play out: development and catastrophe can often be measured by nothing clumsier than the moment-hand" (6). Nevertheless, the participants in that drama are resigned to see themselves as pawns of a higher power, a power whose transformative magic can instantaneously give them a self-understanding unlike anything they had ever possessed. Indeed, it takes no time at all before Gwendolen begins to see herself as a woman commanding supremacy and deserving worship: "She had begun to believe in her luck, others had begun to believe in it: she had visions of being followed by a *cortege* who would worship her as a goddess of luck and watch her play as a directing augury. Such things had been known of male gamblers; why should not a woman have a like supremacy?" (ibid.). Thus at the very beginning Gwendolen identifies with the goddess of luck whom Burne-Jones represented in his *Wheel of Fortune* as an "implacable goddess against the helpless mortal figures" (Wildman and Christian 52).

Burne-Jones took years to complete *The Wheel of Fortune* (1875–1883). It is quite possible that Eliot had seen early sketches of the painting or the eponymous watercolor painted in 1871 since she became acquainted with Georgiana and Edward Burne-Jones in February of 1868.[7] Indeed Edward Burne-Jones's words about the painting capture Eliot's sentiment expressed in her last novel: "My Fortune's Wheel is a true image, and we take our turn at it, and are broken upon it" (Fitzgerald 245). The figures of the slave at the top, the king in the center, and the poet below, all strapped to Fortune's wheel, which she turns, oblivious and indifferent to their predicament, look vulnerable and helpless next to the powerful but blind goddess. The 1871 watercolor of the same title with the figure of Fortune blindfolded and placed within the wheel on which the figures of the slave, king, and poet are attached, represents Fortune herself as powerless as her victims.[8] In another pencil drawing, "Study for 'The Wheel of Fortune,' " (1872) Fortune is depicted with her eyes closed. "The artist here considers the equal potency of revealing the figure's full profile, echoing the idealized beauty of her male victims, while rendering the sense of implacability by showing her with closed eyes" (Wildman and Christian 155). During her friendship with Edward Burne-Jones, Eliot visited his studio on numerous occasions between 1869 and 1876 (the publication of Daniel Deronda) when she would have seen the studies for *The Wheel of Fortune*, including the watercolor and the aforementioned study (*Letters* 5:246, 9:148).

No doubt Eliot would have most likely agreed with John Ruskin's interpretation of *The Wheel of Fortune* in his "Mythic Schools of Painting" (delivered in May 1883), in which he extolled the "gradual and irresistible motion of rise and fall,—the *tide* of Fortune, as distinguished from instant change or catastrophe, . . . of the connection of the fates of men with each other, the yielding and occupation of high place, the alternately appointed and inevitable humiliation" (*Works* 33:293). Like the British Empire, Gwendolen's life is swept by the "irresistible motion of rise and fall,—the tide of Fortune." When we first meet her, she carries herself like "an awful majesty" (66); in the hands of her tyrannical husband, however, she later becomes a "galley-slave" (595). Yet her indirect involvement in her husband's death, her consciously unconscious decision not to help him while he is drowning, annihilates his "empire of fear." Though Burne-Jones's painting depicts a deterministic universe, in her novel Eliot demonstrates that people also play a crucial role in shaping their own destiny.

In Eliot's notebooks of *Daniel Deronda,* among several entries on history, a quotation by Herodotus encapsulates the cyclical nature of historical movements, the inevitable fall following the rise of people and empires: "If you know that you and those who rule you are but men, then I must first teach you this: men's fortunes are on [a] wheel which in its turning suffers not the same man to prosper forever."[9] Even a cursory look at Herodotus's *History* reveals concerns quite similar to those Eliot voices in her criticism of the expansion of the British Empire. Indeed Herodotus's lengthy narratives documenting the rise and fall of tyrants convey a call to reflection: In their tyrannical conduct toward their allied city-states, the Athenians must keep in mind that, even though their empire continues to expand triumphantly, no tyranny can ever remain immune to the whimsical turns of fate. A contextual study of his history further reveals that, at a time when the consolidation of the democratic polis had already taken place, Herodotus's work also addressed the need to refigure the self. Lengthy descriptions of Asiatic manners and customs seek to fulfill a purpose integral only to discourses designed to promote self-understanding: To know themselves as Greeks, the Athenians must learn about the barbarian others. In Burne-Jones's *Wheel of Fortune,* then, Eliot found a contemporary image from classical, medieval, and Elizabethan ages that also captured a Victorian anxiety. In the spirit of Herodotus, Eliot traces through history the turns of Fortune's wheel. Like Herodotus, she uses the turning of Fortune's wheel to adjust the story she tells to the contemporary demands of political advocacy. In *Daniel Deronda* she exposes the implications for both the political and social spheres that decisions on the expansion of the British Empire entail.

On the day following the gambling incident of the opening scene, Fortune's wheel turns once again for Gwendolen, who finds her family impoverished as a result of a national (possibly international) gamble, the speculations of Grapnell and Company, which her mother tries in vain to explain to the outraged Gwendolen: "No, dear, you don't understand. There were great speculations: he meant to gain. It was all about mines and things of that sort. He risked too much" (199). Here then we see Gwendolen on the other side of the spectrum—the successful gambler losing to a bigger gamble. Yet we may also read Gwendolen's confusion and desperation as symptomatic of a collective anxiety about the British economy. Though we cannot ascertain that Grapnell and Company speculated in colonial investments, we may assume that was the case, since, soon after Gwendolen hears about her family's financial disaster, we are told that Gwendolen "had no notion how her maternal grandfather got the fortune inherited by his two daughters; but he had been a West Indian—which seemed to exclude further question" (17).

Thus Eliot's redrawing of Burne-Jones's *Wheel of Fortune* casts Gwendolen to the vicissitudes of fortune; her supremacy shatters as quickly as it is established. Throughout the novel Gwendolen desperately seizes opportunities that may restore her supremacy. In the process she becomes entangled in the colonialist mentality, which defines supremacy through material acquisition and the subjugation of others. Through Gwendolen and Grandcourt, respective representatives of the middle class and aristocracy, Eliot undermines the prevalent idea of British supremacy, the right to rule over others, and underscores its attendant catastrophic results. Eliot suggests Gwendolen's colonialist bent by briefly sketching it in her early life and later developing it in her perspective on marriage. At home with her mother and her sisters in her "domestic empire" (32), she is often "an awful majesty" (66). Described from the start as "an empress of luck," Gwendolen drives herself by the "hunger of the inner self for supremacy" (43) and "the possibility of winning empire" (52). The impoverishment of her family (due to someone else's gambling) forces her to see Grandcourt's renewal of courtship as her chance to get "a sort of empire over her own life" (247). Thus her motive for marriage becomes money, the most basic, imperialist incentive. On that momentous occasion in her life, she is confident about her playing "at the game of life," fully conscious that she is "daring everything to win much" (299). However, her early conviction that Grandcourt would not have "the slightest power over her" (89) is soon smashed as Gwendolen discovers herself a victim in "her husband's empire of fear" (364).

In both Gwendolen and Grandcourt we witness emotional rather than territorial imperialism, an attempt to expand one's sovereignty by subjugating others.[10] Thus in his courtship of Gwendolen, Grandcourt anticipates "the pleasure in mastering reluctance" (269). Similarly, Lydia Glasher, the mother of his children, whom he forsakes for Gwendolen, represents "his delight in dominating" (289). In fact, Gwendolen becomes his colony, which he masters by "the force of his own words. If this white-handed man . . . had been sent to govern a difficult colony, he might have won reputation among his contemporaries. He had certainly ability, would have understood that it was safer to exterminate than to cajole superseded proprietors . . ." (507). Certainly Grandcourt becomes a spokesperson for British supremacy on more than one occasion in the novel. When, for instance, the conversation at a social gathering turns to the Jamaican governor's brutal handling of the native insurrection, Grandcourt contemptuously responds, "the Jamaican Negro was a beastly sort of baptist Caliban" (279).[11] Ironically, before his drowning, for which Gwendolen is partly responsible in her unwillingness to rescue him, Grandcourt relishes "the courage and confidence that belong to domination, and he was feeling perfectly satisfied that he held his wife with bit and bridle" (582). Like Croesus, the protocolonialist made infamous by Herodotus throughout Greece for having counted his blessings too early, Grandcourt is the subject of a catastrophic fall from prosperity. Laden with the rhetorical thrust of an argument, the private narrative becomes the carrier of a public statement against imperialist ideology.

As the novel progresses, we become aware that Gwendolen's gambling and the sense of supremacy it fuels is paradigmatic of the colonialist ideology dominating the mid-Victorian years (preceding the publication of *Daniel Deronda*). Thus the germ of the novel encompasses not just Gwendolen's future but also the contemporary, sociopolitical scene. Several historians have seen that period as crucial to the history of British expansion overseas. Bernard Porter, for instance, argues that in the early 1870s the popular mood in Britain became "more enthusiastic towards the extension of the empire for its own sake" (63), and he goes on to reflect that "Britain's expansion into the world in the 1860s and '70s was only partly territorial and political. Mainly it was economic and cultural" (65). Arguments in favor of territorial and cultural expansion are voiced in the writings of Victorian intellectuals such as John Ruskin and Alfred, Lord Tennyson, and notable politicians such as Benjamin Disraeli, whose works Eliot knew quite well. Invariably these writers extolled the grandeur, power, and supremacy of the empire and argued for its consolidation, preservation, and expansion. So much so, in fact, that the idea of the supremacy of the empire is the sentiment that fuels most of the arguments in that era. In his "Future of England" (1869), for instance, John Ruskin exhorts "the more adventurous and ambitious" of young Englishmen to found "new seats of authority, and centres of thought, in uncultivated and unconquered lands" (*Works* 18:514). Similarly, Tennyson in 1872 in the "Epilogue to the Queen," which he added to the new edition of the *Idylls of the King*, praises the "ocean-empire with her boundless homes/for ever-broadening England, and her throne/In our vast Orient and one isle, one isle,/that knows not her own greatness" (1755).

Disraeli's famous Crystal Palace speech of 1872 seems to crystallize the sentiments of the time regarding British supremacy. Attacking Gladstonian separatist foreign policy and asserting the necessity of the colonies, Disraeli connects the concepts of British supremacy and power:

In my opinion no minister in this country will do his duty who neglects an opportunity of reconstructing as much as possible our colonial empire, and of responding to those distant sympathies which may become the source of incalculable strength and happiness to this land. . . . The issue is not a mean one. It is whether you will be content to be a comfortable England modeled and molded upon continental principles and meeting in due course an inevitable fate, or whether you will be a great country, an imperial country, a country where your sons, when they rise, rise to paramount positions and obtain not merely the esteem of their countrymen, but command the respect of the world. (Monypenny and Buckle 2:535–36)

Thus Disraeli connected individual ambition and self-fulfillment with the expansion of the British Empire.

Perhaps the force of these arguments on the supremacy of the British Empire, its rise, and its glory led Eliot to record in her notebooks the history of other empires that once luxuriated in their supremacy. Entries in her notebooks range from notes on the fall of the Athenian, Babylonian, and Persian Empires to that of the Roman Empire and include the Arthurian legend (the story of national glory and its disintegration) and the French Revolution and its disastrous aftermath (Baker *Notebooks* 1:15–40). Instead of joining her contemporaries in celebrating the rise and supremacy of the British Empire, Eliot adumbrates its inevitable fall in her last novel.[12]

In effect, as the novel progresses, Eliot demonstrates that colonialists, like gamblers, are betting mindlessly on future gains, but if history is any lesson, they too will ultimately lose.

Eliot's Reconfigurations of Legendary and Mythological Women

In Rossetti's *Pia dé Tolomei* (1868–80) (plate 11) Eliot must have seen yet another deplorable change of fortune. In this painting we once again find the wheel of fortune, this time in miniature, painted in the background. The subject is from Dante's *Purgatorio* (Canto v, lines 130–36) about the wife who, confined by her husband in the fortress of Maremma, pines away and dies of malaria (or perhaps poison). Rossetti inscribed these lines from Dante's poem in the frame of his painting:

Remember me who am La Pia; me
Siena, me Maremma, made, unmade.
This in his inmost heart well knoweth he
With whose fair jewel I was ringed and wed.

Plate 11. Dante Gabriel Rossetti, *La Pia dé Tolomei*, 1868–1881. Oil on canvas, 41$^1/_2$ x 47$^1/_2$ in (104.8 x 120.6 cm), Spencer Museum of Art, University of Kansas. Reproduced by permission.

Eliot captures all of the elements and qualities of Rossetti's *Pia dé Tolomei* in her representation of Gwendolen at the opening of chapter 54, where we find her a pitiful prisoner, "a galley-slave" (595) in her husband's yacht. Like Pia, who was incarcerated in a tower, Gwendolen finds herself a prisoner in her husband's luxurious yacht, ironically surrounded by the vast space of the sea and the sky, associated with unrestrained freedom:

> MADONNA PIA, whose husband, feeling himself injured by her, took her to his castle amid the swampy flats of the Maremma and got rid of her there, makes a pathetic figure in Dante's Purgatory. . . . We know little about the grounds of mutual discontent between the Siennese couple, but we may infer with some confidence that the husband had never been a very delightful companion. . . . And thus, without any hardness to the poor Tuscan lady who had her deliverance long ago, one may feel warranted in thinking of her with a less sympathetic interest than of the better known Gwendolen who, instead of being delivered from her errors on earth and cleansed from their effect in purgatory, is at the very height of her entanglement in those fatal meshes which are woven within more closely than without. (572)

Wiesenfarth sees Gwendolen's condition at this stage as the result of the arrival of the diamonds on Gwendolen's wedding day, which, he believes, "signals the beginning of her moral renewal through intense remorse and emotional anguish. She becomes an image of Pia" (xxxvii). Pia's predicament, then, seems to represent that of Gwendolen. Unlike Pia, however, Gwendolen is both a victim and a victimizer, in this respect a victim of her own choices. In marrying Grandcourt, she becomes not only his victim but also the victimizer of Lydia Glasher (Grandcourt's mistress and mother of his children). Ultimately, Grandcourt becomes Gwendolen's victim, for she hesitates, or perhaps refuses, to come to his rescue when he is drowning. George Eliot then by modifying Pia's story implies that the roles of the victimizer and victim, superior and inferior, colonizer and colonized are easily reversible, for oppression breeds desperation, which in turn fuels abusive power.

Both Gwendolen and Lydia initially become victims of a patriarchal society that overlooks and implicitly condones a man's criminal and victimizing conduct. But Lydia herself, after becoming Grandcourt's and Gwendolen's victim, exercises her power by enclosing a letter with the diamonds that Grandcourt had originally given her and later asks her to relinquish to Gwendolen: "I am the grave in which your chance of happiness is buried as well as mine. . . . He would have married me at last, if you had not broken your word. You will have your punishment. I desire it

with all my soul" (363). Thus Lydia at this point relishes the prospect of
retribution.

In this scene, as Gwendolen opens the box of diamonds, she resembles
Rossetti's *Pandora* (1869), a mythological figure conventionally seen as the
victim of her own unrestrained drive for self-aggrandizement, heedless of
the dire consequences. Eliot had seen a drawing of this painting during her
first visit to Rossetti's studio, as we have seen. A year later Rossetti refers
to her viewing of this drawing in a letter in which he enclosed the sonnets on *Mary Magdalene* and *Pandora*, adding a note "in case they add anything to the drawings" (*Letters* 5:78). Rossetti's ambivalence toward his
portrayal of the well-known myth is disclosed in his choice of J.
Lemprière's classical dictionary, which he used for his mythological pictures: "The woman was Pandora which intimates that she had received
every necessary gift" (cited by Faxon 189). By opening the box Pandora
lets a cloud of mischief escape, yet the focal point in all of the drawings
and later paintings is on the box containing Hope. In this painting
Rossetti seems to blend Christian and pagan mythology, for the light
around Pandora's hair, along with her vulnerable and wistful gaze, casts her
into a martyrlike figure rather than into the alleged mythical wrongdoer.
Like the painting, which merges the dialectical opposites of the victimized Christian martyr and the victimizing pagan goddess, the questions
raised, but not answered, in the sonnet Rossetti wrote for the painting at
once destabilize the mythological meaning of the painting that incrimi-
nates Pandora and highlight conflicting qualities, thus underscoring the
era's contradictory attitudes toward women:

> What of the end, Pandora? Was it thine,
> The deed that set these fiery pinions free?
> Ah! wherefore did the Olympian consistory
> In its own likeness make thee half divine?
> Was it that Juno's brow might stand a sign
> For ever? and the mien of Pallas be,
> A deadly thing? and that all men might see
> In Venus' eyes the gaze of Proserpine?
>
> What of the end? These beat their wings at will,
> The ill-born things, the good things turned ill,—
> Powers of the impassioned hours prohibited.
> Aye, hug the casket now! Whither they go
> Thou mayst not dare to think: nor canst thou know
> If Hope still pent there be alive or dead.

As in the case of several of the sonnets Rossetti wrote to accompany his paintings, the woman represented in the painting, in this case Pandora, remains silent even in her verbal rendition. The reader of the sonnet has replaced the spectator who gazes at Pandora but knows nothing about her thoughts concealed behind her wistful gaze. Yet the series of questions invites the reader to see Pandora beyond the stereotypical constraints that cast her as the source of evil, prompted by her supposedly thoughtless feminine curiosity. Casting Pandora as the victim of absolute authority, "the Olympian consistory," Rossetti revises a mythological representation of a human impulse into an individual woman trapped in an oppressive society that continues to exploit her victimization. Pandora, Rossetti implies, has been held responsible for an action whose consequences she could not have foreseen. In this respect Gwendolen seems but Pandora's individual manifestation.

It is interesting to note the transformation of this painting a few years later, a painting of which Eliot might have seen a sketch or a preliminary drawing. In this later painting, *Pandora* (1874–1878) (plate 12), the central figure appears as stupendously androgynous, devoid of her earlier feminine traits. Her strong shoulders and muscular arms (concealed by a feminine robe in the earlier version), as well as her direct, transfixed, and defiant gaze, unlike that of the earlier Pandora, conveys no remorse; instead, "the drapery and cloud of 'ill borne things' twist and writhe with a life of their own. Menace and frenzied movement have replaced the lethargic gloom of the earlier version" (Grieve in Parris, *The Pre-Raphaelites,* 309). Yet like the earlier version, this painting also captures contradictory qualities. The focus of the picture seems to be not on impending disaster but on the box, which now bears the inscription VLTIMA [MANET] SPES (Hope remains at last).

As in Rossetti's painting, in Eliot's redrawing the subject's gaze becomes the focus of the scene when Gwendolen, like Pandora, opens the box ("the casket") of diamonds, and the potential gift turns into terror: "It seemed at first as if Gwendolen's eyes were spell-bound in reading the horrible words of the letter over and over again as a doom for penance" (303). Lydia's letter becomes the most ominous detriment: "But in opening the case, in the same instant that she saw their gleam she saw a letter lying above them. . . . It was as if an adder had lain on them" (302). Eventually, the words of Lydia's letter generate more mischiefs, as they "nestled their venomous life within her" (363). Like Rossetti, who sees in Pandora's eyes "the gaze of Proserpine," Eliot associates Pandora with Proserpine. Likewise, Lydia's letter becomes the "grave" in which Gwendolen's chance of happiness is buried, and indeed her marriage to Grandcourt seems but a version of Proserpine's marriage to Pluto. It is

Plate 12. Dante Gabriel Rossetti, *Pandora*, 1874–1878. Chalks, 38¹/₂ x 25¹/₂ in (97.8 x 64.8 cm), Merseyside County Council, Lady Lever Art Gallery, Port Sunlight. Reproduced by permission.

entirely possible that Eliot had seen Rossetti's *Proserpine* (1873–1877) (plate 13). In a letter to W. A. Turner, Rossetti describes the subject of this painting: "The figure represents Proserpine as an Empress of Hades. . . . She is represented in a gloomy corridor of his palace, with the fatal fruit in her hand. As she passes, a gleam strikes on the wall behind her from some inlet suddenly opened, and admitting for a moment the light of the upper world; and she glances furtively towards it, immersed in thought" (Sharp 236). On the frame of the painting, Rossetti inscribed the English version of the sonnet "Proserpina":

> Afar away the light that brings cold cheer
> Unto this wall,—one instant and no more
> Admitted at my distant palace-door.
> Afar the flowers of Enna from this drear,
> Dire fruit, which, tasted once, must thrall me here.
> Afar those skies from this Tartarean grey
> That chills me; and afar, how far away,
> The nights that shall be from the days that were.
>
> Afar from mine own self I seem, and wing
> Strange ways in thought, and listen for a sign;
> And still some heart unto some soul doth pine,
> (Whose sounds mine inner sense is fain to bring,
> Continually together murmuring,)—
> "Woe's me for thee, unhappy Proserpine!"

Although Rossetti wrote his own sonnet to accompany his painting, Alicia Faxon conjectures that he may have been inspired by a poem on Proserpine by Audrey De Vere (which he refers to in a letter to Allingham) with the haunting refrain:

> Must I languish here forever
> In this empire of Despair? (Faxon 191)

Unlike most of Rossetti's sonnets, which present the subject's experience from the viewer's perspective, this sonnet captures the subject's own voice and poignantly expresses her sorrow. Perhaps Rossetti's imaginative projection in Proserpine's plight originated in his intense passion for his beloved Jane, whom he also saw as a captive of her marriage. In the process he transforms a mythological stereotype into a victimized person whose plight was overlooked by Ovid and those following the classical version of mythology.

Plate 13. Dante Gabriel Rossetti, *Proserpine*, 1874. Oil on canvas, 49³/₄ x 24 in (126.4 x 61 cm), Tate Gallery. Reproduced by permission.

Believing in rendering the truth in change, Eliot does not represent Gwendolen as a modern Proserpine in a single moment; instead, she draws parallels between Gwendolen's disastrous marriage and Proserpine's ordeal. Throughout the novel Eliot seems to paint Gwendolen's portrait as Proserpine brushstroke by brushstroke. This painting reaches its completion at the end of the novel. Once again Eliot uses a classical myth for its modern relevance and modifies it considerably in an attempt to show the cultural contradictions it represents. Though scattered throughout the novel, the affinities between Gwendolen and Proserpine seem unmistakable. Like Proserpine, Gwendolen sees herself as an empress. Her family's impoverishment, for instance, forces Gwendolen to see Grandcourt's renewed courtship as her only chance to get a "sort of empire over own her life" (247). Like Proserpine, who is forced by Pluto into an "empire of despair," Gwendolen, through her marriage, begins to reside in an "empire of fear" (364), a "painted gilded prison," (504); thus she is reduced to an "obvious prisoner, with her husband barring the door" (510). Occasionally Gwendolen's prison, like Proserpine's "Tartarean grey," is illuminated: "Suddenly from out the grey sombre morning there came a stream of sunshine, wrapping her in warmth and light where she sat in stony stillness" (503). Remorse and regret for her wrongdoing often become moments of spiritual illumination in her poignant ordeal: "[T]he vision of her past wrong-doing, and what it had brought on her, came with a pale ghastly illumination over every imagined deed that was a rash effort at freedom, such as she had made in her marriage" (576). At this point, in the abyss of despair, Gwendolen seems to have reached the understanding Deronda had earlier suggested: "Take the present suffering as a painful letting in of light" (388).

As the novel reaches its close, we see the final brushstrokes of Gwendolen's portrait as Proserpine. Soon after Grandcourt's drowning, when her mother arrives, Gwendolen leaves Genoa, which she perceives as a dreadful place. "For what place, though it were the flowery vale of Enna, may not the inward sense turn into a circle of punishment where the flowers are no better than a crop of flame-tongues burning the soles of our feet?" (646). Like Rossetti's Proserpine, who in her despair wistfully recalls the "flowers of Enna" (where she was abducted by Pluto while gathering them), Gwendolen is here also associated with the mythological site—"the flowery vale of Enna." And like Proserpine, who is kept away from her mother, Gwendolen has also been kept at a distance. Yet in this positive turn of the myth, she is finally reunited with her beloved mother after Grandcourt's death. At this point, Gwendolen sees herself responsible for his death, thus becoming the victimizer of her oppressor.

The narrative threads documenting the imperialist theme of rise and fall, gain and loss, find thematic closure with Gwendolen's realization that one's gain is made possible only through someone else's loss. Her marriage to Grandcourt, along with the social prestige and the economic affluence such marriage signifies, gives her the very thing it has taken away from Mrs. Glasher and her children. Furthermore, she admits to Deronda her collusion, bringing to mind the imperialist's mission: "I have thrust out others—I have made my gain out of their loss—tried to make it—tried" (386). Long before her realization, Deronda had exposed the logic of Fortune's wheel and the participants' complicity with that logic. He remarks to Gwendolen, "there is something revolting to me in raking a heap of money together, and internally chuckling over it, when others are feeling the loss of it. . . . There are enough inevitable *turns of fortune* which force us to see that our gain is another's loss:—that is one of the ugly aspects of life" (284, my emphasis). Deronda's remarks express his critique of the materialist ideology propelling the British culture. By extension, Gwendolen's ability to take up that critique as a springboard from which to read and understand her own past may very well constitute an indication of thematic closure. "I wronged some one else," Gwendolen says in reference to her marriage, "I wanted to make my gain out of another's loss—you remember?—it was like roulette—and the money burnt into me. And I could not complain. It was as if I had prayed that another should lose and I should win. And I had won" (593). Gwendolen's epiphany connects her once again to the imperialist paradigm that Eliot expresses through her reconfiguration of Edward Burne-Jones's *Wheel of Fortune*.

Yet Deronda's destiny heralds a new logic that breaks the rise/fall, gain/loss binaries maintained by Gwendolen's predicament. His ambiguous heritage represents a stance on the world by someone who is at once both an insider and an outsider. Deronda's stance emerges all too clearly in his devotion to Hans Meyrick, whose inflamed eyes prevent him from having a chance at a scholarship he desperately needs. Likewise, Deronda's readiness to give selflessly questions the logic of the gain and loss paradigm: "This crushing trouble called out all Deronda's readiness to devote himself, and he made every other occupation secondary to that of being companion and eyes to Hans, working with him and for him at his classics, that if possible his chance of the classical scholarship might be saved" (154). When Meyrick gets the scholarship and Deronda does not, the gesture of giving marks a space in the novel that remains unaffected by and exceeds the paradigm of the turning wheel, whose logic has managed to control all else. Furthermore, in his expression of solidarity, Deronda criticizes British supremacy that fosters racism.

The Self and the Colonized Other

The novel's attempt to criticize notions of self-supremacy as so many justifications for racism finds analogue in Eliot's personal struggles to speak out in her other writings against the prevalent attitudes of the times. In writing "The Modern Hep! Hep! Hep!" included in *Theophrastus Such* (published three years after *Daniel Deronda*), Eliot must have been aware of the public impact of advocates of colonial expansion such as Charles Dilke, whose popular *Greater Britain* praised British supremacy and defined progress in terms of the exploitation of "backward" and "inferior" races, thus justifying racism. Other notable intellectuals shared his opinion. Henry James, for instance, in his reviews of travelogues in exotic lands where England had imperialist interests, adopts the "white man's burden" discourse popular at the time and endorses racism. In his review of Sir Samuel Baker's *Ismailia: A Narrative of the Expedition to Central Africa for the Suppression of the Slave trade, Organized by Ismael, Khedive of Egypt,* James remarks that the native population "consists of naked and blood-thirsty savages, and the beautiful trees on the lawn-like slopes are very apt to have one of these gentry lurking behind them" (733). Even Herbert Spencer, Eliot's intimate friend, who disapproved of imperialism as "the unscrupulous greed of conquest cloaked by the blessing of British rule and British religion" (1:217), nevertheless (in a work ironically titled *The Principles of Ethics*) endorses racist attitudes in comments like the "lesser development" of sympathy in "the Negro who jeers at a liberated companion because he has no master to take care of" (2:28).

Indeed the discourse in such works reveals what Edward Said maintains in *Culture and Imperialism*: "[N]either imperialism nor colonialism is a simple act of accumulation and acquisition. Both are supported and perhaps even impelled by impressive ideological formations that include notions that certain territories and people *require* and beseech domination, as well as forms of knowledge affiliated with domination: the vocabulary of classic nineteenth-century imperial culture is plentiful with words and concepts like 'inferior' or 'subject races,' 'subordinate peoples,' 'dependency,' 'expansion,' and 'authority' " (1993, 9).

Accounts of African exploration in the 1860s by explorers like David Livingstone, Richard Burton, and Winwood Reade (of which Eliot was aware) are also permeated by similar "ideological formations." Such accounts abounded in sensational stories of African barbarism, savagery, and evil. According to Livingstone, for instance, Africans are "inured to bloodshed and murder, and care for no god except being bewitched" (Jeal 146).[13] For Richard Burton in *The Lake Regions of Central Africa* (1861), "the African is inferior to the active-minded and objective . . . European. . . . He partakes largely of the worst characteristics of the lower Oriental types—stagnation of mind, indolence of body, moral deficiency, superstition, and childish passion" (490). In the same vein, Winwood Reade in *Savage Africa* (1863) spins tales of African cannibalism (54, 136).[14]

We have seen that the gambling scene includes aspects of rationality and magic, reason and superstition. Faithful to its origin and center, the novel develops the gambling scene around the binaries of superiority and inferiority, civilization and savagery. Yet these binaries do not remain neatly distinct, for the novel progresses by transgressing and blurring distinct boundaries, blending and weaving together concepts ordinarily considered as separate and distinct. We have seen that an aura of superstition permeates the gambling events, giving the scenes an otherworldly atmosphere. This same impression often recurs. Throughout the novel, facets of a primitive world protrude, rupturing its civilized, polished surface. Thus we may not be unjustified in speaking about Eliot's struggle to cope with otherness and to decode her discursive blending of binaries as her way of problematizing the self by means of the other. When we accept the terms "colonizing and colonized" and "civilized and savage" as natural designations of the real, the only thing left to do may be to break the oppositions and show how one expression partakes of its opposite. As David Spurr maintains, "members of a colonizing class will insist on their radical difference from the colonized as a way of legitimizing their own position in the colonial community." Paradoxically, they will also insist "on the colonized people's essential identity with them—both as preparation for the domestication of the colonized and as a moral and philosophical precondition for the civilizing mission" (7). It may very well be that Eliot is willing to grant the qualities attributed to the colonized barbarian so long as those same qualities are also ascribed to the colonizing self. Eliot's way of coping with the colonized others may be to bring them home to England. In this respect Eliot seems to articulate the tendency of modern literature and science of locating "the savage within us, in our historical origins and in our psychic structure" (ibid.).

This conflation may explain why Gwendolen's character from time to time displays aspects of the demonic. "Roulette was not a good setting for her," says Deronda in response to Sir Hugo's inquiry about her: "[I]t brought out something of the demon" (304). In addition, when unable to justify his attraction to her, Deronda resorts to a discourse of sense perception that confirms Gwendolen's alliance with something otherworldly: "Strange and piteous to think what a centre of wretchedness a delicate piece of human flesh like that might be, wrapped around with fine raiment, her ears pierced for gems, her head held loftily, her mouth all smiling pretence, the poor soul within her sitting in sick distaste of all things! But what do I know of her? There may be a demon in her to match the worst husband, for what I can tell" (354). At once a fine representative of the rising middle class and a demon, Gwendolen is the site of a double set of qualities that most of the novel goes to great pains to keep separate and opposite. She is at once a calculating person, looking out for her self-interest, seizing the opportune moment to gain an advantage, *and* a cannibal, "a Lamia beauty" (7), a sorceress who supposedly lives by sucking children's blood. Thus Gwendolen's representation reveals Eliot's awareness of the impossibility of distinguishing the domestic space from the colonial realm, a concept articulated by recent theorists on the colonial discourse (Gikandi 60). Gwendolen's thoughts, as she reminisces about her past, partake of her ascent to aristocracy (representative of civilization) and her entrance into the diabolic (representative of contemporary attitudes toward primitive tribes): "a lure through a long Satanic masquerade, which she had entered on with an intoxicated belief in its disguises, and had seen the end of in shrieking fear lest she herself had become one of the evil spirits who were dropping their human mummery and hissing around her with serpent tongues" (652).

Such passages reveal deep-seated convictions exposing the complicity of the self with attributes assigned exclusively to the other. This explains why Eliot elsewhere tells the history of the Anglo-Saxon Christian in terms of the invading savage who massacres natives in the name of progress:

> The men who planted our nation were not Christians, though they began their work centuries after Christ; and they had a decided objection to Christianity when it was first proposed to them: they were not monotheists, and their religion was the reverse of spiritual. But since we have been fortunate enough to keep the island-home they won for us, and have been on the whole a prosperous people, rather continuing the plan of invading and spoiling other lands than being forced to beg for shelter in them, nobody has reproached us because our fathers thirteen hundred years ago worshipped Odin, massacred Britons, and were with difficulty persuaded to accept Christianity, knowing nothing of Hebrew history. . . . The red Indians, not liking us when we settled among them, might have been willing to fling such facts in our faces, but they were too ignorant, and besides their opinions did not signify, because we were able, if we liked, to exterminate them. The Hindoos also have doubtless had their rancour against us and still entertain enough ill-will to make unfavorable remarks on our character, especially as to our historic rapacity and arrogant notions of our own superiority . . . but though we are a small number of

an alien race profiting by the territory and produce of these prejudiced people, they are unable to turn us out; at least when they tried we showed them their mistake. (*Theophrastus* 263–64)[15]

In this passage Eliot seems to disclose what Deidre David believes are "the rhetorical and ideological moves that displace the unquestionable link between empire building and commercial profit into political fictions of a barbarism waiting at the gates" (1995, 7). Responding to the binaries of superiority and inferiority, civilization and savagery, endorsed by contemporary explorers in future colonies, George Eliot, like Herodotus, blurs the boundaries between the civilized and the savage, shows how one designation partakes of its opposite, and underlines the need to understand the self through the other.

Evidently Eliot sees otherness as a critical domain from which to refigure the self. Like Herodotus, she seems convinced that the initial conflation of self with other is a prerequisite to critical self-understanding and a first step to the process of refiguring the self. Gwendolen, the gambler, must see the "mean, money-making demon" in herself before she can transcend the logic of rise and fall or before she can position herself outside the imperatives of gain and loss that circumscribe the boundaries of her existence. Fluctuating between seemingly distinct categories, victim and victimizer, good and evil, Eliot seems to blend these categories through the classical myths she chooses and interprets. In representing a Victorian woman as versions of mythological subjects, she grants herself the license to freely criticize her culture's contradictory attitudes toward women and to underscore the detrimental effects of oppression. Indeed, the novel begins with the question of good and evil, and the answer appears to depend on the viewer who poses it.

"Was she beautiful or not beautiful? and what was the secret of form or expression which gave the dynamic quality to her glance? Was the good or the evil genius dominant in those beams?" (3). A close reading of the novel's opening questions reveals that it is Daniel Deronda's gaze that ascribes contradictory attributes, the good and evil, to Gwendolen. Gwendolen's youthful face concentrating on the movements of the spinning roulette becomes the focus of his gaze. Thus Eliot seems to endorse the traditional binaries of the male as surveyor and female as surveyed. In her discussion of this scene, Evelyne Ender contends that it "sets the stage for a specularization of the heroine. . . . Gwendolen can be said to 'exist' as surface projection of the images held in the gaze and in the mind of the men who shape her destiny: Deronda, Klesmer, Grandcourt and a more undifferentiated group (made up of Mallinger, Gascoigne and their likes)" (234). Yet Deronda's inquisitive gaze in the opening of the novel does not subdue Gwendolen's "dynamic glance." Moreover, although Gwendolen is acutely aware of the patriarchal dynamics of the gaze that cast a woman as the inferior of a man's scrutinizing glance, she resists them and haughtily defies them. When her eyes meet Deronda's, instead of averting them "as she would have desired to do, she is unpleasantly conscious that they were arrested—how long?" Driven by "an inward defiance" Gwendolen subverts conventional feminine behavior (6). In adopting the role of the spectator in the opening scene as well as throughout the novel, Gwendolen assumes a traditionally masculine prerogative. In this scene Gwendolen's defiant gaze and her other facial features, as well as her lavishly green garments, recall Rossetti's somewhat androgynous *Astarte Syriaca* (1877) (plate 14), the self-aggrandizing Assyrian goddess, an early malign version of Venus, whose unflinching gaze overpowers and disturbs the viewer. Certainly the reconfiguration of this primitive goddess, "the powerful ancient Semitic goddess of Syria-Palestine in the pre-Greek era," as Gwendolen is extreme-ly appropriate, for this goddess at once underscores Gwendolen's primitive nature and is consistent with the Semitic subject of the novel (Barbara Bryant in Wilton and Upstone 159). Astarte Syriaca's incongruous nature—she is both a priestess and a seductress—is also manifested in con-temporary perceptions of women that Gwendolen's character represents.

It is entirely possible that Eliot had seen preliminary sketches of Astarte, which Rossetti had started drawing in 1875. Like Astarte Syriaca, who appears in classical drapery of intense and lavish green hues, adorned with a girdle "in silver sheen," as Rossetti describes it in the sonnet he wrote for the painting (3), Gwendolen is depicted as a "Nereid in sea-green robes and silver ornaments," "a sort of a serpent now, all green and silver" (7). Struck by her dazzling appearance, the onlookers in the casino focus on Pre-Raphaelite features such as her "light-brown hair," her "delicate nose with its gradual little upward curve," which one of the Vandernoodt group finds "distracting," and "her mouth—there never was a prettier mouth, the lips curl backward so fine-ly," which looks "so self-complacent, as if it knew its own beauty—the curves are so immovable" (8). A close look at Astarte Syriaca's fea-tures—the luxuriant light-brown hair, the idealized rosebud mouth, the feminine nose with the "upward turn"—reveals the striking resemblance between the Assyrian goddess and Gwendolen. In her "sea-green robes and silver ornaments," Gwendolen is repeatedly compared to a serpent, her alluring and irresistible beauty becoming a threatening attribute to the other gamblers in the casino, who see her as the *"ensemble du serpent."* The "dynamic quality" of Gwendolen's gaze seems identical to Astarte's "all penetrative spell" (12) or the "absolute eyes that wean/The pulse of hearts" (7–8).[16]

Plate 14. Dante Gabriel Rossetti, *Astarte Syriaca*, 1875–1877. Oil on canvas, 72 x 42 in (183 x 106.7 cm), Manchester City Art Galleries. Reproduced by permission.

No doubt, at least when Daniel first meets Gwendolen, what he defines as evil is Gwendolen's refusal to abide by conventional feminine strictures such as lowering her gaze when her eyes meet his or displaying traditionally feminine modesty. Unable to contain or explain his intense attraction to Gwendolen's fascinating beauty, Deronda labels it evil: "Was the good or the evil genius dominant in those beams? Probably the evil; else why was the effect that of unrest rather than of undisturbed charm? Why was the wish to look again felt as coercion and not as a longing in which the whole being consents?" (3). In this context the choice of the word "beams" is also interesting, perhaps an allusion to the rays of light emitted by the sun and the moon above Astarte Syriaca's head. Deronda's unsettled response to Gwendolen's beauty resembles the negative reactions of Victorian as well as modern critics to some of Rossetti's representations of highly sexualized women like *Astarte Syriaca*. "In those unforgotten, unforgettable faces, so appealing in several senses," Jerome McGann comments in *Dante Gabriel Rossetti*, "a disturbing male gaze turns to look back at itself, at us, men and women both. The event seems the more significant and moving exactly because it has hardly been recognized or translated as an important moment in the history of art" (154). In time Deronda's gaze also turns "to look back at itself," as we shall see.

In the beginning as well as throughout the novel, Gwendolen is represented as a self-aggrandizing femme fatale, like Astarte Syriaca, a malign version of Venus. And like the androgynous Assyrian goddess with her massive shoulders and masculine arms, Gwendolen is somewhat androgynous in her bold and defiant, conventionally masculine qualities. Like Rossetti, who depicts the Assyrian Venus as simultaneously attractive and lurid, feminine and masculine, throughout the novel the narrator presents Gwendolen as a "problematic sylph" reified by a culture that glorifies feminine beauty at once worshiping and condemning it.

Deronda's fear of Gwendolen, translated at times into misogynist words, seems but representative of the patriarchal perspective of the day. Indeed his perspective on Gwendolen as "the demon" echoes one of Burne-Jones's statements, capturing the gynophobic attitude of the day: "A woman at her best, self-denying and devoted, is pathetic and lovely beyond words; but once she gets the upper hand and flaunts, she's the devil" (Lago 11). In adopting the role of the spectator, however, in the opening scene as well as throughout the novel, Gwendolen assumes a dominant position traditionally granted to men. Her transgression of patriarchal boundaries transforms her into a monster, a witch, a Medusa figure. As Nina Auerbach explains, "these serpent-women, terrestrial cousins of the hybrid mermaid in their secret transformations, their power over social life and its laws, exude a power that withers patriarchs. George

Eliot's lamialike Rosamund and Gwendolen . . . all find their greatest triumphs in displacing male authorities" (8).

Certainly images of Medusa in her many disguises of serpents, lamias, and mermaids proliferate in Gwendolen's depiction throughout the novel, bringing to mind what seems to be her iconographic, spectacular representation in *The Beguiling of Merlin* (1873–1874) (plate 15). This painting captures the catastrophic results of Nimue's "spellbinding gaze," depicted here as a Medusa figure, her hair entwined with snakes. We see Merlin, the sorcerer, lying at the enchantress's feet, "transfixed by the spell she is reciting from his ancient book of charms" (Marsh 114). Harrison and Waters observe that the painting portrays an interesting reversal of traditional male and female roles. Nimue, her Medusa hair the focal point of her face, occupies "the main vertical plane usually a symbol of the active male, whilst Merlin lies passive, relaxed, his power ebbing away" (113). Ironically, in explaining the significance of the painting to Mrs. Gaskell, Burne-Jones saw himself as the victim (not the victimizer) of his lover, Mary Zambaco, whom he forsook after an extramarital affair with her: "Yet you did say it was a nasty woman the head of Nimue in the picture called 'the enchanting of Merlin' was painted from that poor traitor, & was very like—all the action is like—the name of her was Mary. . . . She was born at the foot of Olympus and looked and was primeval but that's the head & the way of standing and turning . . . and I was turned into a hawthorn tree in the forest of Broceliande the spell is on him for ever—Arthur will come back out of his restful sleep but Merlin's face can never be undone."[17]

Referring to Burne-Jones's comments about this painting, Poulson remarks that by identifying Mary Zambaco with Viviane and himself with Merlin, he absolved himself of moral responsibility: "[I]f Merlin's love for Viviane was predestined, then so was Mary's for him. . . . Zambaco is a force of nature, amoral, 'primaeval' " (151). Depictions of woman as "elemental enchantress," Jan Marsh explains, reveal attempts to fathom feminine mystery and to come to terms with otherness (1987 114). At the same time, the power that Nimue's stance conveys, traditionally relegated to men, may also be construed as a transgression of conventional gender boundaries and therefore a threat to male identity.

Before her marriage to Grandcourt, Gwendolen relishes her power over him, believing in her "divine right to rule" (346), driving herself by the "hunger of the inner self for supremacy" (43). Though she loses that power after her marriage, she nevertheless looks powerful and intractable when, standing in the yacht, she towers over the drowning Grandcourt. Indeed her glance here becomes Medusa's petrifying gaze: "I saw him sink, and my heart gave a leap as if it were going out of me. I think I did not move. I

Plate 15. Edward Burne-Jones, *The Beguiling of Merlin*, 1874. Oil on canvas, 73¹/₄ x 43³/₄ in (186 x 111 cm), National Museums and Galleries on Merseyside (Lady Lever Art Gallery, Port Sunlight). Reproduced by permission.

kept my hands tight. It was long enough for me to be glad, and yet think it was no use—he would come up again. And he *was* come. . . . It was all like lightning. 'The rope!' He called out in a voice—not his own—I hear it now—and I stooped for the rope—I felt I must—I felt sure he could swim, and he would come back whether or not, and I dreaded him. That was in my mind—he would come back. . . . And he cried again—and I held my hand, and my heart said, 'Die!' and he sank" (596).

The scene becomes an isomorphic verbal equivalent of *The Beguiling of Merlin*, Gwendolen (like Nimue) towering over Grandcourt, whose sinking figure reminds us of Merlin's swooning, cowering glance. Like Merlin swooning under Nimue's intense gaze, Grandcourt literally sinks under Gwendolen's "dynamic glance." In this respect Gwendolen's glance becomes Medusa's gaze. Yet Eliot has taken pains throughout the novel to show that Medusa's destructive power is the product of an oppressive patriarchal society. By marrying Grandcourt, Gwendolen becomes the victim of his sadistic exercise of power—a prisoner without escape. This inequitable distribution of power, condoned by the Victorian legal system, becomes one of Eliot's targets of scathing critique. After all, Gwendolen's decision to marry Grandcourt, prompted by her desire to support her impoverished family, follows her discovery that she cannot earn an independent living, that her education has not provided her with such power.

As in *Adam Bede*, in her last novel Eliot concentrates on Medusa's victimization and further demonstrates that the borderline between victimizer and victim, colonizer and colonized is a hazy one. Gwendolen becomes Grandcourt's victimizer after having endured years of abuse. Whereas George Eliot's novels at times seem to endorse the unequal dynamics of power represented by the gaze, most often they challenge such conceptions by presenting Medusa figures as representative of Victorian anxieties about the emerging roles of women or as paradigmatic of the culture's incongruous perspectives on women. In the notebooks of *Adam Bede* Eliot records the tragic aspect of Medusa's myth, an aspect often overlooked in traditional versions that present Medusa as a victimizer of men: "Her story is a tragic account of the acute jealousy of the ancient gods directed against all splendor and beauty in mankind. . . . According to another version of the story—one which the Roman poet Ovid followed—Medusa's fate was yet more undeserved. The wild god Poseidon raped the incomparably beautiful princess in Athena's temple. . . . Athena's punishment, moreover, fell on the innocent victim, because she was powerless to punish the guilty god" (Wiesenfarth 153). Though traditionally seen as a victimizer, Medusa, in Eliot's understanding, is the victim of absolute, oppressive authority and she is portrayed as such in various of her novels.[18] Unlike Hetty and Maggie, however, who are also seen as Medusa figures and perish at the end of the novel, seemingly for their transgressions of conventional gender boundaries, Gwendolen survives. Perhaps in her last novel Eliot suggests that if a woman is to survive in a highly competitive patriarchal world she must usurp authority and tradition and must, as she herself did, find the means to undermine oppression and extend those conventional gender boundaries that constrain her power and relegate her to the status of the underprivileged and unauthorized.

As the novel progresses, Daniel's gaze moves beyond the established gendered categories, for he cultivates a nurturing friendship with Gwendolen beyond the superior/inferior binaries that erotic desire often establishes. Indeed the last exchange between them demonstrates the defusion of the unequal power relations, fostered by the traditional dynamics of the gaze. Bitterly inconsolable in response to Daniel's announcement that he is to marry, Gwendolen exclaims, "I said I should be forsaken. I have been a cruel woman. And I am forsaken." Deronda's response thwarts traditional expectations: "He seized her outstretched hands and held them together and kneeled at her feet. She was the victim of his happiness. 'I am cruel, too, I am cruel,' he repeated, with a sort of groan, *looking up at her imploringly.* His presence and touch seemed to dispel a *horrible vision,* and she met his *upward look* of sorrow with something like the return of consciousness after fainting" (690, my emphasis). Tremblingly wavering between the erotic and the empathic, this intense farewell scene destabilizes the traditional binaries of the gaze—subject/object, surveyor/surveyed, superior/inferior: "Sobs rose, and great tears fell fast. Deronda would not let her hands go—held them still with one of his, and himself pressed her handkerchief against her eyes. . . . She bent forward to kiss his cheek, and he kissed hers. Then they *looked at each other* for an instant with clasped hands, and he turned away" (690–91, my emphasis). Shattering the hierarchical gendered ambivalences of the gaze, this scene creates consummate reciprocity.

As her novels and letters reveal, George Eliot was keenly aware of contemporary fears of the social and sexual status of women, which seem to have culminated in the 1870s (the years of the composition of *Daniel Deronda*), when women's suffrage and women's rights became major issues. Edward Burne-Jones's response to women's changing roles seems to represent the patriarchal voice of the era. "It's a pity to educate women, only spoils them takes away all their charm, to make them into tenth-rate men." On another occasion, in a conversation with Thomas Rooke, his studio assistant, he articulates his opposition to women's franchise: "Tiresome the modern woman is. I like women when they're good and kind and pretty—agreeable objects in the landscape of existence—give life to it—and pleasant to look at and think about. What do they want with votes?"[19]

The knowledge of contemporary patriarchal resistance to the women's equal rights movement compelled Eliot to expose her culture's gender incongruities in her own redrawings of stereotypical representations of women endorsed by a revival of classical mythological figures in Victorian fiction and painting. In revising mythological or gender stereotypes, Eliot sought to represent women as people, thus undermining the unequal dynamics of power that reduced them to objects. A letter to Mrs. John Nassau, dated October 4, 1869, explicitly records what her novels subtly convey—Eliot's strong and eloquent conviction in the importance of mutual understanding and respect:

> But on one point I have a strong conviction, and I feel bound to act on it, so far as my retired way of life allows of public action. And that is, that women ought to have the same fund of truth placed within their reach as men have; that their lives (i.e. the lives of men and women) ought to be passed together under the hallowing influence of a common faith as to their duty and its basis. And this unity in their faith can only be produced by their having each the same store of knowledge. It is not likely that any perfect plan for educating women can soon be found, for we are very far from having a perfect plan for educating men. But it will not do to wait for perfection. (*Letters* 5:58)

Eliot's contradictory images of Gwendolen, representative of incongruous attitudes toward women, may also be construed as the era's struggle to cope with otherness, a way of problematizing the self by means of the other. At the very beginning of the novel, as we have seen, Gwendolen appears to others in the gambling as "a Lamia beauty," a cannibal. Eliot masterfully captures deep-seated convictions and exposes the complicity of the self with attributes assigned exclusively to the other.

Jewish Idealism versus British Individualism

With the resolution of Deronda's ambiguous identity comes the consequent clearing of the confusion that the novel carefully sustains all along between self and other, civilized and uncivilized people, "superior" and "inferior" races. In the light of this determination, Jewish religion and culture no longer constitute a site for self-critique or a possibility for some alternative logic. Rather they become an alternative to British individualism, colonial expansionism, and Anglo-Saxon supremacy. The idealistic manifestations of the gambling paradigm appear through Mordecai's vision of a Jewish homeland that does not entail the gain of one nation at the expense of another:

There is [a] store of wisdom among us to found a new Jewish polity, grand, simple, just, like the old—a republic where there is equality of protection, an equality which shone like a star on the forehead of our ancient community, and gave it more than the brightness of Western freedom amid the despotisms of the East. . . . And the world will gain as Israel gains. For there will be a community in the van of the East which carries the culture and the sympathies of every great nation in its bosom; there will be a land set for a halting-place of enmities, a neutral ground for the East as Belgium is for the West. (456)

At this point, the Jewish other is no longer a source of critique leveled against the British self but a locus for glorification. Contemporary cultural theorists like to use the phrase "benevolent racism." Indeed some critics have accused Eliot of endorsing "proto-fascist ideas" (Myers 123) or of sublimating social conflicts to "universal" humanity (Cottom 30). More recently, critics have criticized the Zionist plot for fostering the very anti-Semitism Eliot seems to attack. Katherine Linehan, for instance, posits that "Eliot's theoretically democratic racialism and nationalism are shaded by hierarchical views of higher and lower races and more or less advanced civilization" (325). Similarly, Susan Meyer maintains that "the novel is rife with anti-Semitism" (1996, 180). Such allegations, however, disregard Eliot's response to the adverse criticism of the Jewish "element" of *Daniel Deronda*. In a letter to Harriet Beecher Stowe in October 29, 1876, she defends her novel in terms of what it both criticized and affirmed, thus responding not only to Victorian but also to future critics:

But precisely because I felt that the usual attitude of Christians towards Jews is—I hardly know whether to say more impious or more stupid when viewed in the light of their professed principles, I therefore felt urged to treat Jews with such sympathy and understanding as my nature and knowledge could attain to. Moreover, not only towards Jews, but towards all Oriental peoples with whom we English come in contact, a spirit of arrogance and contemptuous dictatorialness is observable which has become a national disgrace to us. There is nothing I should care more to do . . . than to rouse the imagination of men and women to a vision of human claims in those races of their fellow-men who most differ from them in customs and beliefs. . . . To my feeling, this deadness to the history which has prepared half our world for us, this inability to find interest in any form of life that is not clad in the same coat-tails and flounces as our own lies very close to the worst kind of irreligion. . . . [I]t a sign of the intellectual narrowness . . . which is still the average mark of our culture. (*Letters* 6:301–2)

As this passage shows, Eliot's primary intention in *Daniel Deronda* was to expose the hierarchical relations of social existence that organize human beings in terms of opposition and domination, a cultural logic that colonialism abroad and patriarchy at home is based upon. Nevertheless, the critical thrust of her novel is not without its affirmative counterpart, a vision that organizes human beings in terms of equality and cooperation.

Critics who denounce Eliot's presumably anti-Semitic notions seem to assume that Eliot lacked a clear understanding of her own intentions. Yet Eliot clearly stated these intentions in the earlier letter and in *Theophrastus Such*. At the zenith of her career, she could "gamble," take a risk with a subject that she knew would be highly controversial. In the same letter to Harriet Beecher Stowe, she states that she had anticipated the negative criticism her novel received: "As to the Jewish element in 'Deronda,' I expected from first to last in writing it, that it would create much stronger resistance and even repulsion than it has actually met with. . . . But I was happily independent in material things and felt no temptation to accommodate my writing to any standard except that of trying to do my best" (*Letters* 6:301–2).

Anyone familiar with Eliot's career knows about her acute sensitivity to adverse criticism, a sensitivity that George Henry Lewes protected by concealing letters with negative remarks about her work. Yet Eliot risked such criticism, for, as her other works reveal, she believed in fighting social inequities. In this case, she personally knew Jewish intellectuals who suffered discrimination. Emmanuel Deutsch, who served as the model for Mordecai, is a notable case. Furthermore, in accusing Eliot of anti-Semitism critics seem to overlook the contemporary Jewish response to the novel. David Kaufmann, for instance, celebrates the novel as a "glorious exaltation" (95), and other Jewish critics share his admiration (Martin 90–106).

Unlike her other novels, *Daniel Deronda* takes place in the previous decade. As such it addresses not one but several contemporary sociopolitical and aesthetic issues, some of which cannot possibly be fathomed by our own remote perspective. I have explored only a few of the strands of the novel's multiplicity that involve the intersection of Pre-Raphaelite techniques, subjects, and preoccupations with sociopolitical issues. By evoking classical subject paintings, Eliot entered into contemporary debates on art, mythography, anthropology, historiography, colonialism, and legislation. As *Daniel Deronda* and her other novels reveal, she was aware that the contemporary interest in classical Greece and Rome dovetailed with colonialist and patriarchal ideologies. At a time when women's status was gradually improving through legislative measures and the women's movement, the turn to classical gender constructs by influential intellectuals such as Walter Pater and John Ruskin expressed the contemporary resistance to women's evolving roles.

Mythological representations of women in paintings as contemporary images further reinforced the belief in their universally inferior status and endorsed the double standard as "natural" rather than cultural. As Kestner has already demonstrated, "the history of classical-subject painting as it relates to women is a product of the rise of mythology and the fervor for the Greco-Roman world intersecting with the history of women's political development in the nineteenth century. . . . The power of mythological pictorial ideograms of women as mad, abandoned, deceiving, sensuous, and intimidating derived force from the seemingly unchanging nature and continuous relevance of myth. Mythic eternality was a basis for resisting the progress of women" (1989, 32). Like John Stuart Mill, who in *The Subjection of Women* (1869) refuted arguments in favor of the eternal, universal, and natural status of women, Eliot in *Daniel Deronda* demonstrates the importance of cultural forces in shaping and changing gender constructs.

Eliot was perhaps willing to grant the qualities attributed to the colonized "barbarian" so long as those same qualities are also attributed to the colonizing self. Her way of coping with the colonized others may be to bring them home to England. Evidently in her last novel Eliot saw otherness as a critical domain from which to refigure the self; she seemed convinced that the initial conflation of the self with the other is a prerequisite to critical self-understanding and a first step in the process of refiguring the self. In this respect Eliot seems to articulate the tendency of modern literature and science to locate "the savage within us, in our historical origins and in our psychic structure" (Spurr 7).

CHAPTER FIVE

Beyond Gender Boundaries:
Edward Burne-Jones and Thomas Hardy

Edward Burne-Jones, the friend, admirer, and successor of Dante Gabriel Rossetti, was recognized as the leader of the second generation of Pre-Raphaelites, who, starting in the late 1860s, created sensuous and dazzling paintings placing primary importance on form and color. Since his first exhibition at the opening of the Grosvenor Gallery in 1877, Burne-Jones achieved unprecedented success and was recognized as the leader of the Aesthetic school.[1] After a long absence from the London galleries, Burne-Jones exhibited eight of his most brilliant paintings in the new and striking Grosvenor Gallery: *The Beguiling of Merlin* (1873–1874), *The Mirror of Venus* (1870–1876), *The Days of Creation* (1870–1876), *Temperantia* (1872–1873), *Fides* (1872), *Spes* (1871–1877), *A Sibyl* (1877), and *Saint George* (1873–1877). At the same exhibit appeared paintings of his followers, Spencer Stanhope, J. M. Strudwick, Walter Crane, Marie Spartali, and Evelyn Pickering. "In other words, an entire school suddenly seemed to have emerged, with Burne-Jones as its undisputed leader. No other artist on display could compete. Overnight he was famous, the star of the Grosvenor and the doyen of aestheticism in its fully developed form" (Wildman 192).

Brainchild of Sir Coutts Lindsay and his wife, Blanche, a talented painter, the Grosvenor Gallery was intended as a challenge to the Royal Academy and as a venue for young artists, whom the Royal Academy might have rejected; nevertheless, Royal Academicians were also invited to exhibit. The astounding success of the Grosvenor Gallery was partly due to the lack of high-quality pictures exhibited in the Royal Academy at the time. Henry James, for instance, in his "Picture Season in London," in 1877 commented, "The Royal Academy is, I believe, this year pronounced a rather poor academy; but such, I also believe, is the regular verdict." The reason for such failure, James believed, was partly the willingness of the academy to please an "unimaginative and unaesthetic" audience—"the British merchant and paterfamilias and his excellently regulated family" (147–48).

By contrast, the Grosvenor Gallery—with highly imaginative pictures such as Burne-Jones's *Le Chant d'Amour* (1868–1877), *The Beguiling of Merlin*, *The Mirror of Venus*, *Laus Veneris*, and *The Days of Creation*—offered seductive alternatives and at the same time expressed and depicted the mood and the atmosphere of the Aesthetic movement by then prevalent in art and poetry. Such pictures lacked the detailed realism and narrative content of early Pre-Raphaelitism. "One of the most hauntingly beautiful works, the composition of *Le Chant d'Amour*," John Christian explains, "moves beyond narrative: the musical theme, the emotional tension between the figures, the romantic landscape, and the evening light combine to create a mood of nostalgia and yearning which he [Edward Burne-Jones] often aims for but seldom captures in so intense a form" (Wildman and Christian 212). Rather than seeking the meaning of Burne-Jones's paintings, admiring critics like Henry James celebrated their enchanting colors and the expressions of their figures. Referring to *Laus Veneris* and *Le Chant d'Amour* in his review of the 1878 Grosvenor exhibition, James declared, "As a brilliant success in the way of colour it is hard to know which picture to place first; each of them, at any rate, bears in this respect the great stamp— the stamp of the master for whom the play of colour is a freedom, an invention, a source of thought and delight." As in the early Pre-Raphaelite paintings, expression rather than beauty was the distinct characteristic of Edward Burne-Jones's figures. James singled out the expression of the main figures as the "strongest point" when he discussed *Laus Veneris,* for instance, and focused on "the grand weariness and, at the same time, absorption of posture of the medieval Venus, and the beautiful, rapt dejection of the mysterious young warrior" ("The Grosvenor Gallery" 163).

By the late 1870s the Pre-Raphaelite influence was not limited within the walls of art galleries but extended into the social realm. In 1879 Justin McCarthy noted the pervasiveness of the Pre-Raphaelite spirit in just about every aspect of Victorian culture and society: "We have now in London pre-Raphaelite painters, pre-Raphaelite poets, pre-Raphaelite novelists, pre-Raphaelite young ladies; pre-Raphaelite hair, eyes, complexion, dress, decorations, window curtains, chairs, tables, knives, forks, and coal-scuttles. We have pre-Raphaelite anatomy, we have pre-Raphaelite music" (1876, 725). Numerous critics, however, did not welcome the Pre-Raphaelite presence in social circles; instead, they resisted and opposed such a prevalent influence that, they believed, destabilized moral values and gender boundaries.

Three decades after their first exhibition as the Pre-Raphaelite Brotherhood, the Pre-Raphaelites once again became the target of hostile critics who described in melodramatic terms the putatively deleterious effect of Pre-Raphaelite paintings on young and old viewers alike. Bewildered by unprecedented modes of representation, art critics of the late 1870s and 1880s, like their predecessors responding to the early Pre-Raphaelite exhibits, decried what they saw as the unintelligible, archaic, deviant style of the aesthetic phase of Pre-Raphaelitism. In response to the glamorous and spectacular 1877 Grosvenor exhibition, the *Times*, for instance, assailed the pictures in terms reminiscent of the vituperative attacks on the first exhibits of the Pre-Raphaelite Brotherhood: "To a great many . . . these pictures are unintelligible puzzles, of which they do not care to attempt the solution; to others they are occasions of angry antagonism or contemptuous ridicule. To a large majority of the crowd who will soon be thronging the Academy galleries, such pictures as these seem unaccountable freaks of individual eccentricity, or the strange and unwholesome fruits of hopeless wanderings in the mazes of mysticism and medievalism."[2]

Similarly, after tracing the roots of aestheticism to the Pre-Raphaelite Brotherhood, Henry Quilter of *Macmillan's Magazine* deprecated aestheticism for its corrupting impact on art and society. Ironically this critic recognized the early Pre-Raphaelitism, which initially was vehemently denounced by contemporary critics as a "healthy" attempt to reform art; by contrast, in his view, late Pre-Raphaelitism, by then identified with aestheticism, was a cause of "corruption":

> [T]hough pre-Raphaelitism, in its pure and original form, has passed away, its dead carcase is still left with us, and is a source of corruption which cannot be too soon fully understood. The claim of the modern gospel of intensity, and the critical theories of pure sensuousness which are proclaimed so loudly just now, have their curiously unfitting root in the pre-Raphaelite movement; and it strangely happens that the action taken by three or four clever art students, towards a reformation in art as healthy as it was needful, has ended in breeding phases of art and poetry, which embody the lowest theory of art-usefulness, and the most morbid and sickly art-results. . . . [T]he evil is spreading from pictures and poems into private life; it has attacked . . . the decoration of our houses, and the dresses of our women. . . . If this hybrid pre-Raphaelitism has not yet erected itself into a rule of conduct, it has become in some sort effective as a standard of manners; and there may now be seen at many a

social gathering young men and women whose lacklustre eyes, dishev-
elled hair, eccentricity of attire, and general appearance of weary passion
proclaim them members of the new school.[3]

Most often the adverse criticism of the Pre-Raphaelite aestheticism was
not aimed merely at the lack of narrative content or the absence of a
moral message. Like the art critics of the early years of the Pre-Raphaelite
movement, reviewers of the 1870s often interwove their objections to
aesthetic innovations with comments on morality, which, in turn
expressed their anxieties over transgressions of conventional gender
boundaries. Almost thirty years after the first Pre-Raphaelite exhibit,
reviewers once again articulated their objections to subversions of gender
boundaries in terms of physical and moral disease and deviance. Frederick
Wedmore, for instance, reviewing Burne-Jones's pictures at the 1877
Grosvenor exhibit, felt compelled "to protest against and to bewail the
prominence of the unhealthy type with which his work has familiarised
us. "Laus Veneris" is an uncomfortable picture, so wan and death-like, so
stricken with disease of the soul, so eaten up and gnawed away with disappointment and desire, is the Queen of Love at Grosvenor. . . . The type
is to many an offensive, to most a disagreeable one, and the Venus is of
that type the most disagreeable, the most offensive example. The very
body is unpleasant and uncomely; and the soul behind it . . . is ghastly."[4]

Henry James, discussing the same painting, concurred, emphasizing the
unhealthy state of figures. Venus "has the face and aspect of a person who
has had what the French call an 'intimate' acquaintance with life; her
companions, on the other hand, though pale, sickly, and wan, in the manner of all Mr. Burne-Jones's young people, have a more innocent and
vacant expression, and seem to have derived their langour chiefly from
contact and sympathy" (The Grosvenor Gallery" 162).

As in the early years of the Pre-Raphaelite movement, adverse criticism
to Pre-Raphaelite art was often fueled by anxieties over the subversion of
conventional gender constructs, already destabilized by then by sociopolitical movements and legislative measures. In reference to *Laus Veneris*, for
instance, Wedmore underscored her androgynous nature: "and then the
hips, narrow and straight—the exaggeration of a beauty which Greek art
recognized—a beauty in which the one sex was not so very far removed
from the other" (339). Similarly the critic of the *Illustrated London News*
in 1879 expressed the same apprehension over Pre-Raphaelite transgressions of conventional gender constructs when he censured Burne-Jones's
pictures of the Pygmalion series in terms of their blurring firmly established
boundaries between femininity and masculinity. For the *Illustrated London
News*, not only was the wholesome definition of gender constructs at stake

but the British national identity as well. Referring to the "ultra-sensual school" Burne-Jones's pictures depicted, the critic proceeded to define it as "a school which in its worst development is the morbid outcome of weakly over-wrought physique—which every man who respects his manhood and every woman who values her honour must regard with disgust, and would destroy everything of value in the national character."[5]

It is interesting to note that the same critic ascribed the origin of Burne-Jones's "super sensuousness" to Rossetti's "queer ideal of womankind—with hollow cheeks and square jawbones, necks like swans . . . hair like Topsy's, lips of the same race, 'stung,' therefore swollen, 'with kisses.' The young are apt to sicken to this sort of thing, like puppies to the distemper." Like the early reviewers, those of the late 1870s equated unorthodox representations of gender with dis-ease and unhealthy states: "a sombre, joyless, unhealthy art," as the same critic of the *Illustrated London News* labeled it (415). Similarly, Harry Quilter traced the putative lack of morality of Burne-Jones's paintings to a disturbing absence of a distinction between masculinity and femininity: "One curious resemblance to Botticelli which belongs to Mr. Burne Jones' work . . . is the assimilation of the types of male and female; it is difficult, if not impossible to tell, in many instances, in either painter's work, the sex of the person represented."[6] In his response to the 1877 Grosvenor exhibit, Henry James was also puzzled over the lack of definite gender boundaries in Burne-Jones's paintings: "Perhaps they are young men; they look indeed like beautiful, rather sickly boys. Or rather, they are sublimely sexless, and ready to assume whatever charm of manhood or maidenhood the imagination desires" (The Picture Season in London" 146–47). Referring to the knight in *Le Chant d' Amour*, James underscored his lack of masculinity and perceived him as characteristic of Burne-Jones's representation of gender: "It must be admitted that the young warrior, with the swimming eyes, has a certain perplexing femininity of expression; but Mr. Burne-Jones does not pretend to paint very manly figures, and we should hardly know where to look for a more delicate rendering of a lovesick swain" (The Grosvenor Gallery" 164). Though James is perplexed by Burne-Jones's unconventional gender constructs, at the same time he implicitly acknowledges their necessity, for he recognizes that certain emotional states cannot possibly be expressed by conventional representations of gender.

A fluid definition of masculinity and femininity that characterized the early Pre-Raphaelites also distinguished those of the second movement, especially the paintings of Solomon and Burne-Jones that at times transgressed and quite often eliminated gender boundaries. Their androgynous, sexless figures elided the ideological distinction between masculinity and femininity in paintings such as Solomon's *Bacchus* and Burne-Jones's *St. George*, *The Mirror of Venus*, and *The Days of Creation*, to mention but a few.[7] Henry James's comment about the important role the viewer's imagination plays in determining the gender of the figures in Burne-Jones's paintings is highly suggestive. In his hazy and indistinct representations of gender, Burne-Jones engaged his viewers in more problematic and puzzling ways than his Pre-Raphaelite predecessors, in whose pictures gender identity was more readily understood. In seductive dreamscapes that seem completely removed from the gender politics of his era, Burne-Jones problematizes gender constructs in indefinite and indeterminate androgyny. As the spectators attempt to establish the subjects' gender, they must, at least temporarily, suspend their own notions of gender and collaborate with the artist's resistance to and transgression of the hegemonic gender ideology. Thus the imaginary world with its suspension of gender boundaries represented in Burne-Jones paintings, though seemingly disengaged from the social, is inextricably interwoven with it. As Francette Pacteau points out, when she discusses the transgression of gender boundaries androgyny represents,

Androgyny can be said to belong to the domain of the imaginary, where desire is unobstructed; gender identity to that of the symbolic, the Law, it is at the nodal point where symbolic and imaginary meet that resistance occurs. The androgynous-looking figure presents me with an impossibility, that of the erasure of difference, that very difference which constructs *me* as a subject. From the instant my biological sex is determined, my identity is defined in difference—I am either a boy or a girl. I shall consequently take up my position in society on the side of the sexual divide, behave according to the genderized codes, reaffirm the difference. The androgynous "position" represents a denial, or a transgression, of the rigid gender divide, and as such implies a threat to our given identity and to the system of social roles which define us. How can I reconcile the observation of *threat* with that of desire? . . . In this context the wish correlative to the androgynous fantasy would be attached to archaic memories of early childhood; the disavowal of sexual difference therefore represents the fantasized re-enactment of an early pleasurable perception. (63)

Whether consciously or unconsciously, in his otherworldly paintings, Burne-Jones transgressed the restrictive, forbidding gender boundaries and reconciled threat with desire. His influence, along with that of other late Pre-Raphaelites, extended beyond the galleries, for it moved from the aesthetic into the sociopolitical. In his lightly facetious essay, "The Pre-Raphaelites in

England," Justin McCarthy states that he was bewildered when it came to distinguish genders in their paintings: "[T]he hero has high cheekbones, the gaunt face, the red hair . . . and only for the dress, I doubt whether you would know one from the other." No longer contained within the frames of paintings, he observes, these sexless Pre-Raphaelite figures can actually be seen in London: "But the strangest thing is that this gaunt, lank, and long-limbed damosel has actually stepped from the canvas into life and is to be found everywhere in certain circles of London society." He poses a rhetorical question: "How did all these pre-Raphaelite girls manage to come to life so suddenly?" It is also interesting to note that this critic's observations about the awkwardness of these figures, whether they be pictorial or human, are reminiscent of similar remarks in antagonistic reviews of early Pre-Raphaelite paintings that underscored the angularity of the figures: "[W]e cheer each other by interchanging illustrations of the stiff and lean young woman in various ungainly attitudes, and seeming to be all angles, joints, and fuzzy red hair."[8] Life imitated art, the Pre-Raphaelites had come full circle. As Bullen has already observed, the aestheticism of Burne-Jones's paintings, which seemed to remove them from the sociopolitical realm, was actually directly engaged in gender politics, more specifically in the subversion of masculinity:

> Burne-Jones's paintings of the 1870s are also political in that they resist the polarized gender divisions of the culture. Meditative rather than active, they were accused of unmanliness; imaginative rather than real, they were accused of femininity. We know that Burne-Jones's views were defiant ones—"the more materialistic Science becomes, the more angels shall I paint"—and knowing how "the Fleshly School" had already been received he must have realized in advance of the opening of the Grosvenor Gallery the likely consequences. In a period which was so fraught with sexual anxiety it is perhaps not surprising that the guilt, the horror, and the sense of personal impurity and national degeneracy, all associated with sexuality, should be projected onto forms of visual art which seemed to contravene the prevailing standards of robust, healthy manliness. (Bullen 1998, 216)

Since the Grosvenor Gallery exhibition of 1877 and the Paris Universal Exposition of 1878, Edward Burne-Jones was recognized as one of the most prestigious British painters whose paintings were highly esteemed during the 1880s and 1890s. Like the founders of the Pre-Raphaelite Brotherhood, Burne-Jones sought inspiration in literature, and quite a few of his paintings, such as *The Beguiling of Merlin* (1874), *Sidonia von Bork, 1560* (1860), *Love among the Ruins* (1894), and *Arthur in Avalon* (1881–1898), made visible and palpable the verbal and uninhibited imaginings of literary artists. In turn, literary artists like George Eliot and Thomas Hardy redrew his highly symbolic and suggestive paintings in their own novels thus creating a common ground with the readers who had also been viewers of Burne-Jones's masterpieces. In the process, these novelists also participated in sociopolitical issues of their era and engaged their readers in questioning prevalent gender norms.

Thomas Hardy and the Visual Arts

"If he had been a woman he must have screamed under the nervous tension which he was now undergoing. But that relief being denied to his virility, he clenched his teeth in misery, bringing lines about his mouth like those in the Laocoön, and currugations between his brows."[9] Thus the narrator shapes Jude's devastation into the form of a well-known classical statue, shortly after his lifelong dream of attending the university in Christminster has been shattered by a detached letter of rejection with "sensible advice": "I have read your letter with interest; and, judging from your description of yourself as a working-man, I venture to think that you will have a much better chance of success in life by remaining in your own sphere and sticking to your trade" (120).

By the end of the nineteenth century the famous statue of Laocoön did not merely evoke the terror of Apollo's priest carved in marble, but the sculpture had also become paradigmatic of Lessing's distinctions between the boundaries of spatial and temporal arts. Furthermore, as we have seen, aesthetic distinctions were not simply based on the laws of genre but were also often dictated by the laws of gender. Consciously or unwittingly, the narrator in *Jude the Obscure* also interweaves aesthetic with gender boundaries in the preceding description, a tendency that is not limited to the aforementioned passage but pervades the entire novel. Throughout the novel allusions to contemporary paintings evoke conventional and unconventional gender boundaries. Convention is often represented only to be quickly undermined by the unique idiosyncrasies of Jude and Sue, who though representative of their era, continually struggle against the constraints conventional gender boundaries impose on them, yet are ultimately defeated and destroyed by them. As in his other novels, rather than maintaining the limitations between the different arts, in *Jude the Obscure* Thomas Hardy draws on their affinities, often relying on implicit and subtle allusions to contemporary paintings that express intense emotions or elide established gender boundaries.

In his last novel as well as his other works, Hardy quite often transforms painterly methods into narrative techniques in an attempt to express intense emotions or as a way of engaging in contemporary debates on aesthetics and sociopolitical issues. In an entry in his *Notebooks* some of the goals of his narrative art and those of Pre-Raphaelite art, though he refers to Crivelli and Bellini, seem to dovetail, for he, like the Pre-Raphaelites, is interested in depicting intense emotion: "Jan 3 [1885]. My art is to intensify the expression of things, as is done by Crivelli, Bellini, & so that the heart and inner meaning is made vividly visible" (Millgate, *Life and Works of Thomas Hardy* 183). In another entry the same year he talks about his efforts to make novels visible: "4th, March. Novel-writing as an art cannot go backward. Having reached the analytic stage it must transcend it by going still further in the same direction. Why not by rendering as visible essences, spectre, & the abstract thoughts of the analytic school?" (ibid.). In essence here Hardy seems to describe some of the goals of the Aesthetic movement in Pre-Raphaelite art, which often rendered visible, abstract concepts in paintings such as Burne-Jones's *Days of Creation, Temperantia, Fides,* and *Spes*. In Pre-Raphaelite art Hardy must have seen the means of making his narratives memorable and meaningful to diverse audiences.

Allusions to paintings abound in Hardy's journals and novels, reflecting his profound knowledge of paintings, which began in his early days in London in 1862, when he began visiting the South Kensington Museum (now the Victoria and Albert Museum) and the National Gallery daily. He himself had a talent for sketching and drawing that he exhibited in his own illustrations of his *Wessex Poems,* published in 1898. Hardy's contemporary reviewers often noted the intersection of the verbal and the visual in his novels. In June 1872 the *Athenaeum,* for instance, referred to the "graphic pictures of rustic life" in *Desperate Remedies*. In his review of *Far from the Madding Crowd,* R. H. Hutton of the *Spectator* discussed "the beauty of its descriptive sketches. Many of them are pictures of the most delicate and vivid beauty—watercolours in words, and very fine ones too."[10] Hardy's knowledge of the visual arts has been extensively documented by several scholars. C. J. Weber, for instance, compiled a long catalog of thirty European artists with whose works Hardy was familiar. It is debatable whether any English novelist, Alistair Smart contends, "possessed so intimate a knowledge of the visual arts. Certainly no other writer of fiction has ever used such knowledge with equal skill or imagination" (263).

More recently, Thomas Hardy's allusions to the visual arts have been the subjects of varied interpretations and critical controversies. Some critics, for instance, contend that Hardy is parading his knowledge (Gittings 141; Page 1977, 66). J. Hillis Miller points out that Hardy's pictorial symbolism is "so blunt and unsubtle . . . that one hesitates to read anything into it"

(211). Other critics consider Hardy's allusions to the visual arts as "incongruous and gratuitous," for, they remark, Hardy suddenly refers to them in his texts and as quickly and without warning abandons them (Byerly 153). Most critics, however, fail to see that Hardy's allusions to art become progressively more sophisticated in the course of his career. Whereas in *The Woodlanders*, *The Return of the Native*, and *Far from the Madding Crowd*, references to art appear suddenly and unexpectedly, in *Tess of the d'Urbervilles*, Hardy represents ordinary people as artistic masterpieces. In both *Tess of the d'Urbervilles* and *Jude the Obscure* Hardy does not merely allude to contemporary paintings but redraws them and in the process participates in contemporary debates on issues such as aesthetics, class, and gender, to mention but a few. As Bullen has already pointed out, Hardy's pictorialism becomes more persuasive when the names of paintings are no longer mentioned in the text of his novels (*The Expressive Eye* 7). Some critics have briefly noted that several of the paintings Hardy reconfigures in his narratives are well-known Pre-Raphaelite masterpieces.[11]

Hardy's Suspension of Gender Boundaries in Burne-Jones's Dreamscapes

As his other novels *Jude the Obscure* is precariously balanced on an uneasy tension between an endorsement and a subversion of gender ideology. I locate this tension in *Jude the Obscure* in subtle reconfigurations of contemporary paintings by Edward Burne-Jones, whose androgynous figures are often cast in dreamlike landscapes, paintings of classical or chivalrous scenes, luxuriant images of a world that never was or could never exist. Contemporary and postmodern art historians have often described Burne-Jones as "a dreamer and a romantic in a prosaic and materialistic world" who "sought to transcend the limits of mundane reality by creating a rarefied realm of beauty in his art" (Mancoff 1998, 7). Most critics would agree that his paintings possess "an irresistibly dream-like and often mysterious and detached quality" (Ash 10). Burne-Jones himself in a letter in 1872 remarked, "I mean by a picture a beautiful, romantic dream of something that never was, never will be—in a light better than any lights that ever shone—in a land no one can define or remember, only desire—and the forms divinely beautiful—and then I wake up" (ibid., plate 9). Like the subjects of Burne-Jones's paintings, Jude and Sue often conjure a world of dreams, a utopian universe seemingly detached from constraining social conventions until conventions obliterate it. In fact, Hardy's initial title for *Jude the Obscure* in its serialized version included the word "dreamer" as a possible choice: "The Simpletons / Part First / Hearts Insurgent / A

Dreamer" (Kramer 165). But unlike Burne-Jones's dreams materialized in exquisitely beautiful canvases, Jude's and Sue's dreams are shattered by Victorian reality. It is interesting to note that as early as April 1883, Havelock Ellis, writing for *Westminster Review* about Hardy's novels preceding *Jude the Obscure*, draws a parallel between Hardy's narratives and the dreamy qualities of Burne-Jones's paintings: "No one, who has once felt the charm of the dream-wrapt faces which Mr. Burne-Jones loves to delineate, has cared that the artist should seek for fresh types of loveliness, and it is equally easy to be content with the type of womanhood which Mr. Hardy gives us in all its delicate variations" (Cox 106).[12]

An entry in his *Notebooks* in January 1887 reveals Hardy's awareness of the limitations of realistic art in meeting or representing the demands of the modern temperament:

> I feel that Nature is played out as a Beauty, but not as a Mystery. I don't want to see landscapes, i.e., scenic paintings of them, because I don't want to see the original realities—as optical effects, that is. I want to see the deeper reality underlying the scenic, the expression of what are sometimes called abstract imaginings. The 'simply natural' is interesting no longer. . . . The exact truth as to material fact ceases to be of importance in art—it is a student's style—the style of a period when the mind is serene and unawakened to the tragical mysteries of life; when it does not bring anything to the object that coalesces with and translates the qualities that are already there—half hidden, it may be—and the two united are depicted as the All. (Millgate 1984, 192)

These statements could very well describe the two most important phases of Pre-Raphaelitism—realism and aestheticism. In the last four decades of the nineteenth century "abstract imaginings" had gradually replaced the intense and accurate representations of reality. By then Hardy had visited the Grosvenor Gallery and had met Edward Burne-Jones. Another entry in the January 1887 *Notebooks* also suggests the elision between dreams and reality, yet another feature of aestheticism: "I was thinking a night or two ago that people are somnambulists—that the material is not the real—only the visible, the real being invisible optically. That it is because we are in a somnambulistic hallucination that we think the real to be what we see as real" (ibid.). Three years later, on August 5, 1890, in an entry titled "Reflections on Art," Hardy rejects realism for aestheticism: "Art is a disproportioning . . . of realities, to show more clearly the features that matter in these realities, which, if merely copied . . . might possibly be observed, but would more probably be overlooked. Hence 'realism' is not Art" (ibid., 239).

The poignant incongruity between soft romantic dreams and brutal reality is a theme on which Hardy's entire novel pivots. He alluded to this theme in a letter to Edmund Gosse on November 10, 1895, after several outraged critics attacked the novel for its alleged obscenity, some of them labeling it *Jude the Obscene:* "The 'grimy' features of the story go to show the contrast between the ideal life a man wished to lead, & the squalid real life he was fated to lead," he explains. "The throwing of the pizzle, at the supreme moment of his young dream, is to sharply initiate this contrast. But I must have lamentably failed, as I feel I have, if this requires explanation & is not self-evident. The idea was meant to run all through the novel. It is, in fact, to be discovered in *every* body's life—though it lies less on the surface perhaps than it does in my poor puppets" (*Letters* 2:93).

Indeed Arabella's first appearance in Jude's life occurs as a disruption of the dream world Jude conjures, immersed as he is in his speculations about his progress in classical works, the knowledge of which he believes will qualify him to matriculate in Christminster: "And then he continued to dream, and thought he might become even a bishop by leading a pure, energetic, wise, Christian life. . . . Euripides, Plato, Aristotle, Lucretius, Epictetus, Seneca, Antoninus. Then I must master other things: the Fathers thoroughly" (34). Engrossed in his dreamy musings, completely detached from the surrounding world, Jude "was now standing quite still, looking at the ground as though the future were thrown thereon by a magic lantern. On a sudden something smacked him sharply in the ear, and he became aware that a soft cold substance had been flung at him, and had fallen at his feet" (35).

Crass reality, in the form of Arabella's phallic missile, suddenly disrupts Jude's academic musings. Even more surprising than the disparity between idealism and sordid reality is Jude's response to Arabella. Though an idealist who repeatedly questions the hierarchical underpinnings of Victorian society, Jude nevertheless appears from the very beginning of the novel to be representative of the patriarchal society he questions and attempts to undermine. Such ideology is registered in his initial glance at Arabella, devoid of any idealism, highlighting gender and hierarchical binaries: "She whom he addressed was a fine dark-eyed girl, not exactly handsome, but capable of passing as such at a little distance, despite some coarseness of skin and fibre. She had a round and prominent bosom, full lips, perfect teeth, and rich complexion of a Cochin hen's egg. She was a complete and substantial female human;—no more, no less; and Jude was almost certain that to her was attributable the enterprise of throwing the lump of offal at him" (36).[13]

Later on Jude's gaze travels from her eyes to her bosom, swiftly appropriating Arabella's body from a distance, reducing her to the object of his desire: "It is scarcely an exaggeration to say that till this moment Jude had

never looked at a woman to consider her as such, but had vaguely regarded the sex as being outside his life and purposes. He gazed from her eyes
to her mouth, thence to her bosom, and to her full round naked arms, wet,
mottled with the chill of the water, and firm as marble" (37–38). In this
scene the gendered hierarchy of the gaze is underscored.

However, what is even more striking is not so much Jude's gaze, which
moves within established gender boundaries, as Arabella's defiance of his
gaze, her returning glance that transgresses those limits: "She brightened
with a little glow of triumph, swept him almost tenderly with her eyes in
turning, and retracing her steps down the broadside grass rejoined her
companions" (38). Arabella's boldness unsettles and disturbs Jude's pleasure, paralyzing his will power and undermining his self-control. Indeed
Jude seems to undergo the terrifying effects of Medusa's power evoked by
her staring eyes, as he experiences the weakening of his resolution: "[T]he
intentions as to reading, working, and learning, which he had so precisely formulated only a few minutes earlier, were suffering a curious collapse
into a corner, he knew not how" (ibid.).

The first encounter between Jude and Arabella, replete with suggestive
narrative hints, evokes the situation strikingly depicted in Edward Burne-
Jones's *Beguiling of Merlin* (1873) (plate 15), which captures the catastrophic results of Nimue's "spellbinding gaze" and sharply registers the
transgression of conventional gender boundaries. Appropriating Merlin's
book of charms, a signifier of his intellectual, and traditionally masculine,
power, Nimue rises above him intransigent and self-assured, whereas the
feminized Merlin looks fearfully into space, averting her direct stare.
Based on the Arthurian legend, the painting depicts Nimue, who has pursued Camelot's wizard into the forest, hoping to learn his secret spells.
"Lulled into submission by her promise to satisfy his every desire, Merlin
relinquishes his ancient book of enchantment. Nimue then betrays him,
using his own magic to drain his powers and imprison him for eternity in
the flowering branches of the hawthorn tree" (Mancoff 1998, 71).

Though depicted as a femme fatale, Nimue in this picture surprisingly
lacks the alluring femininity associated with such a figure. Instead, her
strong and tall fully clothed figure, the snakes in her hair, as well as her
gaze, exude traditionally masculine power and control. In his review of this
painting, F. G. Stephens commented on the reversal of traditional gender
constructs in the picture: "Nimue looks while she works a spell. . . . [H]er
face in its snaky intensity of malice is marvelous, not so the weak and
womanish visage of Merlin."[14] Merlin's immobility, his entrapment within
the hawthorn tree, is contrasted with Nimue's movement away from the
claustrophobic scene, her left foot advancing on a stone bridge over a
stream, a seemingly insignificant detail overtaken by the largeness of the

hawthorn tree that covers the entire canvas and even conceals the background opening of the horizon behind the two figures. Yet the bridge over the stream is about to separate Nimue from Merlin both physically and figuratively; it signifies Nimue's eventual liberation from her mentor's power, while the ensnared Merlin remains behind—abandoned.

Hardy's narrative reconfiguration of this painting includes the seemingly insignificant detail of the stream, which also separates Jude from Arabella and her companions when Jude first becomes aware of their presence: "On the other side of the hedge was a stream, whence, as he now for the first time realized, had come the slight sounds of voices and laughter that had mingled with his dreams" (35). Like Nimue, the narrator implies, Arabella trades her "love" for the power that marriage to Jude would provide her; she entraps the naïve Jude and abandons him, yet we are led to believe that he remains her entrapped victim to the very end of his life. No doubt the evocation of *The Beguiling of Merlin* is somewhat ironic, for Arabella is never interested in Jude's books, often thinking instead that her husband ought to "stick to his trade, and throw aside those stupid books for practical undertakings" (57). Her insolent disregard of his books, when she indifferently smears them with hot grease and furiously tosses them on the floor, triggers Jude's first outrage against his young wife (68).

From the beginning of the novel, when Arabella first meets Jude by attracting his attention through her phallic missile (the offal of a pig), she is associated with another classical enchantress—Circe. Through her scheming, that is, her feigned pregnancy, she induces the nineteen-year-old Jude to marry her and later through her wine to remarry her. Her merciless slaughtering of the pig at the beginning of her marriage alienates Jude from her completely. When Jude confronts Arabella about the deception of her pretended pregnancy and his consequent entrapment, he once again associates Arabella with swine (67). Like the mythological Circe, Arabella is throughout the book associated with deceit, the pigs of her father's farm, and the wine that she uses to ensnare Jude. In *The Wine of Circe*, his 1869 watercolor, Burne-Jones represented Circe preparing her wine for Ulysses and his crew, whose ships approach in the distance. According to John Christian, Ruskin had initially commissioned this watercolor for his *Munera Pulveris*, a series of papers originally published in *Fraser's Magazine* (Parris, *The Pre-Raphaelites*, 303–4). For Ruskin Circe represents "pure Animal life," a comment worth considering in the context of Jude's first description of Arabella as a "female animal." Ruskin continues: "She is . . . indeed an Enchantress . . . but always wonderful. . . . [E]ven the wild beasts rejoice and are softened around her cave. . . . [T]he transforming poisons she gives to men are mixed with . . . wine, milk, and corn. . . . [I]t is their own fault if these make swine of them."[15]

Unlike Arabella, Sue is portrayed as a vulnerable and sensitive, ethereal woman, yet because of her intelligence and sophistication she is presented as even more destructive than her sensuous opposite. On numerous occasions the narrator dwells on the putatively destructive effects of the female gaze, whether it be that of the voluptuous and mindless Arabella or that of the intelligent and highly sophisticated nonconformist Sue. In fact, the narrator implies, Sue's direct gaze galvanizes friendship into sexual desire, eventually destroying Jude's and her own life. When Jude visits Sue at Shaston, eight weeks after her marriage to Phillotson, she confides in him her utter unhappiness and misery: "'I like Mr. Phillotson as a friend, I don't like him—it is a torture to me to—live with him as a husband!'" (223). As in their other encounters, the evening Sue and Jude spend together confiding in each other is erotically charged; the magnetism between them is still intense the morning they part on the "lonely road to Alfredston. . . . They had stood parting in the silent highway, and their tense and passionate moods had led to bewildered inquiries of each other on how far their intimacy ought to go. . . . And then they had turned from each other in estrangement, and gone their several ways, till at a distance of twenty or thirty yards both had looked round simultaneously. That look behind was fatal to the reserve hitherto more or less maintained. They had quickly run back, and met, embracing most unpremeditatedly, kissed close and long. . . . The kiss was a turning point in Jude's career" (227).

Although the glance is mutual, Jude attributes to Sue's gaze the dramatic change in his life. That evening, left alone to his musings, he contemplates women's destructive force (originating in their returning gaze): "Strange that his aspiration—towards academical proficiency—had been checked by a woman, and that his second aspiration—towards apostleship—had also been checked by a woman." Once again Jude sees Sue as his captor. In this sense then, Sue, like Arabella, in Jude's perspective, represents a femme fatale to whose power he surrenders with resignation, without any protest or resistance. "'Is it,' he said, 'that the women are to blame; or is it the artificial system of things, under which the normal sex-impulses are turned into devilish domestic gins and springs to noose and hold back those who want to progress?'" (228).

At no time in his musings does Jude recognize the weakness of his own resolution. His passion for Sue, he reasons, is opposed to his new goal to become a minister. In a sacrificial ritual that night, he burns all his theological and ethical works: "Lighting some loose pamphlets to begin with, he cut the volumes into pieces as well as he could. . . . They kindled, and lighted up the back of the house, the pigsty, and his own face, till they were more or less consumed" (ibid.). Thus Jude once again sacrifices his own aspirations, this time to that "aerial being," the ethereal goddess of his life (227). At no time in his life does he assert his own will power against the spell of the femmes fatales, who paradoxically become such only through the power Jude invests in them.

Known for her iconoclastic views of religion and convention, Sue, since the novel's publication, has been the subject of critical controversy; indeed, she is the most problematic and elusive of Hardy's characters, resisting classification or containment.[16] Contemporary and recent critics have often treated her like a patient desperately needing a diagnosis that might elucidate her problematic psyche. In his review of the novel in *Cosmopolis* on January 4, 1896, Edmund Gosse, for instance, refers to Sue as "the neurotic, semi-educated girl of hyper-sensitive instincts" whose "*vita sexualis* is the central interest of the book, and enough is told about it to fill the specimen tables of a German specialist" (Cox 264, 268). Later in the same review he concludes, "She is a poor, maimed 'degenerate,' ignorant of herself and of the perversion of her instincts, full of febrile, amiable illusions, ready to dramatize her empty life, and play at loving though she cannot love" (ibid., 269).[17]

Surprisingly even recent critics dwell on Sue's "frigidity," one of them believing that it "entangles three men, causes the death of two and the moral corruption of a third," diagnosing Sue's condition as an Attention Deficit Syndrome: "Sue is thus distractible and unfocused in her sexuality" (Taylor xxv, xxvi). Yet even a Victorian critic, Havelock Ellis (himself a psychologist), could perceive the absurdity of the various diagnoses of Sue's seemingly aberrant psychology. In his October 1896 review of *Jude the Obscure* he contends, "Sue is neurotic, some critics say; it is fashionable to play cheerfully with terrible words you know nothing about. 'Neurotic,' these good people by way of dismissing her, innocently unaware that many a charming 'urban miss' of their own acquaintance would deserve the name at least as well" (Cox 311). Surprisingly, Hardy also spoke of Sue's "abnormalism" in a letter to Edmund Gosse on November 11, 1895, but instead of clarifying and specifying the term made it even hazier, thus opening it to further speculation: "There is nothing perverted or depraved in Sue's nature," he states. "The abnormalism consists in disproportion: not in inversion, her sexual instinct being healthy so far as it goes, but unusually weak & fastidious (*Letters* 2:99). Yet his comments also reveal Sue's desperate efforts to be treated as her male partners' equal:

> [T]hough she has children, her intimacies with Jude have never been more than occasional, even while they were living together (I mention that they occupy separate rooms, except towards the end), & one of her reasons for fearing the marriage ceremony is that she fears it wd be breaking faith

with Jude to withhold herself at pleasure, or altogether, after it; though while uncontracted she feels at liberty to yield herself as seldom as she chooses. This has tended to keep his passion as hot at the end as at the beginning, & helps to break his heart. He has never really possessed her as freely as he desired. Sue is a type of woman which has always had an attraction for me—but the difficulty of drawing the type has kept me from attempting it till now. (*Letters* 2:99)

Sue's wish to withhold herself at pleasure is yet another one of her ineffectual attempts to be treated as an equal. A free spirit like Sue experiences even more acutely the social constraints of the patriarchal institutions of Victorian society, including that of marriage, which reduces her, even in the most intimate moments of her life, to an inferior deprived of any power to assert her subjectivity. Again and again she struggles to train her male admirers to treat her as an equal, but each time she fails, for her male pursuers insist on a physical relationship with her. However, Sue is aware of the fact that even the erotic is regulated by established gender boundaries that threaten her autonomy and ultimately destroy her.

When she confesses to Jude her repugnance for Phillotson, she poignantly articulates the humiliation she experiences each time she has to submit to his desire irrespective of her own wishes. Though rebellious against and resistant to the distorted laws that hierarchical gender relations impose on people, Sue has internalized their force and sees her wish to be treated as an equal as "wickedness." "'But it is not as you think,'" she tells Jude. "'There is nothing wrong except my own wickedness, I suppose you'd call it,—a repugnance on my part, for a reason I cannot disclose, and what would not be admitted as one by the world in general! . . . What tortures me so much is the necessity of being responsive to this man whenever he wishes, good as he is morally!—the dreadful contract to feel in a particular way, in a matter whose essence is its voluntariness!'" (223). Caught in a labyrinth of ideological incongruities, Sue struggles alone to resolve them but is ultimately defeated.

A close reading of the narrative reveals that Sue can by no means be held accountable for the death of two men as some critics maintain. When she escapes from the training school for teachers in which she has been persecuted, following her assignation with Jude, she shares with him the story about her relationship with the undergraduate at Christminster. What initiates and propels her friendship with him, Sue explains, is his willingness to treat her as an equal: "'We used to go about together on walking tours, reading tours, and things of that sort—like two men almost. He asked me to live with him, and I agreed to by letter. But when

I joined him in London I found he meant a different thing from what I meant. He wanted to be my lover, in fact, but I wasn't in love with him—and on my saying I should go away if he didn't agree to my plan, he did so'" (153). Even though quite young at the time, only eighteen, Sue knows what she wants and reaches an agreement with her roommate, but he later reneges on his promise. Yet it is Sue who has been blamed by contemporary and recent critics alike for her sexless cruelty. She herself is aware of the image she projects and, anticipating Jude's judgment, defends her behavior: "'People say I must be cold-natured—sexless—on account of it. But I won't have it! Some of the most passionately erotic poets have been the most self-contained in their daily lives'" (154). Indeed Sue resembles Burne-Jones's figures, described by contemporary critics such as Henry James "like beautiful, rather sickly boys. Or rather, they are sublimely sexless, and ready to assume whatever charm of manhood or maidenhood the imagination desires" ("The Picture Season in London" 146–47). Or she is very much like the "gaunt, lank, and long-limbed damosel" Justin McCarthy discusses who "has actually stepped from the canvas into life and is to be found everywhere in certain circles of London society" (727).

Certainly, Sue's ethereal appearance is reminiscent of Burne-Jones's dreamy, androgynous figures situated in an imaginary and fragile universe. When Sue for instance argues that marriage smothers passion, Jude retorts, "'But you, Sue, are such a phantasmal, bodiless creature, one who . . . has so little animal passion in you, that you can act upon reason in the matter'" (272). When she goes to visit the sick Phillotson, she enters his room "in light spring clothing, and her advent seemed ghostly—like the flitting in of a moth" (262). At the agricultural exhibition, we are told, Sue went along by Jude's side "as if she hardly touched the ground, and as if a moderately strong puff of wind would float her over the hedge into the next field" (306). When Arabella sees her then, she remarks to her husband, "'He's charmed by her as if she were some fairy!'" (307). Further, when Jude tries to soothe her anguish following the children's suicide, he exclaims, "'you are absolutely the most ethereal, least sensual woman I ever knew to exist without inhuman sexlessness'"(364). Such descriptions charged with emotional intensity lack the detailed realism of the Pre-Raphaelite reconfigurations drawn by Elizabeth Gaskell, Wilkie Collins, or George Eliot. In his redrawings of Burne-Jones's figures and paintings Hardy follows more closely the principles of aestheticism rather than realism as he concentrates quite often on conveying a mood rather than the physical appearance of the characters and their surroundings.

Sue's intense desire for autonomy and equality is often described as an aspect of her androgynous character. It is for the chance of achieving such

equality that Sue becomes involved with Jude. Frequently during her relationship with him she calls him none of the affectionate names lovers
often use but chooses instead the word "comrade" for its strong connotations of equality. On the night she confides in him about the undergraduate, for instance, she explains what has attracted her to Jude: "'But I did
want and long to ennoble some man to high aims; and when I saw you,
and knew you wanted to be my comrade, I—shall I confess it?—thought
that man might be you. But you take so much tradition on trust that I
don't know what to say'" (158). Even when she is distraught over the
death of her three children, she still holds on to the ideal of equality: "'O
my comrade, our perfect union—our two-in-oneness—is now stained in
with blood!'" (357).

   People around Sue and Jude are often struck by the extraordinary affinity between them and their regard of each other as equals, certainly a
unique relationship for the patriarchal standards of the time. When
Phillotson, for instance, confides in his friend George Gillingham about
his troubled marriage, he exclaims: "'I have been struck with these two
facts: the extraordinary sympathy, or similarity, between the pair. He is her
cousin, which perhaps accounts for some of it. They seem to be one person split in two!'" (240–41). Even Arabella, when from a distance she sees
Jude and Sue holding hands and walking at the agricultural exhibition,
discerns their unique attachment: "That complete mutual understanding,
in which every glance and movement was as effectual as speech for conveying intelligence between them, made them almost the two parts of a
single whole" (306). Such allusions direct our attention to Plato's
Symposium, in particular to Aristophanes' comic narrative of the origin of
Eros, which he situates in the beginning of the universe when, in his
opinion, there were not just two genders but an additional one—the
androgynous. At the time, Aristophanes explains, "The sexes were three
in number, not, as they are now, two, male and female; there was also as
a third the union of the two, having a name corresponding to this double
nature, which had once a real existence, but is now lost, and the word
'androgynous' is preserved as a term of reproach" (229). He continues
with the well-known story of the round, primeval humans, "their backs
and sides forming a circle" until the gods, threatened by the strength of
these creatures, cut them in half, and since then each half has been desperately seeking the other (230–33). It is interesting to note that
Aristophanes locates the origin of heterosexual love in the androgynous:
"Now men who are a section of that double nature that was once called
androgynous are lovers of women" (231). Hardy's allusions to Plato also
evoke several of Edward Burne-Jones's representations of Cupid and
Psyche, most notably *Cupid Finding Psyche, Cupid Delivering Psyche,*

Psyche, Holding the Lamp, Gazes Enraptured on the Face of the Sleeping Cupid; Psyche Kneels, with Arms Held Out in Supplication, as Cupid Flies Away through the Doorway, pictures in which the two deities are depicted as a dyad, two halves of a circular configuration. As we have already seen, Sue is described in spiritual rather than physical terms, as a "phantasmal," "ethereal," "ghostly" figure, a personification of the soul, as it were, the Greek meaning of Psyche's name. Jude defines her as such when he says, "'you spirit, you disembodied creature, you dear, sweet, tantalizing phantom'" (256), and Sue herself directly identifies with Psyche when she asks him to say "those pretty lines from Shelley's 'Epipsychidion,'" meaning in Greek "On the Subject of the Soul."[18]

In 1864 William Morris and Edward Burne-Jones decided to produce a lavish, illustrated folio of Morris's long narrative poem *Earthly Paradise*, the first poem of which is "The Story of Cupid and Psyche." Burne-Jones designed seventy subjects from this story. Beginning in the 1860s, when he drew his first watercolors, *Cupid Finding Psyche* and *Cupid Delivering Psyche*, this theme preoccupied him for the next thirty years, and *The Wedding of Psyche* (1895) is one of his last paintings on the subject (Wildman and Christian 119).[19] In these paintings, gouaches, and oils Burne Jones depicts a sequence of love, betrayal, and rescue, resembling the phases of Jude's and Sue's love story.[20]

When Sue escapes from the Training School for Teachers, she comes to Jude's apartment soaked from her walk through the river. Seeing her in the darkness, Jude "palpitated at the thought that she had fled to him in her trouble as he had fled to her in his" (149). The allusion to Cupid and Psyche is embedded in Jude's thinking and action: "What counterparts they were! He unlatched the door of his room, heard a stealthy rustle on the dark stairs, and in a moment she appeared in the light of his lamp. He went up to seize her hand, and found she was clammy as a marine deity, and that her clothes clung to her like the robes upon the figures in the Parthenon frieze" (ibid.). Jude's lamp casts an enchanting light on Sue's sudden appearance and evokes a similar event in the Cupid and Psyche story. Moreover, lest we missed the allusion to Cupid and Psyche, this important chapter concludes with Jude leaning over the sleeping Sue, observing that "a warm flush now rosed her hitherto blue cheeks, and felt that her hanging hand was no longer cold. Then he stood with his back to the fire regarding her, and saw in her almost a divinity" (150). This scene reconfigures the subject of Burne-Jones's *Cupid Finding Psyche* (1865) (plate 16), which shows Cupid gazing affectionately at the sleeping Psyche, her left arm loosely hanging in the foreground, the two figures forming two halves of a circular configuration. Originating in an illustration of Morris's "Story of Cupid and Psyche," this watercolor depicts the

Plate 16. Edward Burne-Jones, *Cupid Finding Psyche*, 1865. Watercolor, bodycolor, and pastel mounted on linen, 27³/₄ x 19 in (70.3 x 48.3 cm), Yale Center for British Art. Reproduced by permission.

beginning of the story when the goddess Venus has sent Cupid to destroy Psyche, but instead he falls in love with the sleeping princess. The following lines from Morris's tale correspond with the watercolor and the aforementioned scene in the novel:

> As Love cast down his eyes with a half smile,
> Godlike and cruel , that faded in a while,
> And long he stood above her hidden eyes
> With red lops parted in god's surprise. (Wildman and Christian 121)

Startled by Sue's unanticipated appearance, Jude asks in bewilderment: "'Whatever have you done, darling?' he asked, with alarm." Sue retorts, "'walked through the largest river in the county—that's what I've done! They locked me up for being out with you; and it seemed so unjust that I couldn't bear it, so I got out of the window and escaped across the stream!'" (149). Sue emerging from the water in search of Jude evokes yet another painting of the story of Cupid and Psyche, *Pan and Psyche* (1872–1874), which represents Psyche emerging from the water after trying to drown herself following Pan's desertion. Burne-Jones exhibited this painting in the Grosvenor Gallery in 1878, an exhibition that, as we have seen, Hardy had attended.

As in several of Burne-Jones's paintings, the male figure, in this case Cupid—in a flowing classical drapery resembling that of Psyche, his features as feminine as those of Psyche—appears androgynous. Thus the painting extends and transgresses conventional gender boundaries. Hardy, however, in his narrative reconfigurations of the Cupid and Psyche story casts Sue, not Jude as an androgynous figure. Her androgyny is particularly emphasized in the scenes described earlier that reconfigure Burne-Jones's Cupid and Psyche paintings. When Jude's landlady unexpectedly comes to his room and sees Sue in Jude's clothes sleeping by the fireplace, she mistakes her for "a young gentleman" (151). Later on, when Sue asks Jude to be her comrade, Jude "looked away, for that epicene tenderness of hers was too harrowing. . . . If he could only get over the sense of her sex, as she seemed to be able to do so easily of his, what a comrade she would make" (159). In that fleeting moment of the suspension of gender boundaries, Jude sees Sue as his equal, his other half from which he may not be separated under any circumstances: "She was nearer to him than any other woman he had ever met, and he could scarcely believe that time, creed, or absence, would ever divide him from her" (ibid.). The next morning as he gazes at Sue asleep, once again he seems to cherish her androgyny, "looking warm as a new bun and boyish as a Ganymedes" (ibid.).

The Problematics of Androgyny

Scholars interested in situating Sue within a chronological context have debated whether she is representative of "the Girl of the Period" of the 1860s or the "New Woman" of the 1890s. The girl of the period and the English girl of the past, "a creature generous, capable and modest," Eliza Lynn Linton declared in March 1868, have nothing in common. The girl of the period is characterized by "her love of pleasure and indifference to duty" and by "her dissatisfaction with the monotony of ordinary life, and horror of all useful work; in a word, to the worst forms of luxury and self-ishness, to the most fatal effects arising from want of high principle and absence of tender feeling." Men are afraid of her and prefer "the simple and genuine girl of the past."[21] Like the Girl of the Period, the New Woman of the 1890s usurped traditional gender boundaries and sought equality in professions, sports, and relationships. S. R. White's sarcastic tone in "Modern Mannish Maidens" seems representative of the period. Like Linton, he laments the replacement of ideal womanhood with the modern woman known for her "mannish ways": "In former days the sex were wont to appeal to men from their softer, gentler, weaker side. Now, it is the reverse. They appear to aim at meeting men on their own plat-form, and consorting with them as like to like,—from a man's standpoint rather than from a woman's."[22] After a brief overview of the scholarly debate over the novel's temporal setting, Dale Kramer concludes, "If we accept that the novel's two possible times are the 1860s (when Hardy was a young man in London) and the 1890s (when Hardy was moving through a restless stage in his marriage), we can link a psychological involvement with the historical . . . ; but more importantly we can see that substantive issues are not defined by a single time and place" (171).[23] It is possible then that the novel covers a long span of time from the 1860s to the 1890s. In this respect it is highly possible that Hardy took into con-sideration several of Burne-Jones's paintings in an attempt to evoke the aura of the period he tried to create in *Jude the Obscure*.

By reconfiguring in his novel the androgynous figures of Burne-Jones's paintings, Hardy engaged in contemporary debates over the destabilization of gender constructs the women's movement had created since the 1860s. Through the representation of androgynous figures, Burne-Jones suspend-ed gender boundaries in his classical-subject paintings, compelling his critics and viewers to question gender boundaries within not only his paintings but their social sphere as well. As in the dreamscapes of Burne-Jones's paintings peopled by androgynous figures, Thomas Hardy's exper-iments in the suspension of gender boundaries take place in Jude's and Sue's "dreamy paradise" until crass reality completely annihilates their dreams and their lives. Yet Sue's androgyny raises questions that still puzzle critics today. Is absolute equality possible only in the suspension of gender boundaries that androgyny invites? Does Hardy imply that absolute gender equality is impossible? That once lovers, a man and a woman cannot be comrades? Or does Hardy mean that those women who seek perfect and absolute equality lose their femininity and become androgynous in the process of acquiring the power patriarchal society grants to men, thus alienating men?

In the 1912 postscript to *Jude the Obscure*, Hardy once again revisits the issue of Sue's androgyny when he refers to a letter he received from an "experienced reviewer" from Germany (when the novel was published there as a serial story), who claimed that Sue "was the first delineation in fiction of the woman who was coming into notice in her thousands every year—the woman of the feminist movement—the slight, pale, 'bachelor' girl—the intellectualized, emancipated bundle of nerves that modern conditions were producing, mainly in cities as yet: who does not recognize the necessity for most of her sex to follow marriage as a profession" (*Jude the Obscure*, xxxviii). Hardy's response to this reviewer is as evasive as his reactions to contemporary critics of the novel, once again leaving the character open to interpretation: "Whether this assurance is borne out by dates I cannot say. Nor am I able, across the gap of years since the production of the novel, to exercise more criticism upon it of a general kind than extends to a few verbal corrections. . . . And no doubt there can be more in a book than the author consciously puts there, which will help either to its profit or to its disadvantage as the case may be" (ibid., xxxix). Though unwilling to reveal the temporal setting of the novel or to concede to this reviewer's interpretation of Sue's character, yet he singles it out of the vast criticism the novel received and once again alludes to Sue's androgyny—"the bachelor girl." Through Sue's intellectual power and her depiction as an androgynous figure, Hardy sustains feminism, yet through her stereotypically feminine breakdown and eventual capitulation to convention he subverts it.

Unlike Edward Burne-Jones, who suspended gender boundaries by representing both male and female figures as androgynous, thus destabilizing conventional gender constructs, Hardy, in his reconfigurations of Burne-Jones's paintings, represents only Sue as androgynous. As Laura Green remarks, "Hardy seems to imply that women are more able to achieve and maintain an androgynous ideal partly for that most Victorian of reasons—their lesser sexual impulses" (127). Through Jude's masculinity, albeit passive, Hardy holds on to the gender stability that Sue's anarchic nature has threatened and, if we think in terms of the accomplishments of the feminist movement, has forever changed. Yet Sue's sudden change into docile femininity at the end of the novel comes too late. By then the readers of *Jude the Obscure* and viewers of the androgynous figures of Burne-Jones's paintings, which the novel evokes, have already questioned the validity of the established gender boundaries and have toyed with androgyny and its implicit reconciliation of threat and desire and its elusive promise of equality.

Conclusion

After an extensive and thorough discussion of Lessing's *Laocoön*, a work which he deemed indispensable to an understanding of the distinctions between temporal and spatial arts, Walter Pater declares in his *Renaissance* that each art has "an untranslatable charm." Carrying the debate over the distinctions of the arts even further than Lessing, Pater states that at times an art may "pass into the condition of some other art, by what German critics term an *Andersstreben*—a partial alienation from its own limitations, through which the arts are able, not to supply the place of each other, but reciprocally to lend each other forces."[1] Pater's definition of *Andersstreben* may also be applicable to the convergence of the spatial and temporal arts in the Victorian novel—the narrative redrawings of Pre-Raphaelite paintings. Through their intersection, the novels and Pre-Raphaelite paintings extended their own boundaries, added dimensions to each other, and created possibilities that each art lacked. Thus within the temporal dimension of the novel, by means of their narrative redrawings, the subjects of Pre-Raphaelite art acquired a voice and quite often a subjectivity that the spatial essence of painting had denied them.

The verbal portraits or scenes of the novels, on the other hand, were endowed with color and depth. Defying the novel's fictional or temporal constraints, fictional characters seemed to have once inhabited the real world of the galleries, where readers visiting exhibits had first become acquainted with them. Yet the expansion of verbal and visual boundaries, achieved through the coalescence of the two arts, was not merely confined to the aesthetic realm but extended to the social sphere as well. Through their pictorial reconfigurations, narratives obtained a realistic foundation and thus more readily engaged their readers in their construction, in the process involving them in actual, not fictional, sociopolitical concerns. Narrative redrawings of Pre-Raphaelite representations of gender, perhaps more so than their visual counterparts, raised questions over circum-scribed conventional gender roles (no longer relevant to contemporary needs), offered alternatives and possibilities (at the time unavailable in the readers' actual lives), and created the desire for change.

Victorian novelists and Pre-Raphaelite artists, as we have seen, were concerned with the constraining sociopolitical limitations imposed on gender roles and often attempted to extend conventional gender boundaries. Contemporary denunciation of unconventional, Pre-Raphaelite representations of gender revealed intense anxieties over transgressions of traditional gender boundaries, slowly eroding by social protests and legislative measures. Whereas most Victorian novelists approved of the Pre-Raphaelite extension of these boundaries, they also saw and criticized the limitations of their representations.

At times male and women novelists perceived and interpreted these limitations in completely different ways. Women novelists, as their letters and notebook entries reveal, had directly and painfully experienced the crushing effect of conventional gender boundaries. The narrative reconfiguration of Millais's *Mariana* may serve as a case in point. In Collins's *Woman in White* Mariana is redrawn as Marian when Walter first sees her standing by the window gazing outside; from a distance, after erotically appraising her figure, he eagerly anticipates seeing her beautiful face. Like contemporary reviewers responding to Millais's painting, Walter is initially repulsed by her unattractive appearance. In his representation of Marian as Mariana, Collins transforms the Pre-Raphaelite pictorial technique of light and shade into his successful narrative strategy. Though he develops Marian into a more complex individual than the subject of his Pre-Raphaelite friend, Collins in this case does not fundamentally change Millais's *Mariana*. Marian's valiant resistance to conventional femininity throughout the novel ends in a regrettable acquiescence to a conventionally subsidiary role, "the angel" in Laura's and Walter's house. Our last encounter with Marian is beset with regrets over her confinement within the domestic sphere, which deprives her of the affirmation of subjectivity and the opportunity to become an agent of social change.

For Elizabeth Gaskell, however, Millais's *Mariana* becomes the locus of contemporary questions about women's oppression and the role of literary history in contributing to their victimization by entrenching gender stereotypes, thus stifling their individuality and depriving them of possibilities for meaningful social roles and actions. Her choice of Pre-Raphaelite paintings is a deliberate attempt to give voice to figures whose painted silence has promoted stereotypically passive femininity. Unlike Collins, Gaskell does not contain the redrawing of Millais's *Mariana* within a single narrative scene, but brushstroke by brushstroke, as it were, she reconfigures this painting on numerous occasions in the novel, each time for a different purpose. At the very beginning, for instance, Ruth is

Mariana's reflection when we first see her illuminated by the light filtered through the stained-glass window. Shortly after this scene, Ruth, like *Mariana*, stretches wearily, exhausted by the cruel working conditions imposed on her and her fellow workers. In this case, however, Ruth is not Millais's middle-class Mariana luxuriating in a solipsistic cocoon; rather, she becomes representative of thousands of women, seamstresses struggling for a meager living in unbearable conditions, exploited by their employers.[2]

Later, in her transposition of Millais's *Mariana*, Gaskell also alludes to Tennyson's "Mariana," a poem that casts her in the stereotypical role of the abandoned lover who sees death as the only alternative. Unlike either Millais's or Tennyson's Mariana, who would have welcomed the return of their love, Ruth rejects Bellingham's offer of marriage when she meets him years later, overcomes the boundaries of the domestic sphere, even the more pernicious constraints of ostracism, and becomes an agent of social change, "the light of the world." Gaskell does not reconfigure either Mariana or Ophelia merely to establish a rapport with her readers but does so in an attempt to bring to the foreground conditions that both the paintings and the poem conceal. In the process, she underscores obstacles and limitations that, if they were understood as detrimental to social progress, she suggests, they could and should be rectified, for they would benefit not only the victimized but the privileged as well. The typhoid fever that spreads through Eccleston, for instance, eliminates class distinctions and barriers; Ruth, hitherto an outcast, becomes Bellingham's rescuer and is reinstated in the community. Certainly one could argue that Ruth's death at the end of the novel eradicates the possibilities Gaskell has explored; simultaneously, however, we cannot deny that the emotional turmoil at the end implicates the sacrosanct or the complacent readers who, unlike Benson, refuse to make a difference in the lives of the underprivileged and the victimized. Undoubtedly the intense pain the reader experiences at the end of the novel is an unforgettable call for action.

In her reconfigurations of Rossetti's and Burne-Jones's mythological and legendary figures, Eliot, like Gaskell, traces the limitations that art and literature place upon women. Her choice of Rossetti's paintings of women like Proserpine, Pia dé Tolomei, and Astarte Syriaca, at once attractive and lurid, feminine and masculine, as representations of Gwendolen, captures her culture's incongruous perspectives on women, which deny them any possible empowerment. Thus Gwendolen, deprived of education, in a culture that worships beauty, relies on her striking appearance to rescue her family from poverty by marrying Grandcourt, a man she finds repulsive. By juxtaposing Deronda's development with that of Gwendolen's, Eliot highlights the lack of opportunities available to women of her time and the limitations that propelled them to acts of desperation that often turned victims into victimizers. Surprisingly, Gwendolen, unlike Ruth, or Maggie in *The Mill on the Floss*, survives in spite of the transgressions she has incurred. Indeed Eliot's response to the hostile critics of the Jewish element in *Daniel Deronda* could very well also serve as her justification for Gwendolen's triumphant survival: "But I was happily independent in material things and felt no temptation to accommodate my writing to any standard except that of trying to do my best" (*Letters* 6: 301–302).

Though somewhat subdued and dispirited, Gwendolen is still a powerful figure by the end of the novel; the irresolution with which the novel ends, regarding Gwendolen's life, leaves room for speculation. Sue, however, is completely broken when we meet her for the last time. After an intrepid struggle against conventional boundaries of femininity, she collapses into the conventional and the stereotypical—the hysterical, nonsensical woman. Knowledge in the hands of Burne-Jones's Nimue becomes a weapon for Merlin's demise. Similarly, Sue's self-education and by extension education for women, intensely advocated and debated at the time, Hardy intimates, leads to the transgression of gender boundaries, and woman's femininity turns into terrifying androgyny, a psychological aberration, the cause of men's and women's physical and psychological disintegration.

Women and male writers then reconfigured Pre-Raphaelite paintings for various and complex reasons as this study has demonstrated. However, whereas male writers like Collins and Hardy, through their narrative reconfigurations of Pre-Raphaelite paintings, quite often emphasized limitations for women, Eliot and Gaskell frequently explored possibilities. Representations of (stereotypical) literary women by Pre-Raphaelite women artists also depict possibilities rather than limitations for women. I have already intimated the difference between Millais's illustration of *Mariana* and that of Marie Spartali Stillman, whose wistful gaze, by her open window, signals the possibility for self-renewal and liberation, denied to either Millais's or Rossetti's *Mariana*, both claustrophobically enclosed within the domestic sphere. Likewise, Julia Margaret Cameron's *Mariana* is self-possessed and rather irritated by the lengthy wait, somewhat determined to disengage herself from the long ordeal. Unlike Millais's *Ophelia*, who is helplessly drowning, Cameron's looks neither insane nor desperate but rather self-assured.[3] Like women writers of the time, women Pre-Raphaelite artists undermined literary stereotypes and through their works expressed possibilities for women rather than the restrictions their male counterparts often preferred to depict—a subject worth further exploration.

In *The Pre-Raphaelite Body* J. B. Bullen demonstrates the tremendous impact of the Pre-Raphaelites in British art between 1850 and 1880, emphasizing their liberal perspectives on gender issues: "Though from this distance they appear to be quintessentially nineteenth-century in their ideas and attitudes, at the time each phase, in its different way, seemed strangely defiant, and to be perversely working against the grain of contemporary forward-looking, progressive ideology. This sense of shock was enhanced by the fact that their impact extended beyond the canvas and onto the page. The changes they represented had analogues in literature and criticism" (216).

Taking the Pre-Raphaelites' often unconventional representations of gender as their point of departure, Victorian novelists further pursued alternative constructions of gender. Thus Pre-Raphaelite art became an integral part of the Victorian novel, but its presence did not cease at the end of the Victorian era. Modern novelists such as D. H. Lawrence and postmodern ones such as John Fowles and, most recently, Tracy Chevalier in *Falling Angels* have relied on Pre-Raphaelite representations of women to enrich and vivify their literary portraits, leaving indelible memories in the recesses of their readers' imagination.[4] Like Victorian readers, we may still go beyond the temporal boundaries of the Victorian novel and see in galleries today pictorial versions of characters or scenes. Certainly the Victorian novel enjoys a vibrant, dazzling afterlife.

The ever-shifting perspectives Pre-Raphaelite paintings offer within various contexts partly explain their enduring appeal. Such striking renewals take place not only within the walls of galleries but also on the pages of novels as Pre-Raphaelite paintings slowly emerge through the novelists' narrative redrawings. In the process, the Victorian novel, the reading of which is today often seen as a formidable task for postmodern students, acquires the lush colors, the enchanting hues and the mysterious, fascinating expressions of Pre-Raphaelite subjects.[5] Recent film adaptations of Victorian novels continue to establish our connection to the Victorian era, highlighting our preoccupation with similar concerns— identity formation, gender issues, and postcolonialist aggression, to name but a few.[6] We often tend to overlook the fact that the Victorian era, like our own, was a highly visual culture.[7] This book suggests ways of channeling the twenty-first-century desire for the visual into explorations of Pre-Raphaelite paintings in the Victorian novel.

Notes

Notes to Preface

1. "The Royal Academy Exhibition," *Fraser's Magazine* 47 (June 1853): 708.
2. John Eagles, "The Fine Arts and the Public Taste in 1853," *Blackwood's Edinburgh Magazine* 74 (July 1853): 100.

Notes to Introduction

1. John Christian in *Visions of Love and Life: Pre-Raphaelite Art from the Birmingham Collection, England*, ed. Stephen Wildman (Alexandria, Va.: Art Services International, 1995; an exhibition catalog), 27.
2. J. A. V. Chapple and Arthur Pollard, eds. *The Letters of Mrs. Gaskell* (Manchester: Mandolin/Manchester University Press, 1997), 580; October 25 and 30, 1859; hereafter cited in the text as *Letters*.
3. William Baker and William M. Clarke, eds. *The Letters of Wilkie Collins, 1838–1889*, 2 vols. (New York: St. Martin's, 1999), 2:521; July 24, 1886; hereafter cited in the text as *Letters*.
4. Cited by Georgiana Burne-Jones, *Memorials of Edward Burne-Jones*, 2 vols. (London and New York: Macmillan, 1904), 2:31.
5. *The Life and Work of Thomas Hardy*, ed. Michael Millgate (London and Basingstoke: Macmillan, 1984), 124.
6. "Royal Academy Exhibition Notice," *Athenaeum* (June 1, 1850): 590.
7. Some of the works devoted to the interarts studies include the following: Wylie Sypher, *Rococo to Cubism in Art and Literature* (New York: Random House, 1960); Mario Praz, *Mnemosyne: The Parallel between Literature and the Visual Arts* (Princeton: Princeton University Press, 1970); Chauncey Brewster Tinker, *Painter and Poet: Studies in the Literary Relations of English Painting* (Freeport, N.Y.: Books for Libraries Press, 1969); Jeffrey Meyers, *Painting and the Novel* (Manchester: Manchester University Press, 1975); Wendy Steiner, *The Colors of Rhetoric* (Chicago: University of Chicago Press, 1982) and *Pictures of Romances: Form against Context in Painting and Literature* (Chicago: University of Chicago Press, 1988); Göran Sonneson, *Pictorial Concepts* (Sweden: University of Lund, 1989); Richard Altick, *Paintings from Books:*

Art and Literature in Britain, 1760–1900 (Columbus: Ohio State University Press, 1985); Corrado Federici and Esther Raventos-Pons, eds., *Literary Texts and the Arts: Interdisciplinary Perspectives* (New York: Peter Lang, 2003).

Jean Hagstrum discusses the history of ekphrasis in *The Sister Arts: The Tradition of Literary Pictorialism and English Poetry from Dryden to Gray* (Chicago: University of Chicago Press, 1958). See also Henry Markiewicz, "Ut Pictura Poesis: A History of the Topos and the Problem," *New Literary History* 18 (Spring 1987): 535–58; Lawrent Dechery, "Turning Words into Colors: Robbe-Grillet's Visual Language," *Mosaic* 32 (3) (September 1999): 59–74; Grant F. Scott. *The Sculpted Word: Keats, Ekphrasis, and the Visual Arts* (Hanover and London: University Press of New England, 1994).

8. See for instance Richard Altick, *The Presence of the Present: Topics of the Day in the Victorian Novel* (Columbus: Ohio State University Press, 1991) for allusions to the Pre-Raphaelites in the Victorian novel, especially pp. 487–92. For comments on the novelists discussed in this book and the Pre-Raphaelites, see the following: Hilary Schor, "The Plot of the Beautiful Ignoramus: *Ruth* and the Tradition of the Fallen Woman," in *Sex and Death in Victorian Literature*, ed. Regina Barreca (Bloomington: Indiana University Press, 1990), 158–177; Patricia Frick, "Wilkie Collins and John Ruskin," *Victorians Institute Journal* 13 (1985): 11–22; Pamela Didlake Brewer, "Pre-Raphaelitism in *Lady Audley's Secret*," *Publications of the Arkansas Philological Association* 19 (1) (Spring 1993): 1–10; Joseph Nicholes, "Dorothea in the Moated Grange: Millais's *Mariana* and the *Middlemarch* Window Scenes," *Victorians Institute Journal* 20 (1992): 93–124; and Alison Byerly, "Art Works: Thomas Hardy and the Labor of Creation," in *Realism, Representation, and the Arts in Nineteenth-Century Literature* (Cambridge: Cambridge University Press, 1997), 149–83.

9. In 1766 Gotthold Lessing firmly established for subsequent generations the boundaries of poetry and painting. See *Laocoön: An Essay on the Limits of Painting and Poetry*, trans. Edward Allen McCormick (Baltimore: Johns Hopkins University Press, 1962). See also W. J. T. Mitchell. *Iconology: Image, Text, Ideology* (Chicago: University of Chicago Press, 1986).

10. See Kate Flint's *Victorians and the Visual Imagination* (Cambridge: Cambridge University Press, 2000), especially chapter 8, "Criticism, Language, and Narrative," 197–235.

11. "Review of Elizabeth Gaskell's *Ruth*," *Prospective Review* 9 (May 1853): 224–25.

12. "Review of Elizabeth Gaskell's *Ruth*," *North British Review* 19 (May–August 1853): 161.

13. A. C. Swinburne, "Wilkie Collins," *Fortnightly Review* n.s., 275 (November 1, 1889): 589–99, cited in *Wilkie Collins: The Critical Heritage*, ed. Norman Page (London and Boston: Routledge and Kegan Paul, 1974), 255.

14. R. H. Hutton, unsigned review, *Spectator* 44 (September 9, 1876): 1131–33. Cited in *George Eliot: The Critical Heritage*, ed. David Carroll (London and New York: Routledge, 1995), 368.

15. W. H. Mallock on George Eliot, 1879, cited in *George Eliot: The Critical Heritage*, 452.

16. A. V. Dicey, unsigned review, *Nation* 23 (October 19, 1876): 245–46, cited in *George Eliot: The Critical Heritage*, 402.

17. *The Saturday Review* (September 28, 1872), cited in *Thomas Hardy and His Readers*, eds. Laurence Lerner and John Holmstrom (London: Bodley Head, 1968), 19.

18. *The Spectator* (December 19, 1874), cited in *Thomas Hardy and His Readers*, 26.

19. *The Savoy* (October 1896), cited in *Thomas Hardy and His Readers*, 142.

20. Lindsay Smith, *Victorian Photography, Painting, and Poetry: The Enigma of Visibility in Ruskin, Morris, and the Pre-Raphaelites* (Cambridge: Cambridge University Press, 1995), 123.

21. William Holman Hunt, *Pre-Raphaelitism and the Pre-Raphaelite Brotherhood*, 2 vols. (London: Macmillan, 1905), 1:104. Hereafter cited as *Pre-Raphaelitism*.

22. Stephen Spender, "Pre-Raphaelite Literary Painters," *Journal of Pre-Raphaelite Studies* 10 (Spring 2001): 29.

23. Elizabeth Prettejohn, *The Art of the Pre-Raphaelites* (Princeton: Princeton University Press, 2000), 135.

24. For works devoted to William Thackeray and the visual arts, see Stephen Canham, "Art and the Illustration of *Vanity Fair* and *The Newcomes*," *Modern Language Quarterly* 43 (1) (Spring 1982): 43–66; Judith Law Fisher, "The Aesthetic of the Mediocre: Thackeray and the Visual Arts," *Victorian Studies* 26 (1) (Autumn 1982): 65–82, and "Siren and Artist: Contradiction in Thackeray's Aesthetic Ideal," *Nineteenth-Century Fiction* 39 (4) (March 1985): 392–419; Laura Fasick, "Thackeray's Treatment of Writing and Painting," *Nineteenth-Century Literature* 47 (1) (June 1992): 72–90.

For works on George Eliot, see Hugh Witemeyer, *George Eliot and the Visual Arts* (New Haven: Yale University Press, 1979). For works on Thomas Hardy and the visual arts, see John Bullen, *The Expressive Eye: Fiction and Perception in the Work of Thomas Hardy* (Oxford: Clarendon, 1986); Joan Grundy, *Hardy and the Sister Arts* (London: Macmillan, 1979); and Lloyd Fernando, "Thomas Hardy's Rhetoric of Painting," *Review of English Literature* 6 (1965): 62–73.

25. Reviewers did not object to the avant-garde qualities of the first Pre-Raphaelite paintings, Rossetti's *Girlhood of Mary*, Hunt's *Rienzi*, and Millais's *Isabella*, which were exhibited in 1849 with the PRB initials. However, the following year, when the meaning of the initials was revealed, they became vituperative. Michael Rossetti recorded some of them and related the particulars of the divulgence of the PRB meaning. See *Dante Gabriel Rossetti: His Family Letters and a Memoir by William Michael Rossetti*, 2 vols. (London, 1895; rpt. New York: AMS Press, 1970), 1:146, 161.

For the critical reception of the first three Pre-Raphaelite paintings and their avant-garde qualities, see Herbert Sussman, "The Language of Criticism and the Language of Art: The Response of Victorian Periodicals to the Pre-Raphaelite Brotherhood," *Victorian Periodicals Newsletter* 19 (1973): 21–29.

26. Charles Dickens, "Old Lamps for New Ones," *Household Words* 1 (June 15, 1850): 265.

27. Deborah Cherry and Griselda Pollock, "Patriarchal Power and the Pre-Raphaelites," *Art History* 7 (1984): 482.

Notes to Chapter One

1. Mary Elizabeth Braddon, *Lady Audley's Secret*, ed. David Skilton (Oxford and New York: Oxford University Press, 1998), 70.

2. Rossetti's pictures of "highly sexualized" women, with pouty lips and loose hair, beginning with *Bocca Baciata* in 1859, triggered hostile, critical responses. See Tim Barringer, *Reading the Pre-Raphaelites* (New Haven: Yale University Press, 1999), 148–49. In *Lady Audley's Secret*, Pamela Brewer maintains, Rossetti found "the perfect model for his painting *Lady Lilith* and for his companion poem, "Body's Beauty." See "Pre-Raphaelitism in *Lady Audley's Secret*," 8.

3. For contemporary theories of phrenology, physiognomy, and pathognomy that influenced the Pre-Raphaelites' representation of expression see Julie F. Codell, "Empiricism, Naturalism, and Science in Millais's Paintings," in *John Everett Millais beyond the Pre-Raphaelite Brotherhood*," ed. Debra N. Mancoff (New Haven and London: Yale University Press, 2001), 119–47.

4. According to Elizabeth Prettejohn, Pre-Raphaelitism was the first avant-garde movement in British painting (18–19, 64).

5. Cited by Robert Lee Wolff in *Sensational Victorian: The Life and Fiction of Mary Elizabeth Braddon* (New York and London: Garland, 1979), 155.

6. See *Lady Audley's Secret*, 69, 70–71, 294–95.

7. Lecture delivered in New York in 1882. Quoted by S. N. Ghose, *Dante Gabriel Rossetti and Contemporary Criticism* (Geneva: Norwood Editions, 1977), 203.

8. Although Millais, Rossetti, and Holman Hunt were the dominant figures of this originally secret society, Thomas Woolner, James Collinson, Frederic George Stephens, and William Michael Rossetti were also members. Years later Hunt recognized Rossetti and Millais only as the founding members of the Brotherhood. See Hunt, *Pre-Raphaelitism*, 2:437.

At the time, the idea of a brotherhood was not new. Throughout Europe and America artists banded together as early as in the period following the French Revolution in order to limit the power of the academies. See Laura Morowitz and William Vaughan, eds., *Artistic Brotherhoods in the Nineteenth Century* (Burlington: Ashgate, 2000). Over the years, several anecdotes have recounted the choice of the name "Pre-Raphaelite." See Hunt, *Pre-Raphaelitism*, 1:100, 101, 2:437. See also John Ruskin, *The Works of John Ruskin* (library edition), ed. E. T. Cook and Alexander Wedderburn, 39 vols. (London: George Allen, 1903–1912), 12:321, 322, 357.

9. Anthony Harrison, "1848: Revolution and Reform," in *A Companion to Victorian Literature and Culture*, ed. Herbert F. Tucker (Oxford and Malden: Blackwell, 1999), 19.

10. Christine Poulson, *The Quest for the Grail: Arthurian Legend in British Art 1840–1920* (Manchester and New York: Manchester University Press and St. Martin's Press, 1999), 19–20.

11. Though the Pre-Raphaelite Brotherhood lasted only until 1853, it continued to influence British art until the 1920s. See J. B. Bullen, *The Pre-Raphaelite Body: Fear and Desire in Painting, Poetry, and Criticism* (New York: Oxford University Press, 1998), 1.

12. Sir Joshua Reynolds, *Discourses on Art*, ed. Robert R. Wark (London and New Haven: Yale University Press, 1975), 44. William Michael Rossetti explains "slosh" as "a term much in vogue with the Praeraphaelites in their early days, to indicate a hasty, washy, indeterminate manner in painting, neglectful of severe form and accurate detail, and lavish of unctuous vehicle." See William Michael Rossetti, ed., *Collected Works of Dante Gabriel Rossetti*, 2 vols. (London: Ellis, 1886), 1:157 n. 3.

13. Dante Gabriel Rossetti, *Collected Works*, 1:135.

14. Millais's *Christ in the House of His Parents* became the subject of so many debates and disputes that its notoriety attracted the attention of even Queen Victoria, who had it removed from the exhibition and brought to her for a special viewing. See William Fredeman, ed., *The P.R.B. Journal: William Rossetti's Diary of the Pre-Raphaelite Brotherhood 1849–1853* (Oxford: Clarendon, 1975), 71.

15. Julian Treuherz, "A Brief Survey of Victorian Painting," in *Art in the Age of Queen Victoria: Treasures from the Royal Academy of Arts Permanent Collection*, ed. Helen Valentine (New Haven and London: Royal Academy of Arts and Yale University Press, 1999; an exhibition catalog), 17.

16. "The Exhibition of the Royal Academy," *Times* (May 9, 1850): 5.

17. "The Royal Academy," *Athenaeum* (June 1, 1850): 590–91.

18. Ralph M. Wornum, "Modern Moves in Art," *Art Journal* 12 (September 1, 1850): 269–71.

19. "The Pictures of the Season," *Blackwood's Edinburgh Magazine* 68 (July 1850): 82.

20. Charles Dickens, "Old Lamps for New Ones," 265–67, 265. Though as a satirical allusion, Dickens evokes *The Light of the World* in *Little Dorrit*, as Harvey Peter Sucksmith has already demonstrated. See "Dickens among the Pre-Raphaelites: Mr. Merdle and Holman Hunt's 'The Light of the World,' " *Dickensian* 72 (3) (Autumn 1976): 159–62. See also Sucksmith's comments about Millais's reconciliation with Dickens, 161.

21. *Adam Bede,* ed. Valentine Cunningham (Oxford and New York: Oxford University Press, 1998), 176–78.

22. Quoted by Gordon Haight, *George Eliot: A Biography* (Oxford and New York: Oxford University Press, 1968), 107. It is interesting to note that John Ruskin had compared Dutch to Pre-Raphaelite art and deemed it inferior. The Dutch artists, unlike the Pre-Raphaelites, Ruskin pointed out in "Realistic Schools of Painting: D. G. Rossetti and W. Holman Hunt," a lecture delivered at Oxford on March 9, 1883, failed to give "the life and beauty of little things in lower nature" (*Works* 33:290).

23. George Levine, "Introduction: George Eliot and the Art of Realism," in *The Cambridge Companion to George Eliot* (Cambridge and New York: Cambridge University Press, 2001), 7.

24. See Warner in *Pre-Raphaelite Papers*, ed. Leslie Parris (London: Tate Gallery, 1984), 78.

25. See Ruskin, *Works* 12:320 n. 1.

26. George Eliot, *Essays of George Eliot,* ed. Thomas Pinney (London: Routledge and Kegan Paul, 1963), 271.

27. Like other contemporary critics of the novel, George Eliot also used terms borrowed from the visual arts when reviewing other novels. See "History, Biography, Voyages, and Travels," *Westminster Review* 67 (January 1857): 175.

28. See "Art and Belles Lettres," *Westminster Review* 65 (April 1856): 626.

29. According to Prettejohn, *Modern Painters* "was the only substantial original work on art theory that had appeared in England for decades, and arguably since Reynolds's *Discourses* of 1769–90" (58).

30. See "Art and Belles Lettres," *Westminster Review* 65 (April 1856): 626.

31. As Barringer and Prettejohn have already observed, Ruskin's letters to the *Times* marked the turning point in the critical reception of Pre-Raphaelite art (Barringer, 61; Prettejohn, 59).

32. The *Alisma plantago,* made famous by Ruskin's remarks on Collins's *Convent Thoughts,* Elizabeth Deas has recently demonstrated, does not actually appear in the painting. See "The Missing *Alisma*: Ruskin's Botanical Error," *Journal of Pre-Raphaelite Studies* 10 (Fall 2001): 7.

33. Kate Flint also connects *The Awakening Conscience* with the novel, drawing parallels between this painting and Collins's *Basil*. See "Reading *The Awakening Conscience* Rightly," in *Pre-Raphaelites Re-Viewed*, ed. Marcia Pointon (Manchester and New York: Manchester University Press, 1989), 51–52.

34. Richard Stein, *The Ritual of Interpretation* (Cambridge, Mass.: Harvard University Press, 1975), 128.

35. Carol T. Christ, *The Finer Optic: The Aesthetic of Particularity in Victorian Poetry* (New Haven and London: Yale University Press, 1975), 61–64.

36. Chris Brooks, *Signs for the Times: Symbolic Realism in the Mid-Victorian World* (London, Boston, and Sydney: George Allen and Unwin, 1984), 123, 124, 121.

37. Arnold and Ellis, cited by Flint in *The Victorians and the Visual Imagination*, 201.

38. An exhibit held at the Yale Center for British Art, exclusively devoted to Rossetti's "double work of art" intended to "illuminate the symbiotic relationship of Rossetti's art and poetry." See Maryan Wynn Ainsworth, *Dante Gabriel Rossetti and the Double Work of Art* (Hartford: Yale University Art Gallery, 1976; an exhibition catalog), vi. For representations of women in Rossetti's sonnets and paintings see Lynn Pearce, *Woman/Image/Text: Readings in Pre-Raphaelite Art and Literature* (Toronto: University of Toronto Press, 1991).

39. F. G. Stephens, "The Purpose and Tendency of Italian Art," in *The Germ: Thoughts Towards Nature in Poetry, Literature, and Art* (Oxford: Ashmolean Museum, 1992), 60.

40. David Masson, "Pre-Raphaelitism in Art and Literature," *The British Quarterly Review* 16 (August 1852): 203.

41. "The English Pre-Raphaelites," *Eclectic Review* (January 11, 1856): 8–9.

42. "Fine Arts: The Royal Academy," *Athenaeum* (May 7, 1853): 567.

43. Judith Bronkhurst in Leslie Parris, *The Pre-Raphaelites*, 103–4.

44. Cited by Julian Treuherz, "A Brief Survey of Victorian Painting" in Helen Valentine, ed., *Art in the Age of Queen Victoria: Treasures from the Royal Academy of Arts Permanent Collection* (New Haven and London: Royal Academy of Arts and Yale University Press, 1999; an exhibition catalog), 17.

45. William Rathbone Greg is representative of contemporary belief in the double sexual standard. See "Prostitution" in *Westminster Review* 53 (July 1850): 457.

46. Susan Casteras, "Pre-Raphaelite Challenges to Victorian Canons of Beauty," *Huntington Library Quarterly* 55 (February 1992): 27.

47. "The English Pre-Raphaelites," *Eclectic Review* (January 11, 1856): 16, 18.

48. Joseph Kestner, *Masculinities in Victorian Painting* (Aldershoot, England; Brookfield, Vt.: Ashgate, 1995), 92, 189; Jan Marsh, *Pre-Raphaelite Women: Images of Femininity in Pre-Raphaelite Art* (London: Artus Books, 1987), 77, 17, 109.

49. See Susan Casteras, "Pre-Raphaelite Challenges," and Julie Codell, "Expression over Beauty: Facial Expression, Body Language, and Circumstantiality in the Paintings of the Pre-Raphaelite Brotherhood," *Victorian Studies* 29 (Winter 1986): 225–90.

50. Alfred Lord Tennyson, *The Poems*, 2d ed., ed. Christopher Ricks, 3 vols. (Berkeley and Los Angeles: University of California Press, 1987).

51. Hallam Tennyson, *Alfred Lord Tennyson: A Memoir by His Son*, cited by Christine Poulson, *The Quest for the Grail*, 208.

52. Lynda Nead, *Myths of Sexuality: Representations of Women in Victorian Britain* (New York: Basil Blackwell, 1988), 12.

53. E. H. Gombrich, *Art and Illusion: A Study in the Psychology of Pictorial Representation*, 4th ed. (London: Phaidon, 1972), 169.

54. See William Acton, *Prostitution Considered in Its Moral, Social, and Sanitary Aspects in London and Other Large Cities, with Proposals for the Mitigation and Prevention of Its Attendant Evil* (London: John Churchill, 1857).

55. See Nina Auerbach, *Woman and the Demon: The Life of a Victorian Myth* (Cambridge, Mass., and London: Harvard University Press, 1982); Lynda Nead, *Myths of Sexuality*. Judith Walkowitz focuses on the Contagious Disease Acts; see *Prostitution and Society: Women, Class, and the State* (Cambridge: Cambridge University Press, 1980). Amanda Anderson, *Tainted Souls and Painted Faces: The Rhetoric of Fallenness*

in Victorian Culture (Ithaca: Cornell University Press, 1993), and Elsie Mitchie, *Outside the Pale: Cultural Exclusion, Gender Difference, and the Victorian Woman Writer* (Reading Women Writing Series; Ithaca: Cornell University Press, 1993), explore the phenomenon of the fallen woman in literature.

56. Arthur S. Marks, "Ford Madox Brown's *Take Your Son, Sir!*" *Arts Magazine* 54 (January 1980): 139.

57. Lord Cranworth, cited by Lynda Nead, *Myths of Sexuality*, 48.

58. "Fine Arts: Royal Academy," *Athenaeum* (May 1, 1858): 566.

59. Ibid.

60. See Arthur Marks, "Ford Madox Brown's *Take Your Son, Sir!*"

61. Virginia Surtees, *The Paintings and Drawings of Dante Gabriel Rossetti (1828–1882): A Catalogue Raisonné*, 2 vols. (Oxford: Clarendon, 1971), 1:28.

62. Lynn Nead, "The Magdalen in Modern Times: The Mythology of the Fallen Women in Pre-Raphaelite Painting," *Oxford Art Journal* 7 (1984): 39.

63. Alicia Craig Faxon, *Dante Gabriel Rossetti* (New York: Abbeville Press, 1989), 67.

64. Cited by Faxon, 67.

65. F. G. Stephens, "Dante Gabriel Rossetti: Painter and Poet," in *The Portfolio: Monographs on Artistic Subjects*, by Alfred W. Pollard (London: Seeley, 1894), 38.

66. Cited in Stephen Wildman, *Visions of Love and Life*, 188.

67. "Fine Arts: Royal Academy," *Athenaeum* (May 6, 1854): 561.

68. Ruskin interprets in detail the symbolic realism of the visual signifiers in this painting. See *Works* 12:334–35.

69. Cited by George Landow, *William Holman Hunt and Typological Symbolism* (New Haven: Yale University Press, 1979), 48.

70. See Kate Flint, *The Victorians and the Visual Imagination*, 216, and Julie Codell, "Expression over Beauty," 179. For a psychoanalytical reading of the painting, see Caroline Arscott, "Employer, Husband, Spectator: Thomas Fairbairn's Commission of *The Awakening Conscience*," in *The Culture of the Capital: Art, Power, and the Nineteenth-Century Middle Class*, eds. Janet Wolff and John Seed (Manchester: Manchester University Press; New York: St. Martin's Press, 1988), 182–84.

71. In his discussion of Lessing's distinction between poetry and painting, J. T. Mitchell demonstrates that "the most fundamental ideological basis for his [Lessing's] laws of genre" is actually "the laws of gender." See *Iconology*, 109, 110, 112. On the same subject see also his *Picture Theory and Essays on Verbal and Visual Representation* (Chicago: University of Chicago Press, 1994).

72. See James Hefferman, *Museum of Words: The Poetics of Ekphrasis from Homer to Ashbery* (Chicago and London: University of Chicago Press, 1993), 1, 6–7. For Murray Krieger the relationship between the verbal and the visual has evolved into gendered contests, often resulting in the superiority of the word over the image. See *Ekphrasis: The Illusion of the Natural Sign* (Baltimore and London: Johns Hopkins University Press, 1991), 1–28.

73. George Eliot, *Middlemarch*, introd. A. S. Byatt (Oxford and New York: Oxford University Press, 1999), 213. In Eliot's view a verbal portrait empowers the subject of visual art by endowing it with a voice, a quality the pictorial by its nature must deny. Thus Eliot anticipates recent critics, such as James Hefferman and Murray Krieger, who treat the relation between literature and the visual arts as *paragonal*, a conflict for dominance between the word and the image.

Notes to Chapter Two

1. Jenny Uglow, *Elizabeth Gaskell: A Habit of Stories* (New York: Farrar Strauss, 1993), ix.

2. Deirdre D'Albertis, *Dissembling Fictions: Elizabeth Gaskell and the Victorian Social Text* (New York: St. Martin's Press, 1997), 177. Elizabeth Gaskell herself recognized her warring and irreconcilable attributes, often manifested in her fiction. We can see these oppositions in one of her letters to Eliza Fox, in which she describes with humor and piquancy her guilt over the impending purchase of their new house, 42 Plymouth Grove:

> One of my mes is, I do believe, a true Christian—(only people call her socialist and communist), another of my mes is a wife and mother, and highly delighted at the delight of everyone else in the house, Meta and William most especially who are in full extasy [*sic*]. Now that's my "social" self I suppose. Then again I've another self with a full taste for beauty and convenience whh [*sic*] is pleased on its own account. How am I to reconcile all these warring members? I try to drown myself (my *first* self,) by saying it's Wm who is to decide on all these things, and his feeling it right ought to be my rule, and so it is—only that does not quite do. (*Letters*, 108; April 1850)

3. See Laura Hapke, "He Stoops to Conquer: Redeeming the Fallen Woman in the Fiction of Dickens, Gaskell, and Their Contemporaries," *Victorian Newsletter* 69 (1986): 16–22; Peter Stiles, "Grace, Redemption, and the 'Fallen Woman': *Ruth* and *Tess of the d'Urbervilles*," *Gaskell Society Journal* 6 (1992): 58–86.

4. Hilary Schor, "The Plot of the Beautiful Ignoramus," 166.

5. For references to Rossetti see 397, 444, 485, 484b (*Letters*). See also *Further Letters of Mrs. Gaskell*, ed. J. A. V. Chapple and Arthur Pollard (Manchester and New York: Manchester University Press, 2000), 199–201, 221 n. 1, 241–42 n. 2. For references to Millais see 155, 211, 234a (*Letters*); for those to Hunt see 386, 394, 444, 646 (*Letters*); 184 (*Further Letters*).

6. Michael Rossetti, *Dante Gabriel Rossetti*, 2:265.

7. Angus Easson, "Elizabeth Gaskell and the *Athenaeum*: Two Contributions Identified," *Modern Language Review* 85 (October 1990): 829–32.

8. Not all reviews were negative, as Gaskell suggests; in fact, quite a few of them were positive. See the following, for instance: G. H. Lewes, "Review of *Ruth* and *Villette*," *Westminster Review* 3 (April 1853): 245–54; "Review of *Ruth*," *North British Review* 19 (1853): 151–74; "Review of *Ruth*," *Prospective Review* 9 (May 1853): 222–47.

9. Margaret Homans, *Bearing the Word: Language and Female Experience in Nineteenth-Century Women's Writing* (Chicago: University of Chicago Press, 1986), xi. See also Mary Jacobus, *Reading Woman: Essays in Feminist Criticism* (New York: Columbia University Press, 1986); Mary Poovey, *The Proper Lady and the Woman Writer: Ideology as Style in the Works of Mary Wollstonecraft, Mary Shelley, and Jane Austen* (Chicago: University of Chicago Press, 1984).

10. Felicia Bonaparte explains some of the reasons for Gaskell's intense identification with Pasley. Whereas the two women's situations were entirely different, their lives, she notes, shared remarkable similarities: "As Gaskell lost her mother in infan-

cy, so Miss Pasley lost her father. As Gaskell's father then remarried, so in Miss Pasley's case did the mother. Gaskell's father banished Elizabeth. Miss Pasley's mother banished her, sending her to an orphan school. . . . Miss Pasley's mother did not write or visit her while she was in school just as Gaskell's father did not. . . . Here in Miss Pasley, who shared her history, was the very incarnation of an image that had become, in her own imagination, one of the major representations of her own daemonic double." See *The Gypsy Bachelor of Manchester: The Life of Mrs. Gaskell's Demon* (Charlottesville and London: University Press of Virginia, 1992), 83.

11. *Ruth*, chapter VIII. All references to Gaskell's novels are to the Knutsford edition and are cited in the text by chapter numbers.

12. Lynn M. Alexander discusses the plight of seamstresses and their representation in literature and the visual arts in *Women, Work, and Representation: Needlewomen in Victorian Art and Literature* (Athens: Ohio University Press, 2003). See also T. J. Edelstein, "They Sang 'The Song of the Shirt': Visual Iconology of the Seamstress," *Victorian Studies* 23 (2) (Winter 1980): 183–210.

13. Alaistair Grieve in the *Pre-Raphaelites* catalog notes that Rossetti had inscribed on the original frame his sonnet explaining the symbolism, while a second sonnet, referring to the picture's subject, was printed in the catalogue of the Free Exhibition of 1849 (Parris, 65). This latter sonnet was revised for the 1870 edition of his poems. The lines I have quoted were changed to the following:

> This is that blessed Mary, pre-elect . . .
> Unto God's will she brought devout respect,
> Profound simplicity of intellect,
> And supreme patience. From her mother's knee
> Faithful and hopeful; wise in charity;
> Strong in grave peace. ("Mary's Girlhood," 1, 4–8)

14. Barringer notes the underlying sexual overtones of the *Ecce Ancilla Domini!*: "The improbably small, haloed dove, representing the holy spirit, and the half-hearted fire burning at Gabriel's heels, are not sufficient to convince the viewers that this is a spiritual, rather than a sexual, encounter" (42). As Gaskell's redrawing of this painting indicates, she was aware of its erotic quality. Anna Unsworth notes Gaskell's unconventional acceptance of Ruth's sexuality: "The apparent contradiction in Ruth's character between her 'living with her lover in North Wales and positively enjoying it' compared with the nobility and spiritual maturity she later shows, without there having been any process of 're-adjustment,' still puzzles modern critics, as it enraged Mrs. Gaskell's contemporary critics." See *Mrs. Gaskell: An Independent Woman* (Montreaux, London, and Washington: Minerva Press, 1996), 89. Commenting on the same issue, Malcolm Pittock observes, "Mrs. Gaskell is undercutting the basis of that sexual morality which no doubt she believed herself to be upholding. For what she is implying is that sexual relations outside marriage are not innately sinful, it is only society which makes us think they are. . . . Perhaps the furore the novel aroused had a more complex origin than mere disapproval of its subject matter." See "The Dove Ascending: The Case for Elizabeth Gaskell," *English Studies* 81 (6) (2000): 537.

15. Elaine Showalter, "Representing Ophelia: Women, Madness, and the Responsibilities of Feminist Criticism" in *Shakespeare's Middle Tragedies*, ed. David Young (Englewood Cliffs: Prentice-Hall, 1993), 63.

16. "Royal Academy," *Athenaeum* (May 22, 1852): 581.

17. Hughes recalled that "on the morning of the varnishing, as I was going through the first room, before I knew where I was, Millais met me. . . . [H]e said he had just been up a ladder looking at my picture and that it gave him more pleasure than any picture there, but adding also very truly that I had not painted the right kind of stream." John Guille Millais, *The Life and Letters of Sir John Everett Millais* (London: Methuen, 1899), 1:146.

18. Shirley Foster, *Victorian Women's Fiction: Marriage, Freedom, and the Individual* (London and Sydney: Croom Helm, 1985), 155.

19. T. J. Wise and J. A. Symington, eds., *The Brontës: Their Lives and Correspondence*, 4 vols. (Oxford: Oxford University Press, 1933), 3:332.

20. In her interpretation of *Ruth*, Kate Flint points out that the ending of the novel, rather than being didactic as various critics have assumed, is an attempt to turn the reader's disappointment into the motivation for challenging "the assumptions which lie behind such conventions." See *Elizabeth Gaskell* (Plymouth: Northcote Publishers, 1995), 28.

21. Quoted by Uglow, 217; Thomas Carlyle to ECG, November 8, 1848, John Rylands, MS 730/14 (ibid., 642 n. 5).

Notes to Chapter Three

1. Wilkie Collins brought to literature his unique background in law and art. His very first work, his father's biography, *Memoirs of the Life of William Collins, Eq. R.A.* (1848), deals with the life and art of his father, a successful landscape painter. His godfather, Sir David Wilkie, R.A., was also a renowned painter. Wilkie Collins himself studied art for several years; as William Clarke has observed, he "would have found it as easy to drift into painting as into writing; and without his father's somewhat oppressive personality, and his own independent streak, he might have done so." See *The Secret Life of Wilkie Collins* (Chicago: Ivan R. Dee, 1991), 9.

As early as 1851 Collins wrote for *Bentley's Miscellany* pieces connected with the visual arts. See Catherine Peters, *The King of Inventors: A Life of Wilkie Collins* (Princeton: Princeton University Press, 1991), 102. The figure of the artist is a recurrent character in his short stories and novels. See, for instance, *Hide and Seek* (1854) and *The Law and the Lady* (1875).

In Collins's letters we perceive his active interest not only in his Pre-Raphaelite friends' paintings but also in the reception of their work as well. At times the same journals, like the *Athenaeum*, for instance, published reviews of books and paintings. In a letter to Edward Pigot, where he suggests altering the arrangement of *The Leader* to include more space for the fine arts, he comments regretfully that Millais "is cut up in last week's *Athenaeum*, along with me." See *Letters* 1:80 (January 12, 1852). For additional references to Millais, see *Letters*, 1:xxvi, 77 and note, 116, 117, 135, 140 and note; to Hunt, see *Letters* 1:184, 185n, 192, 202, 218, 255–56, *Letters* 2:302, 307, 365, 366, 485–86, 518, 521–22, 534, 550.

2. Wilkie Collins, "The Exhibition of the Royal Academy," *Bentley's Miscellany* 29 (June 1851): 624–25. In *Pre-Raphaelitism* Hunt mentions Wilkie Collins's intention to write an article about the Pre-Raphaelites (1:304). In the same work Hunt gives an intimate portrait of Wilkie Collins in his own home (2:186–87).

3. Patricia Frick, "Wilkie Collins and John Ruskin," *Victorians Institute Journal* 13 (1985): 12–13.

4. "Unsigned Review of *The Woman in White*," *Saturday Review* 252 (August 25, 1860): 249–50, in *Wilkie Collins: The Critical Heritage*, ed. Norman Page, 83–84.

5. The Pre-Raphaelite women in white must have been particularly significant to Wilkie Collins, who met his own woman in white, Caroline Graves, in circumstances as sensational and mysterious as those surrounding Hartright's meeting with Anne Catherick. Ironically, Caroline Graves, who had Collins's children out of wedlock, was also considered a fallen woman by Victorian standards of morality. In his father's biography published in 1895, John Everett Millais's son relates the dramatic incident of Caroline's sensational appearance (*Life and Letters of Sir John Everett Millais,* 1:278–81)

Wilkie Collins's early biographers, Nuel Pharr Davis and Kenneth Robinson, conjecture that Collins's extraordinary meeting with Caroline Graves served as the germ for the novel. William Clarke, however, is more skeptical. Catherine Peters, on the other hand, suggests that Caroline's double identity might have suggested to Collins the merging of Laura's and Anne's identities (219). Davis, *The Life of Wilkie Collins* (Urbana: University of Illinois Press, 1956), 163; Robinson, *Wilkie Collins: A Biography* (New York: Macmillan, 1952), 131; Clarke, *Secret Life of Wilkie Collins,* 92.

6. Like his Pre-Raphaelite friends, Collins created and shaped fallen women as distinct, individual figures rather than as types, ranging from the unrepentant Margaret Sherwin to the victimized Mary Grice, the repentant Sarah Leeson, the bewildered Lydia Gwilt, and the respectable Mrs. Anne Catherick.

7. *The Woman in White,* ed. John Sutherland (Oxford and New York: Oxford University Press, 1998), 282. All further references to the novel are cited in the text.

8. Commenting on Rossetti's "ominous nuptual drawing, *How They Met Themselves,* Elisabeth Bronfen remarks on the ambivalent meaning the picture conveys. Bronfen, *Over Her Dead Body: Death, Femininity and the Aesthetic* (New York: Routledge, 1992), 176.

9. "Fine Arts: Royal Academy," *Athenaeum* (June 2, 1849): 575.

10. "Exhibition of the Royal Academy, Second Notice," *Times* (May 7, 1851): 8.

11. "Fine Arts: Royal Academy," *Athenaeum* (May 10, 1856): 590.

12. See Susan Balee, "Wilkie Collins and Surplus Women: The Case of Marian Halcombe," *Victorian Literature and Culture* 20 (1992): 197–215; Stephen Bernstein, "Reading in Blackwater Park: Gothicism, Narrative, and Ideology in *The Woman in White,*" *Studies in the Novel* 25 (1993): 291–305; Diane Elam, "White Narratology: Gender and Reverence in Wilkie Collins's *The Woman in White,*" in *Virginal Sexuality and Textuality in Victorian Literature,* ed. Lloyd Davis (Albany: State University of New York Press, 1993), 49–63; Laurie Langbauer, "Women in White, Men in Feminism," *Yale Journal of Criticism* 2 (1989): 219–43; Kellen M. Williams, " 'Traced and Captured by the Men in the Chaise': Pursuing Sexual Difference in Wilkie Collins's *The Woman in White,*" *Journal of Narrative Technique* 28 (1998): 91–110.

13. In *The Sensation Novel and the Victorian Family Magazine* (London: Palgrave, 2001), Deborah Wynne points out that the serialization of *The Woman in White* underscored the intersection of the real and the fictional through the publication of sensational crimes along with the installments of the novel (54).

14. Unsigned review, *Critic* 21 (August 25, 1860): 233–34, cited in *Wilkie Collins: The Critical Heritage,* 82.

15. Christopher Wood, *The Pre-Raphaelites* (New York: Crescent Books, 1981), 43.

16. Critics were outraged by the representation of Christ as a common man rather than a glorified figure. *The Eclectic Review,* for instance, denounced the painting as an example of the Pre-Raphaelites' "utter neglect of form and elevation of type; that preference, in fact, for the revolting" (8). For details regarding the composition of the

popular and famous *Light of the World*, see Jeremy Maas, *Holman Hunt and the Light of the World* (Aldershot, Hants: Scolar, 1984).

17. Balee considers the Crimean war as the cause of this popular demand for a new ideal of womanhood: "Sensation fiction, and Marian's creation, had everything to do with a social dilemma that had begun in England in the 1850s. This dilemma centered on a proliferation of single women, who, as men emigrated to the colonies or were killed in the Crimea, would never find mates, would never have the chance to become those maternal angels beloved by Victorian iconography. Something had to be done for and about England's 'surplus women,' and Collins began to do it in the medium most likely to influence the millions—the serial novel" (199).

18. In "Breaking the Laws about Ladies: Wilkie Collins's Questioning of Gender Roles," Kathleen O'Fallon demonstrates that Collins's treatment of Marian Halcombe and Walter Hartright "shows the most significant beginnings of Collins' struggle to rethink gender roles" (231). According to O'Fallon, "the progress of the Collins heroine from novel to novel suggests that Collins became increasingly intrigued by the possibilities of his female characters and, at the same time, he seemed to lose interest in his male characters" (229–30). O'Fallon, in *Wilkie Collins to the Forefront*, ed. Nelson Smith and R. C. Terry (New York: AMS Press, 1995).

19. In *Telling Tales* (Columbus: Ohio State University Press, 2002) Elizabeth Langland points out that the very quality, "asexual childishness," that leads to the idealization of Laura Fairlie also facilitates her condemnation as madwoman (74–75).

20. Cited by Joseph A. Kestner, *Mythology and Misogyny: The Social Discourse of Nineteenth-Century British Classical-Subject Painting* (Madison: University of Wisconsin Press, 1989), 5.

21. Carl G. Jung, *Aspects of the Feminine*, trans. R. F. C. Hull (Princeton: Princeton University Press, 1982), 78.

Notes to Chapter Four

1. *Daniel Deronda*, ed. Graham Handley (Oxford and New York: Oxford University Press, 1998), 96. All further references are cited in the text.

2. Fredeman, *The P.R.B. Journal*, 122.

3. The germs of her first two works, for instance, were based on indirect impressions, narratives she had heard. In retrospect, Eliot seemed to be dissatisfied with *Scenes of Clerical Life*, in which she fictionalized the lives of actual clergymen; see John W. Cross, ed., *George Eliot's Life as Related in Her Letters and Journals* (New York: Harper, 1885), 2:85. Eliot traces the genesis of *Adam Bede* to another indirect experience, a narrative she had heard, which also conjured the image of woman torn by a "collision" (ibid., 2:48–49). The germs of Eliot's later works, however, were not stories she had heard, and they did not come with ready-made plots. For the germinal image of *Silas Marner* see *Letters* 2:427. A vivid visual experience in the British Museum, some fragments of glass "with dyes of sunset in them" (ibid., 3:70) most likely served as the germ of *Middlemarch;* see Andres, "The Germ and the Picture in *Middlemarch*" in *English Literary History* 55 (1988). The germ of *The Spanish Gypsy* most directly demonstrates the amalgamation of the visual and the verbal, for, as Eliot recalls, the story originated in Titian's "small picture" of the Annunciation in the Scuola di San Rocco in Venice (Cross 2:30).

4. Haight, in *George Eliot: A Biography*, notes that "the germ of *Daniel Deronda*,

planted in September 1872 when George Eliot was watching Miss Leigh at the roulette table in Homburg, began to grow at once." He also remarks that Eliot made notes on "Gambling superstitions from an article in the *Cornhill*" (469); see R. A. Proctor, "Gambling Superstitions," *Cornhill Magazine* 25 (1872). For more references to gambling in Eliot's notebooks see *George Eliot's* Daniel Deronda *Notebooks* (Jane Irwin, ed. Cambridge and New York: Cambridge University Press, 1996, 282–83). Mary Wilson Carpenter connects the Book of Esther to "the emblematic theme of gambling in the novel"; see "The Apocalypse of the Old Testament: *Daniel Deronda* and the Interpretation of Interpretation" in *Publications of the Modern Language Association* 99 (1) (January 1984): 60.

5. Contemporary paintings reveal the extent of the Victorian interest in the young woman gambling. Three popular paintings may have confirmed for Eliot the germ's popular appeal. See, for instance, Alfred Elmore's *On the Brink* (1865), William Powell Frith's *The Salon d'Or, Homburg* (1871), and Millais's *Hearts Are Trumps* (1872).

6. The opening of the novel, Baker points out, invites the reader to a "primeval world of nature worship of the elements—the sun, the moon, the stars, the planets, light and darkness" (*Some George Eliot Notebooks: An Edition of the Carl H. Pforzheimer Library's George Eliot Holograph Notebooks,* 4 vols. MSS 707, 708, 709, 710, 711. Salzburg: Universität Salzburg, 1976–1985; 1:39).

7. See Eliot's *Letters* 5:3, 56–57, 77, 105–6, 246, 390–92.

8. Robert Upstone observes that the subject of the watercolor, *The Wheel of Fortune* (1871), first appeared in Edward Burne-Jones's designs for the *Troy Triptych* (1870) and notes that "in the wake of his destructive affair with Maria Zambaco, he perhaps identified with the story of Paris, Helen and the burning of Troy" (132). See Upstone's "Symbolism in Three Dimensions" in *The Age of Rossetti, Burne-Jones, and Watts: Symbolism in Britain 1860–1910,* ed. Andrew Wilton and Robert Upstone, 83–92 (New York, London, Paris: Flammarion, 1997. Tate exhibition catalogue).

9. This is Croesus's advice to Cyrus, king of the Medes (Baker *Notebooks* 3:191). Croesus's career is for Herodotus an illustration of "nemesis or divine retribution for pride over prosperity"; see *Herodotus,* trans. George Rawlinson (New York: Modern Library, 1921, xii). At the zenith of his power Croesus had a conversation with Solon, who warned him about the mutability of human happiness (ibid., 19). Disregarding Solon's advice, Croesus attacked the Persians, was defeated and taken as Cyrus's slave (ibid., 48). Cyrus, in turn, disregarded Croesus's warnings, attacked the Messagetae, and was killed (ibid., 114).

10. Critics such as David, Linehan, and Meyer note Gwendolen's and Grandcourt's imperialist tendencies. Both Meyer and Linehan concentrate on Zionism and the gender politics in the novel. Neither writer, however, deals with the novel as George Eliot's response to prevalent contemporary arguments on imperialism or as her attempt to interweave the sociopolitical and the artistic—one of the tasks of this chapter. Deirdre David, *Fictions of Resolution in Three Victorian Novels: North and South, Our Mutual Friend, Daniel Deronda* (New York: Columbia University Press, 1981, 176); Katherine Bailey Linehan, "Mixed Politics: The Critique of Imperialism in *Daniel Deronda*" in *Texas Studies in Literature and Language* 34 (Fall 1992): 324.

11. According to Rylance, Blacks were associated with subhumans like Caliban "and therefore the Eyre arguments touched scientific controversy in the context of the evolutionary debates." Rick Rylance, *Victorian Psychology and British Culture 1850–1880* (Oxford and New York: Oxford University Press, 2000, 156).

12. The comparison of the British Empire to the Roman and Persian Empires was a favorite one, as Dilke's popular *Greater Britain* reveals (Sir Charles Wentworth Dilke, *Greater Britain: A Record of Travel in English-Speaking Countries*, 2d ed., 2 vols. London: Macmillan, 1869, 2:405–406). For Eliot's awareness of Dilke's work, see *Letters* 5:39, 305, 7:13, 9:219.

13. George Eliot refers to David Livingstone's *Missionary Travels and Researches in South Africa* (1857) in a letter to Sara Sophia Hennell, dated March 2, 1858 (*Letters* 2:439). See Brantlinger for contemporary imperialist and racist attitudes toward Africa.

14. In her recent work, *George Eliot and the British Empire*, Nancy Henry discusses Eliot's reviews of travel and exploration narratives, including Burton's work. Both Eliot and Lewes, according to Henry, through their reviews of such travel narratives, contributed to "the centralizing process by which information arrived from the margins of [the] empire to be assessed and assimilated as colonial knowledge" (Cambridge and New York: Cambridge University Press, 2002, 35).

15. "The Modern Hep! Hep! Hep!"—the title of this essay in *Theophrastus Such*—alludes to the anti-Semitic riots and demonstrations known as the "Hep! Hep!" riots of 1819—"the German reaction to the defeat of Napoleon and hence the defeat of Jewish hopes for early emancipation"; see William Baker, *George Eliot and Judaism*, ed. James Hogg. Romantic Reassessment Series, no. 45 (Salzburg: Universität Salzburg, 1975, 35). Eliot alludes to the Indian mutiny in this essay. For allusions to contemporary historical events in *Daniel Deronda* see Erwin Hester, "George Eliot's Use of Historical Events in *Daniel Deronda*," *English Language Notes* 4 (1966): 115–18. Neil McCaw, in *George Eliot and Victorian Historiography: Imagining the National Past*, notes the significance of Theophrastus's argument against the modern English citizen's failure to "recognize and acknowledge a defined national consciousness as a positive aspect of Jewish history and culture" (New York: St. Martin's Press, 2000, 60).

16. In her interpretation of the sonnet Rossetti wrote for this painting Faxon notes that the first word "mystery" also begins his sonnet "For a Virgin and Child: by Hans Memmelinck," written in 1849 (194–95). Eliot also blurs the demarcation line between good and evil in her opening question referring to Gwendolen's gaze: "Was the good or evil genius dominant in those beams?" (3).

17. Edward Burne-Jones, "Letters to Mrs. Gaskell," Department of Western Manuscripts, British Library, London. Unpublished. Cited by Kestner, *Mythology and Misogyny*, 85.

18. Eliot's fascination with the myth of Medusa is evident in her major novels, where she reinterprets it moving away from the conventional meaning adopted by other contemporary writers and painters. In *Adam Bede*, as in the myth of Medusa, the victim, Hetty, not the victimizer, Arthur, is punished for transgression of social boundaries (430). Dark skinned, with "gleaming black eyes," the precocious young Maggie Tulliver in *The Mill on the Floss*, early on refuses to abide by Victorian standards of femininity by cutting her unruly hair, "looking like a small Medusa with snakes cropped" (161). Later in the novel, when the magnetism between Stephen and Maggie becomes overwhelming, Stephen attributes his attraction to the power of Maggie's defiant look and relies on the conventional dominant/subordinate binaries of the gaze to reason his way out of the labyrinth of desire (489–90, 522–23). Even Dorothea becomes a Medusa figure in Casaubon's eyes when she innocently asks him when he intends to publish his work (139).

19. Edward Burne-Jones and Thomas M. Rooke, "Conversations." Private collection. Unpublished. Quoted by Kestner, 78, 107.

Notes to Chapter Five

1. Christopher Wood notes that Edward Burne-Jones "could never really accept the aesthetic philosophy that art existed only for art's sake, and for no other purpose" (*The Pre-Raphaelites*, 112). The term "aesthetic," as Sussman succinctly defines it, describes "an art practice in which self-contained formal qualities are privileged over social and ethical signification"; see *Victorian Masculinities: Manhood and Masculine Poetics in Early Victorian Literature and Art* (New York: Cambridge University Press, 1995, 175). In his review of the 1877 Grosvenor exhibit, Henry James, referring to Burne-Jones's paintings, distinguishes between the mimetic and the aesthetic by underscoring the lack of realism in the latter; see "Picture Season in London, 1877," in *The Painter's Eye*, ed. John L. Sweeney (London: Rupert Hart-Davis, 1956, 144).

2. "The Grosvenor Gallery Exhibit," *Times* (May 1, 1877): 10.

3. Henry Quilter, "The New Renaissance; or, the Gospel of Intensity," *Macmillan's Magazine* 42 (September 1880): 392–93.

4. Frederick Wedmore, "Some Tendencies in Recent Painting," *Temple Bar* 53 (July 1878): 339.

5. "The Grosvenor Gallery Exhibition," *Illustrated London News* 74 (May 5, 1879): 415.

6. Henry Quilter, "The New Renaissance," 395.

7. According to Christopher Wood, "Androgynous, almost sexless figures were to become a feature of Burne-Jones's mature style, so there can be no doubt that both Swinburne and Solomon influenced his work in this direction. Burne-Jones converted it into something quite different, and quite his own, but it is an important element in his highly complex, eclectic style"; see *Burne-Jones: The Life and Works of Sir Edward Burne-Jones, 1833–1898* (London: Weidenfeld and Nicolson, 1998, 41).

8. Justin McCarthy, "The Pre-Raphaelites in England," *Galaxy* 21 (June 1876): 727.

9. *Jude the Obscure*, ed. Patricia Ingham (Oxford and New York: Oxford University Press, 1998), 128. All further references are cited in the text.

10. These reviews are cited in Cox, *Thomas Hardy: The Critical Heritage* (New York: Barnes and Noble, 1970, 9, 26).

11. See, for instance, L. M. Findlay's "D. G. Rossetti in *Jude the Obscure*" in *Pre-Raphaelite Review* 2 (1978). Winnifred J. Assmann notes that Fancy Day's physical appearance in *Under the Greenwood Tree* resembles that of the women of Pre-Raphaelite art and concedes: "As a Pre-Raphaelite beauty in a painting of the Dutch school, however, she seems out of place"; see "A Pre-Raphaelite Beauty in 'Rural Painting of the Dutch School': The Characterization of Fancy Day," *Thomas Hardy Year Book* 25 (1988, 4). In "Hardy's Dutch Painting," Norman Page also claims that Fancy Day's representation "strongly recalls the kind of Pre-Raphaelite type of female beauty that Hardy might have encountered . . . on the canvases of the Pre-Raphaelite Brotherhood"; see *Thomas Hardy Year Book* 5 (1975, 41). More recently, Bullen points out that Eustacia Vye's appearance resembles that of *Astarte Syriaca* (*The Pre-Raphaelite Body* 170). Hardy also identifies Sue with early Pre-Raphaelite representations of women when he describes her on the morning she is to wed Phillotson: "The bride was waiting, ready; bonnet and all on. She had never in her life looked so much like the lily her name connoted as she did in that pallid morning light" (445).

12. Cox recognizes Havelock's essay as the most important article written on Hardy before the publication of *Tess of the D'Urbervilles* "and one of the most notable during his lifetime" (103).

13. In the 1903 and 1912 editions of the novel Hardy revised "female human" of the 1895 edition to "female animal." Arabella in Jude's eyes is below the human species, yet he marries her. Ironically, by the end of the novel, she appears more perceptive than Sue herself about the nature of Sue's attachment to her cousin. When Mrs. Edin informs Arabella that Sue claims to have "found peace," Arabella astutely responds, " 'She may swear that on her knees to the holy cross upon her necklace till she's hoarse, but it won't be true! . . . She's never found peace since she left his arms, and never will again till she's as he is now!' " (408).

14. Frederick George Stephens, "The Grosvenor Gallery Exhibition," *Athenaeum* (May 5, 1877): 584.

15. John Ruskin (*Works* 17:213), cited by John Christian, catalog entry in Parris, *The Pre-Raphaelites* (304).

16. Critics have long debated the question of whether Sue or Jude is the protagonist of the novel. Though the story is told from Jude's perspective and we know Sue only through others' observations, quite a few critics privilege Sue as the leading character. Hardy himself seemed to shift the focus of the work when in 1897 he chose the titles "The New Woman" and "A Woman with Ideas" for the dramatic version of the novel; see Millgate, *Thomas Hardy: Career as a Novelist* (New York: St. Martin's Press, 1994, 312).

17. Dale Kramer explains Gosse's comments in terms of Sue's possible homosexuality: "With present-day awareness of the psychological anguish caused by suppression of homosexual feelings, this potential aspect of Sue's situation will reward a more coherently addressed scrutiny than any I have seen yet"; see "Hardy and Readers: *Jude the Obscure*" in *The Cambridge Companion to Thomas Hardy* (Cambridge and New York: Cambridge University Press, 1999, 173). Shanta Dutta, however, suggests that Hardy was probably aware that by the end of the century sexologists were defining the New Woman as lesbian, but he takes care "to protect Sue from the charge of lesbianism"; see *Ambivalence in Hardy: A Study of His Attitude to Women* (London and New York: Macmillan and St. Martin's Press, 2000, 114).

18. Kevin Moore comments that in this scene "Sue characterizes herself as [an] Epipsychidion mother-wife figure from whom Jude drinks a nourishing intellectual beauty." He also contends that Hardy casts Jude as a Shelleyan type, identifying him with Alastor and Prometheus. Considering the allusions to Cupid and Psyche, Shirley Stave's arguments that in *Jude the Obscure* "the mystical glimpses into the other world which the other novels offered have disappeared" and that Sue lacks "mythic grandeur" do not seem valid. Moore, *The Descent of the Imagination: Postromantic Culture in the Later Novels of Thomas Hardy* (New York and London: New York University Press, 1990), 229; Stave, *The Decline of the Goddess: Nature, Culture, and Women in Thomas Hardy's Fiction* (Westport and London: Greenwood Press, 1995), 123, 133.

19. The Cupid and Psyche series eventually became a mural frieze commissioned by George Howard for his new home at Kensington. The story of Cupid and Psyche was popular with late-Victorian artists, particularly with J. W. Waterhouse, but the themes Edward Burne-Jones represented are most closely related to the scenes in the novel. To my knowledge there are no references to Waterhouse in either Hardy's letters or notebooks. See Stephen Wildman and John Christian, *Edward Burne-Jones: Victorian Artist-Dreamer* (New York: Metropolitan Museum of Art, 1998), 122–27).

20. See Kestner (*Mythology and Misogyny* 91) for a detailed account of the myth of Cupid and Psyche.

21. Eliza Linn Linton, "The Girl of the Period," *Saturday Review* (March 16, 1868): 339–340.

22. S. P. White, "Modern Mannish Maidens," *Blackwood's Edinburgh Magazine* (February 1890): 253, 259, 261.

23. For an overview of the scholarly dispute over the novel's temporal setting, see Kramer ("Hardy and Readers," 169–71, 180). Whereas most critics argue for the 1860s or the 1890s as the temporal setting of the novel, Robert Gittings maintains that Sue is representative of the Comtean woman of the 1870s, not the feminist of the 1890s; see his *Young Thomas Hardy* (London: Heinemann, 1975), 93–95.

Notes to Conclusion

1. Walter Pater, *The Renaissance: Studies in Art and Poetry: The 1893 Text,* ed. Donald L. Hill, (Berkeley: University of California Press, 1980), 105.

2. See Lynn Alexander, *Women, Work, and Representation: Needlewomen in Victorian Art and Literature.*

3. Cameron's Ophelia, Sylvia Wolf suggests, has a questioning rather than a crazed gaze. See *Julia Margaret Cameron's Women* (Chicago: Art Institute of Chicago, 1998), 49–50.

4. See Karen Z. Sproles, "D. H. Lawrence and the Pre-Raphaelites: 'Love among the Ruins,' " *The D. H. Lawrence Review* 22 (3) (Fall 1990): 299–305; Margaret Bozenna Goscillo, "John Fowles's Pre-Raphaelite Woman: Interart Strategies and Gender Policies," *Mosaic* 26 (1) (Spring 1993): 63–82. Chevalier's *Falling Angels* is set in Edwardian London in the early years of the twentieth century, between 1901 and 1910, dates of the death of Queen Victoria and of her son Edward VII. Early in the novel the Colemans and the Waterhouses meet at the cemetery, where they have adjacent plots. The story revolves around Kitty Coleman and her daughter Maude and Gertrude Waterhouse and her daughter Lavinia. Whereas Kitty represents the New Woman, who desperately attempts to extricate herself from the stifling conventions of the Victorian age, Gertrude rigidly abides by its strictures. At the very beginning of the novel, Kitty, referring to her recent acquaintance with the Waterhouses, comments: "no relation to the painter . . . (Just as well—I want to scream when I see his overripe paintings at the Tate. The Lady of Shalott in her boat looks as if she has just taken opium)" (13). Like the Lady of Shalott, Kitty also dies when later on she ventures into the public sphere and joins the women's movement. Rather than following a Sir Lancelot like her Pre-Raphaelite counterpart, Kitty becomes one of the leaders of (a fictional version of) the largest rally of the Women's Social and Political Union, which took place in Hyde Park in 1908 and dies from the injuries she sustains when the horse she is leading, frightened by a firecracker, kicks her. For information about this historical meeting at Hyde Park, which was attended by a quarter-million people, see Sandra Stanley Holton, *Feminism and Democracy: Women's Suffrage and Reform Politics in Britain 1900–1918* (Cambridge and New York: Cambridge University Press, 1986), 38, 46.

5. In "Revisiting the Serial Format of Dickens's Novels; or, *Little Dorrit* Goes a Long Way," David Barndollar and Susan Schorn voice the concern of teachers of the Victorian novel over the reluctance of students to read these books. Phoebe Wray, who teaches in a private college of high standards, for instance, protests, "It's as if these middle-class, rather privileged kids . . . are from the mines of the 19th century. They do not read. Some of them do not know how to read. They have not a clue about HOW to read in a close way." See *Functions of Victorian Culture at the Present Time,* ed. Christine Krueger (Athens: Ohio University Press, 2002), 174.

6. See John Kucich and Dianne F. Sadoff, eds., *Victorian Afterlife: Postmodern Culture Rewrites the Nineteenth Century* (Minneapolis and London: University of Minnesota Press, 2000).

7. Kate Flint thoroughly explores the visual aspects of the Victorian culture in her recent book, *The Victorians and the Visual Imagination*.

Bibliography

Primary Works

Acton, William. *Prostitution Considered in Its Moral, Social, and Sanitary Aspects in London and Other Large Cities, with Proposals for the Mitigation and Prevention of Its Attendant Evil.* London: John Churchill, 1857.

Anonymous. "Free Exhibition of Modern Art." *Athenaeum* (April 7, 1849): 362.

———. "Fine Arts: Royal Academy." *Athenaeum* (June 2, 1849): 575.

———. "The Exhibition of the Royal Academy." *Times* (May 9, 1850): 5.

———. "Royal Academy Exhibition Notice." *Athenaeum* (June 1, 1850): 590–91.

———. "The Pictures of the Season." *Blackwood's Edinburgh Magazine* 68 (July 1850): 77–93.

———. "Exhibition of the Royal Academy, Second Notice." *Times* (May 7, 1851): 8.

———. "Pre-Raphaelitism." *The Art-Journal* 13 (November 1, 1851): 285–86.

———. "Royal Academy." *Athenaeum* (May 22, 1852): 581–83.

———. "Fine Arts: The Royal Academy." *Athenaeum* (May 7, 1853): 567–68.

———. "Review of Elizabeth Gaskell's *Ruth*." *North British Review* 19 (May–August 1853): 151–74.

———. "Review of Elizabeth Gaskell's *Ruth*." *Prospective Review* 9 (May 1853): 222–47.

———. "The Royal Academy Exhibition." *Fraser's Magazine* 47 (June 1853): 707–13.

———. "Fine Arts: Royal Academy." *Athenaeum* (May 6, 1854): 559–62.

———. "The English Pre-Raphaelites." *Eclectic Review* (January 11, 1856): 1–20.

———. "Fine Arts: Royal Academy." *Athenaeum* (May 10, 1856): 589–90.

———. "Fine Arts: Royal Academy." *Athenaeum* (May 1, 1858): 565–67.

———. "The Grosvenor Gallery Exhibit." *Times* (May 1, 1877): 10.

———. " 'Meglip,' Royal Academy and Grosvenor Gallery." *Vanity Fair* 17 (1877): 281.

———. "The Grosvenor Gallery Exhibition." *Illustrated London News* 74 (May 5, 1879): 415.

Bjork, Lennart A., ed. *The Literary Notebooks of Thomas Hardy.* 2 vols. New York: New York University Press, 1985.

Braddon, Mary Elizabeth. *Lady Audley's Secret*, ed. David Skilton. Oxford and New York: Oxford University Press, 1998.

Burne-Jones, Georgiana. *Memorials of Edward Burne-Jones.* 2 vols. London and New York: Macmillan, 1904.

Burton, Richard F. *The Lake Regions of Central Africa*. St. Clair Shores, Mich.: Scholarly Press, 1971.

Chapple, J. A. V., and Arthur Pollard, eds. *The Letters of Mrs. Gaskell*. Manchester: Mandolin/Manchester University Press, 1997.

———, eds. *Further Letters of Mrs. Gaskell*. Manchester and New York: Manchester University Press, 2000.

Chevalier, Tracy. *Falling Angels*. New York and London: Dutton, 2001.

Collins, Wilkie. "The Exhibition of the Royal Academy." *Bentley's Miscellany* 29 (June 1851): 617–27.

———. *Hide and Seek*. New York: Dover, 1981.

———. *The Woman in White*, ed. John Sutherland. Oxford and New York: Oxford University Press, 1998.

———. *The Law and the Lady*, ed. Jenny Bourne Taylor. Oxford and New York: Oxford University Press, 1999.

———. *The Letters of Wilkie Collins, 1838–1889*, ed. William Baker and William M. Clarke. 2 vols. New York: St. Martin's, 1999.

Cox, R. G., ed. *Thomas Hardy: The Critical Heritage*. New York: Barnes and Noble, 1970.

Cross, John W., ed. *George Eliot's Life as Related in Her Letters and Journals*. 3 vols. New York: Harper, 1885.

Dickens, Charles. "Old Lamps for New Ones." *Household Words* 1 (June 15, 1850): 265–67.

Dilke, Sir Charles Wentworth. *Greater Britain: A Record of Travel in English-Speaking Countries*, 2d ed. 2 vols. London: Macmillan, 1869.

Eagles, John. "The Fine Arts and the Public Taste in 1853." *Blackwood's Edinburgh Magazine* 74 (July 1853): 89–104.

Eliot, George. Review of John Ruskin's *Lectures on Architecture and Painting*. *Leader* 10 (1854): 545–46.

———. "Art and Belles Lettres." *Westminster Review* 65 (April 1856): 625–33.

———. "History, Biography, Voyages, and Travels," *Westminster Review* 67 (January 1857): 158–78.

———. *Theophrastus Such*. London: William Blackwood, 1879.

———. *The George Eliot Letters*, ed. Gordon S. Haight. 9 vols. New Haven: Yale University Press, 1954–1978.

———. *Essays of George Eliot*, ed. Thomas Pinney. London: Routledge and Kegan Paul, 1963.

———. *Some George Eliot Notebooks: An Edition of the Carl H. Pforzheimer Library's George Eliot Holograph Notebooks*, ed. William Baker. 4 vols. MSS 707, 708, 709, 710, 711. Salzburg: Universität Salzburg, 1976–1985.

———. *George Eliot: A Writer's Notebook 1854–1879. And Uncollected Writings*, ed. Joseph Wiesenfarth. Charlottesville: University Press of Virginia, 1981.

———. *George Eliot: The Critical Heritage*, ed. David Carroll. London and New York: Routledge, 1995.

———. *George Eliot's Daniel Deronda Notebooks*, ed. Jane Irwin. Cambridge and New York: Cambridge University Press, 1996.

———. *Adam Bede*, ed. Valentine Cunningham. Oxford and New York: Oxford University Press, 1998.

———. *Daniel Deronda*, ed. Graham Handley. Oxford and New York: Oxford University Press, 1998.

———. *The Journals of George Eliot*, ed. Margaret Harris and Judith Johnston. Cambridge and New York: Cambridge University Press, 1998.

———. *The Mill on the Floss*, ed. Gordon S. Haight. Oxford and New York: Oxford University Press, 1998.

———. *Middlemarch*. Introd. A. S. Byatt. Oxford and New York: Oxford University Press, 1999.

Fredeman, William E., ed. *The P.R.B. Journal: William Michael Rossetti's Diary of the Pre-Raphaelite Brotherhood 1849–1853*. Oxford: Clarendon, 1975.

Gaskell, Elizabeth. *The Works of Mrs. Gaskell*, ed. A. W. Ward. 8 vols. Knutsford edition. New York: G. P. Putman; London: Smith, Elder, 1906.

Germ, The: Thoughts towards Nature in Poetry, Literature, and Art. Four issues published January–May 1850 (nos. 3 and 4 retitled *Art and Poetry: Being Thoughts toward Nature: Conducted Principally by Artists*). Reprinted with an introduction by William Michael Rossetti. Oxford: Ashmolean Museum, 1992.

Greg, William Rathbone. "Prostitution." *Westminster Review* 53 (July 1850): 448–506.

Hardy, Thomas. *Jude the Obscure*, ed. Patricia Ingham. Oxford and New York: Oxford University Press, 1998.

Herodotus. Trans. George Rawlinson. New York: Modern Library, 1921.

Hunt, William Holman. *Pre-Raphaelitism and the Pre-Raphaelite Brotherhood*. 2 vols. London: Macmillan, 1905.

James, Henry. "The Grosvenor Gallery, 1878." In *The Painter's Eye*, ed. John L. Sweeney, 161–71. London: Rupert Hart Davis, 1956.

———. "The Picture Season in London, 1877." In *The Painter's Eye*, ed. John L. Sweeney, 130–51. London: Rupert Hart-Davis, 1956.

———. "Review of *Ismailia* by Sir Samuel Baker." In *Essays on Literature, American Writers, English Writers*, ed. Leon Edel, 732–36. New York: Library of America, 1984.

Jung, Carl G. *Collected Works of C. G. Jung*, ed. H. Read, Michael Fordham, and Gerhard Adler. Trans. R. F. C. Hull. 20 vols. Princeton: Princeton University Press, 1953–1977.

———. *Aspects of the Feminine*. Trans. R. F. C. Hull. Princeton: Princeton University Press, 1982.

Lago, Mary, ed. *Burne-Jones Talking*. Columbia: University Press of Missouri, 1981.

Lerner, Laurence, and John Holmstrom, eds. *Thomas Hardy and His Readers*. London: Bodley Head, 1968.

Lessing, Gotthold Ephraim. *Laocoön: An Essay on the Limits of Painting and Poetry*. Trans. Edward Allen McCormick. Baltimore: Johns Hopkins University Press, 1962.

Lewes, G. H. "Review of *Ruth* and *Villette*." *Westminster Review* 3 (April 1853): 245–54.

Linton, Eliza Lynn. "The Girl of the Period." *Saturday Review* (March 14, 1868): 339–40.

Masson, David. "Pre-Raphaelitism in Art and Literature." *The British Quarterly Review* 16 (August 1852): 197–220.

Mayhew, Henry, and Bracebridge Hemyng. "Prostitutes." *London Labour and the London Poor*. 4 vols. New York: Dover, 1968. Vol 4: 35–273.

McCarthy, Justin. "The Pre-Raphaelites in England." *Galaxy* 21 (June 1876): 725–32.

Millais, John Guille. *The Life and Letters of Sir John Everett Millais*. 2 vols. London: Methuen, 1899.

Morris, William. *Prose and Poetry 1856–1870*. London and New York: Oxford University Press, 1913.

Page, Norman, ed. *Wilkie Collins: The Critical Heritage*. London and Boston: Routledge and Kegan Paul, 1974.

Pater, Walter. *The Renaissance: Studies in Art and Poetry: The 1893 Text,* ed. Donald L. Hill. Berkeley: University of California Press, 1980.

Plato. "Symposium." *Selected Dialogues of Plato.* Trans. Benjamin Jowett. Rev. and introd. Hayden Pelliccia. New York: Modern Library, 2000, 199–277.

Proctor, R. A. "Gambling Superstitions." *Cornhill Magazine* 25 (1872): 707–17.

Purdy, Richard, and Michael Millgate, eds. *The Collected Letters of Thomas Hardy.* 7 vols. Oxford: Oxford University Press, 1978–1988.

Quilter, Harry. "The New Renaissance, or the Gospel of Intensity." *Macmillan's Magazine* 42 (September 1880): 392–95.

Reade, Winwood. *Savage Africa: Being the Narrative of a Tour in Equatorial, Southwestern, and Northwestern Africa.* New York: Harper, 1864.

Reynolds, Sir Joshua. *Discourses on Art,* ed. Robert R. Wark. New Haven: Yale University Press, 1975.

Rossetti, Dante Gabriel. *Collected Works of Dante Gabriel Rossetti,* ed. William Michael Rossetti. 2 vols. London: Ellis, 1886.

———. *Letters of Dante Gabriel Rossetti,* ed. Oswald Doughty and John Robert Wahl. 4 vols. Oxford: Clarendon, 1965–1967.

———. *Collected Writings,* ed. Jan Marsh. Chicago: New Amsterdam Books, 2000.

Rossetti, William Michael. *Fine Art, Chiefly Contemporary.* London, 1867; rpt. New York: AMS Press, 1970.

———. *Dante Gabriel Rossetti: His Family Letters and a Memoir by William Michael Rossetti.* 2 vols. London, 1895; rpt. New York: AMS Press, 1970.

Ruskin, John. *The Works of John Ruskin,* ed. E. T. Cook and Alexander Wedderburn. 39 vols. London: George Allen, 1903–1912.

Spencer, Herbert. *The Principles of Ethics.* 2 vols. New York: Appleton, 1898.

Spender, Stephen. "The Pre-Raphaelite Literary Painters." *Journal of Pre-Raphaelite Studies* 10 (2001): 27–34.

Stephens, Frederic George. *William Holman Hunt and His Works: Memoir of the Artist's Life, with Description of His Pictures.* London: Nisbet, 1860.

———. "The Grosvenor Gallery Exhibition." *Athenaeum* (May 5, 1877): 583–84.

———. "Dante Gabriel Rossetti: Painter and Poet." In *The Portfolio: Monographs on Artistic Subjects,* by Alfred W. Pollard. London: Seeley; New York, Macmillan, 1894, 5–96.

Taylor, Tom. "The Exhibition of the Royal Academy." *Times* (May 9, 1850): 5

———. "The Exhibition of the Royal Academy." *Times* (May 3, 1851): 8.

Tennyson, Alfred Lord. *The Poems,* 2d ed. Ed. Christopher Ricks. 3 vols. Berkeley and Los Angeles: University of California Press, 1987.

Tennyson, Hallam. *Alfred Lord Tennyson: A Memoir by His Son.* 2 vols. London: Macmillan, 1897.

Thackeray, William Makepeace. *Vanity Fair,* ed. J. I. M. Stewart. New York: Penguin, 1985.

Trollope, Anthony. *Barchester Towers,* ed. Robin Gilmour. Hammondsworth: Penguin, 1988.

Wedmore, Frederick. "Some Tendencies in Recent Painting." *Temple Bar* 53 (July 1878): 334–48.

White, S. P. "Modern Mannish Maidens." *Blackwood's Edinburgh Magazine* (February 1890): 252–64.

Wornum, Ralph M. "Modern Moves in Art." *Art Journal* 12 (September 1, 1850): 269–71.

Secondary Sources

Ainsworth, Maryan Wynn. *Dante Gabriel Rossetti and the Double Work of Art.* Hartford: Yale University Art Gallery, 1976. An exhibition catalog.

Alexander, Lynn M. *Women, Work, and Representation: Needlewomen in Victorian Art and Literature.* Athens, Ohio: Ohio University Press, 2003.

Altick, Richard. *Paintings from Books: Art and Literature in Britain, 1760–1900.* Columbus: Ohio State University Press, 1985.

———. *The Presence of the Present: Topics of the Day in the Victorian Novel.* Columbus: Ohio State University Press, 1991.

Amor, Anne Clark. *William Holman Hunt: The True Pre-Raphaelite.* London: Constable, 1989.

Anderson, Amanda. *Tainted Souls and Painted Faces: The Rhetoric of Fallenness in Victorian Culture.* Reading Women Writing Series. Ithaca: Cornell University Press, 1993.

Andres, Sophia. "The Germ and the Picture in *Middlemarch*." *English Literary History* 55 (Winter 1988): 853–68.

———. "George Eliot's Challenge to Medusa's Gendered Disparities." *Victorian Newsletter* 95 (Spring 1999): 27–33.

Ardis, Ann L. *New Women, New Novels: Feminism and Early Modernism.* New Brunswick, N.J. and London: Rutgers University Press, 1990.

Armstrong, Nancy. *Fiction in the Age of Photography: The Legacy of British Realism.* Cambridge, Mass.: Harvard University Press, 1999.

Arscott, Caroline. "Employer, Husband, Spectator: Thomas Fairbairn's Commission of *The Awakening Conscience*." In *The Culture of Capital: Art, Power, and the Nineteenth-Century Middle Class,* ed. Janet Wolff and John Seed, 59–190. Manchester: Manchester University Press; New York: St. Martin's Press, 1988.

Ash, Russell. *Sir Edward Burne-Jones.* New York: Harry Abrams, 1993.

Assmann, Winnifred J. "A Pre-Raphaelite Beauty in 'Rural Painting of the Dutch School': The Characterization of Fancy Day." *Thomas Hardy Year Book* 25 (1988): 3–10.

Auerbach, Nina. *Woman and the Demon: The Life of a Victorian Myth.* Cambridge, Mass., and London: Harvard University Press, 1982.

Baker, William. *George Eliot and Judaism,* ed. James Hogg. Romantic Reassessment Series, no. 45. Salzburg: Universität Salzburg, 1975.

———, and Kenneth Womack, eds. *A Companion to the Victorian Novel.* London and Westport, Conn.: Greenwood Press, 2002.

Balee, Susan. "Wilkie Collins and Surplus Women: The Case of Marian Halcombe." *Victorian Literature and Culture* 20 (1992): 197–215.

Bandelin, Susan Ball. " 'Allegorizing on One's Own Hook.' " In *Dante Gabriel Rossetti and the Double Work of Art,* ed. Maryan Wynn Ainsworth, 37–72. Hartford: Yale University Art Gallery, 1976. An exhibition catalog.

Barndollar, David, and Susan Schorn, "Revisiting the Serial Format of Dickens's Novels; or, *Little Dorrit* Goes a Long Way." In *Functions of Victorian Culture at the Present Time,* ed. Christine Krueger, 157–70. Athens: Ohio University Press, 2002.

Barnes, Rachel. *The Pre-Raphaelites and Their World.* London: Tate Gallery, 1998.

Barringer, Tim. *Reading the Pre-Raphaelites.* New Haven: Yale University Press, 1999.

Bashant, Wendy. "Redressing Androgyny: Hermaphroditic Bodies in Victorian England." *Journal of Pre-Raphaelite Studies* 4 (Fall 1995): 5–26.

Bauer, Dale M. *Feminism, Bakhtin, and the Dialogic*. New York: State University of New York Press, 1991.

Bayard, Jane. " 'Lustral Rites and Dire Portents': Works from 1871 to 1882." In *Dante Gabriel Rossetti and the Double Work of Art*, ed. Maryan Wynn Ainsworth, 95–102. Hartford: Yale University Art Gallery, 1976. An exhibition catalog.

Beer, Gillian. "Myth and the Single Consciousness: *Middlemarch* and the Lifted Veil." In *This Particular Web*, ed. Ian Adam, 91–115. Toronto: University of Toronto Press, 1973.

Berger, John. *Ways of Seeing*. London: Penguin, 1972.

Bernstein, Stephen. "Reading in Blackwater Park: Gothicism, Narrative, and Ideology in *The Woman in White*." *Studies in the Novel* 25 (September 1993): 291–305.

Bodelsen, C. A. *Studies in Mid-Victorian Imperialism*. New York: Howard Fertig, 1968.

Bonaparte, Felicia. *The Gypsy-Bachelor of Manchester: The Life of Mrs. Gaskell's Demon*. Charlottesville and London: University Press of Virginia, 1992.

Brantlinger, Patrick. "Victorians and Africans: The Genealogy of the Myth of the Dark Continent." In *"Race," Writing and Difference*, ed. Henry Louis Gates Jr., 185–222. Chicago: University of Chicago Press, 1985.

———. *Rule of Darkness: British Literature and Imperialism, 1830–1914*. Ithaca: Cornell University Press, 1986.

Brewer, Pamela Didlake. "Pre-Raphaelitism in *Lady Audley's Secret*." *Publications of the Arkansas Philological Association* 19 (1) (Spring 1993): 1–10.

Brittan, Arthur. *Masculinity and Power*. Oxford: Blackwell, 1989.

Bronfen, Elisabeth. *Over Her Dead Body: Death, Femininity and the Aesthetic*. New York: Routledge, 1992.

Brooks, Chris. *Signs for the Times: Symbolic Realism in the Mid-Victorian World*. London, Boston, and Sydney: George Allen and Unwin, 1984.

Brooks, Peter. *Body Work: Objects of Desire in Modern Narrative*. Cambridge, Mass.: Harvard University Press, 1993.

Bullen, John B. *The Expressive Eye: Fiction and Perception in the Work of Thomas Hardy*. Oxford: Clarendon, 1986.

———. *The Pre-Raphaelite Body: Fear and Desire in Painting, Poetry, and Criticism*. New York: Oxford University Press, 1998.

———. "Dante Gabriel Rossetti and the Mirror of Masculine Desire." *Nineteenth-Century Contexts* 21 (3) (1999): 329–52.

———, ed. *The Sun Is God: Painting, Literature, and Mythology in the Nineteenth Century*. Oxford: Clarendon, 1989.

Busst, A. J. L. "The Image of the Androgyne in the Nineteenth Century." In *Romantic Mythologies*, ed. Ian Fletcher, 1–96. London: Routledge, 1967.

Byerly, Alison. "Art Works: Thomas Hardy and the Labor of Creation." In *Realism, Representation, and the Arts in Nineteenth-Century Literature*, 149–83. Cambridge: Cambridge University Press, 1997.

Canham, Stephen. "Art and the Illustration of *Vanity Fair* and *The Newcomes*." *Modern Language Quarterly* 43 (1) (Spring 1982): 43–66.

Carpenter, Mary Wilson. "The Apocalypse of the Old Testament: *Daniel Deronda* and the Interpretation of Interpretation." *Publications of the Modern Language Association* 99 (1) (January 1984): 56–71.

Casteras, Susan. "The Double Vision of Portraiture." In *Dante Gabriel Rossetti and the Double Work of Art*, ed. Maryan Wynn Ainsworth, 9–36. New Haven: Yale University Art Gallery, 1976.

————. *Images of Victorian Womanhood in English Art*. London: Associated University Press, 1987.

————. "Pre-Raphaelite Challenges to Victorian Canons of Beauty." *Huntington Library Quarterly* 55 (February 1992): 13–35.

————. "Pre-Raphaelite Portraiture: A Strangely Disordered Vision." In *Collecting the Pre-Raphaelites: The Anglo-American Enchantment,* ed. Margaretta Frederick Watson, 139–48. Brookfield: Ashgate, 1997.

Chatterjee, Ranita. "*Matilda*: Mary Shelley, William Godwin, and the Ideologies of Incest." In *Iconoclastic Departures: Mary Shelley after Frankenstein*, ed. Syndy M. Conger, Frederick S. Frank, and Gregory O'Dea, 130–49. Madison: Fairleigh Dickinson University Press, 1997.

Cherry, Deborah. *Painting Women: Victorian Women Artists*. London and New York: Routledge, 1993.

————, and Griselda Pollock. "Patriarchal Power and the Pre-Raphaelites." *Art History* 7 (4) (1984): 480–95.

Christ, Carol T. *The Finer Optic: The Aesthetic of Particularity in Victorian Poetry*. New Haven and London: Yale University Press, 1975.

Cixous, Hélène. "The Laugh of the Medusa." Trans. Keith Cohen and Paula Cohen. *Signs* (1976): 875–94. Rpt. in *New French Feminisms*, ed. Elaine Marks and Isabelle de Courtivron, 245–64. Amherst: University of Massachusetts Press, 1980.

Clarke, William M. *The Secret Life of Wilkie Collins*. Chicago: Ivan R. Dee, 1991.

Codell, Julie F. "Expression over Beauty: Facial Expression, Body Language, and Circumstantiality in the Paintings of the Pre-Raphaelite Brotherhood." *Victorian Studies* 29 (Winter 1986): 255–90.

————. "The Dilemma of the Artist in Millais's Lorenzo and Isabella: Phrenology, the Gaze, and the Social Discourse." *Art History* 14 (1) (Spring 1991): 51–66.

————. "Empiricism, Naturalism, and Science in Millais's Paintings." In *John Everett Millais beyond the Pre-Raphaelite Brotherhood*, ed. Debra N. Mancoff, 119–47. Studies in British Art Series, no. 7. New Haven and London: Yale University Press, 2001.

Cottom, Daniel. *Social Figures: George Eliot, Social History, and Literary Representation*. Minneapolis: University of Minnesota Press, 1987.

D'Albertis, Deirdre. *Dissembling Fictions: Elizabeth Gaskell and the Victorian Social Text*. New York: St. Martin's Press, 1997.

David, Deidre. *Fictions of Resolution in Three Victorian Novels: North and South, Our Mutual Friend, Daniel Deronda*. New York: Columbia University Press, 1981.

————. *Rule Britannia: Women, Empire, and Victorian Writing*. Ithaca: Cornell University Press, 1995.

Davis, Nuel Pharr. *The Life of Wilkie Collins*. Urbana: University of Illinois Press, 1956.

Dawson, Terence, ed. *The Cambridge Companion to Jung*. Cambridge: Cambridge University Press, 1997.

Deas, Elisabeth. "The Missing *Alisma*: Ruskin's Botanical Error." *Journal of Pre-Raphaelite Studies* 10 (Fall 2001): 4–13.

Dechery, Laurent. "Turning Words into Colors: Robbe-Grillet's Visual Language." *Mosaic* 32 (3) (September 1999): 59–74.

Dutta, Shanta. *Ambivalence in Hardy: A Study of His Attitude to Women*. London and New York: Macmillan and St. Martin's Press, 2000.

Easson, Angus. "Elizabeth Gaskell and the *Athenaeum*: Two Contributions Identified." *Modern Language Review* 85 (October 1990): 829–32.

Edelstein, T. J. "They Sang 'The Song of the Shirt': Visual Iconology of the Seamstress." *Victorian Studies* 23 (2) (Winter 1980): 183–210.

Elam, Diane. "White Narratology: Gender and Reference in Wilkie Collins's *The Woman in White*." In *Virginal Sexuality and Textuality in Victorian Literature*, ed. Lloyd Davis, 49–63. Albany: State University of New York Press, 1993.

Eldridge, C. C. *Victorian Imperialism*. New Jersey: Humanities Press, 1978.

Ender, Evelyne. *Sexing the Mind: Nineteenth-Century Fictions of Hysteria*. Ithaca: Cornell University Press, 1995.

Fasick, Laura. "Thackeray's Treatment of Writing and Painting." *Nineteenth-Century Literature* 47 (June 1992): 72–90.

Faxon, Alicia Craig. *Dante Gabriel Rossetti*. New York: Abbeville Press, 1989.

Federici, Corrado, and Esther Raventós-Pons, eds. *Literary Texts and the Arts: Interdisciplinary Perspectives*. New York: Peter Lang, 2003.

Fernando, Lloyd. "Thomas Hardy's Rhetoric of Painting." *Review of English Literature* 6 (1965): 62–73.

Findlay. L. M. "D. G. Rossetti in *Jude the Obscure*." *Pre-Raphaelite Review* 2 (1) (November 1978): 1–11.

Fisher, Judith Law. "The Aesthetic of the Mediocre: Thackeray and the Visual Arts." *Victorian Studies* 26 (1) (Autumn 1982): 65–82.

———. "Siren and Artist: Contradiction in Thackeray's Aesthetic Ideal." *Nineteenth-Century Fiction* 39 (4) (March 1985): 392–419.

Fitzgerald, Penelope. *Edward Burne-Jones: A Biography*. London: Michael Joseph, 1975.

Flaxman, Rhoda L. *Victorian Word-Painting and Narrative: Toward the Blending of Genres*. Ann Arbor: University of Michigan Press, 1987.

Fleming, Gordon H. *That Ne'er Shall Meet Again: Rossetti, Millais, Hunt*. London: Michael Joseph, 1971.

Flint, Kate. "Reading *The Awakening Conscience* Rightly." In *Pre-Raphaelites Re-Viewed*, ed. Marcia Pointon, 45–65. Manchester and New York: Manchester University Press, 1989.

———. *Elizabeth Gaskell*. Plymouth: Northcote House, 1995.

———. "Blindness and Insight: Millais's *The Blind Girl* and the Limits of Representation." *Journal of Victorian Culture* 1 (1) (1996): 1–15.

———. "Portraits of Women: On Display." In *Millais: Portraits*, ed. Peter Funnell, 181–215. Princeton: Princeton University Press, 1999.

———. *The Victorians and the Visual Imagination*. Cambridge: Cambridge University Press, 2000.

Fontana, Ernest. "Mary Magdalene and the Pre-Raphaelites." *Journal of Pre-Raphaelite Studies* 9 (Fall 2000): 88–100.

Foster, Shirley. *Victorian Women's Fiction: Marriage, Freedom, and the Individual*. London and Sydney: Croom Helm, 1985.

Foucault, Michel. *The History of Sexuality*. Vol. 1: An Introduction, trans. Robert Hurley. London: Harmondsworth, 1981.

Frick, Patricia. "Wilkie Collins and John Ruskin." *Victorians Institute Journal* 13 (1985): 11–22.

Funnell, Peter, ed. *Millais: Portraits*. Princeton: Princeton University Press, 1999.

Ghose, S. N. *Dante Gabriel Rossetti and Contemporary Criticism*. Geneva: Norwood Editions, 1977.

Gikandi, Simon. "Englishness, Travel, and Theory: Writing the West Indies in the Nineteenth Century." *Nineteenth-Century Contexts* 18 (1) (1994): 49–70.

Gittings, Robert. *Young Thomas Hardy*. London: Heinemann, 1975.

Gombrich, E. H. *Art and Illusion: A Study in the Psychology of Pictorial Representation*. 4th ed. London: Phaidon, 1972.

Goscillo, Margaret Bozenna. "John Fowles's Pre-Raphaelite Woman: Interart Strategies and Gender Politics." *Mosaic* 26 (1) (Spring 1993): 63–82.

Green, Laura Morgan. *Educating Women: Cultural Conflict and Victorian Literature*. Athens: Ohio University Press, 2001.

Grundy, Joan. *Hardy and the Sister Arts*. London: Macmillan, 1979.

Hacking, Juliet. Introduction. In *Essential Pre-Raphaelites*, by Lucinda Hawksley, 6–15. London: Dempsey Parr, 1999.

Hagstrum, Jean. *The Sister Arts: The Tradition of Literary Pictorialism and English Poetry from Dryden to Gray*. Chicago: University of Chicago Press, 1958.

Haight, Gordon. *George Eliot: A Biography*. Oxford and New York: Oxford University Press, 1968.

———. "George Eliot's 'Eminent Failure,' Will Ladislaw." In *This Particular Web*, ed. Ian Adam, 22–42. Toronto: University of Toronto Press, 1973.

Hapke, Laura. "He Stoops to Conquer: Redeeming the Fallen Woman in the Fiction of Dickens, Gaskell, and Their Contemporaries." *Victorian Newsletter* 69 (Spring 1986): 16–22.

Harding, Ellen, ed. *Re-Framing the Pre-Raphaelites: Historical and Theoretical Essays*. Brookfield: Ashgate, 1996.

Harrison, Anthony. "1848: Revolution and Reform." In *A Companion to Victorian Literature and Culture*, ed. Herbert F. Tucker, 19–34. Oxford and Malden: Blackwell, 1999.

Harrison, Martin, and Bill Waters. *Burne-Jones*, 2d ed. London: Barrie and Jenkins, 1989.

Hawksley, Lucinda. *Essential Pre-Raphaelites*. London: Dempsey Parr, 1999.

Hefferman, James A. W. *Museum of Words: The Poetics of Ekphrasis from Homer to Ashbery*. Chicago and London: University of Chicago Press, 1993.

Henry, Nancy. *George Eliot and the British Empire*. Cambridge and New York: Cambridge University Press, 2002.

Hester, Erwin. "George Eliot's Use of Historical Events in *Daniel Deronda*." *English Language Notes* 4 (December 1966): 115–18.

Hilton, Timothy. *The Pre-Raphaelites*. London: Thames and Hudson, 1970.

Hinz, Evelyn. "Introduction: The Sisterly Arts?" *Mosaic* 31 (1998): iii–vii.

Holton, Sandra Stanley. *Feminism and Democracy: Women's Suffrage and Reform Politics in Britain 1900–1918*. Cambridge and New York: Cambridge University Press, 1986.

Homans, Margaret. *Bearing the Word: Language and Female Experience in Nineteenth-Century Women's Writing*. Chicago: University of Chicago Press, 1986.

Hughes, Linda K., and Michael Lund. *Victorian Publishing and Mrs. Gaskell's Work*. Charlottesville and London: University Press of Virginia, 1999.

Ingham, Patricia. "Jude the Obscure." In *The Language of Gender and Class: Transformation in the Victorian Novel*, 160–82. London and New York: Routledge, 1996.

Jacobus, Mary. *Reading Woman: Essays in Feminist Criticism*. New York: Columbia University Press, 1986.

Jeal, Tim. *David Livingstone*. New York: G. P. Putman, 1973.

Johnson, Patricia E. "The Gendered Politics of the Gaze: Henry James and George Eliot." *Mosaic* 30 (March 1997): 39–54.

Kane, Stephen. *Eyes of Love: The Gaze in English and French Painting, 1840–1900*. New York: New York University Press, 1996.

Kaplan, E. Ann. *Women and Film: Both Sides of the Camera*. New York: Methuen, 1983.

Kaufmann, David. *George Eliot and Judaism: An Attempt to Appreciate* Daniel Deronda. 2d ed. Trans. J. W. Ferrier. New York: Haskell House, 1970.

Kestner, Joseph A. *Mythology and Misogyny: The Social Discourse of Nineteenth-Century British Classical-Subject Painting*. Madison: University of Wisconsin Press, 1989.

———. *Masculinities in Victorian Painting*. Aldershot, England; Brookfield, Vt.: Ashgate, 1995.

Kramer, Dale, ed. *The Cambridge Companion to Thomas Hardy*. Cambridge and New York: Cambridge University Press, 1999.

———. "Hardy and Readers: *Jude the Obscure*." In *The Cambridge Companion to Thomas Hardy*, ed. Dale Kramer, 164–82. Cambridge and New York: Cambridge University Press, 1999.

Krieger, Murray. *Ekphrasis: The Illusion of the Natural Sign*. Baltimore and London: Johns Hopkins University Press, 1991.

Krueger, Christine L., ed. *Functions of Victorian Culture at the Present Time*. Athens: Ohio University Press, 2002.

Kucich, John, and Dianne F. Sadoff, eds. *Victorian Afterlife*. Minneapolis and London: University of Minnesota Press, 2000.

Lambourne, Lionel. *Victorian Painting*. London: Phaidon, 1999.

Landow, George P. *William Holman Hunt and Typological Symbolism*. New Haven. Yale University Press, 1979.

———. *Victorian Types, Victorian Shadows: Biblical Typology in Victorian Literature, Art, and Thought*. Boston: Routledge, 1980.

———. "Shadows Cast by *The Light of the World*: William Holman Hunt's Religious Paintings, 1893–1905." *Art Bulletin* 65 (3) (September 1983): 471–84.

Langbauer, Laurie. "Women in White, Men in Feminism." *Yale Journal of Criticism* 2 (2) (April 1989): 219–43.

Langland, Elizabeth. *Telling Tales*. Columbus: Ohio State University Press, 2002.

Ledger, Sally. *The New Woman: Fiction and Feminism at the Fin de Siècle*. Manchester: Manchester University Press, 1997.

Leng, Andrew. "Dorothea's *Awakening Consciousness* and the Pre-Raphaelite Aesthetic in *Middlemarch*." *Journal of the Australasian Universities Language and Literature Association* 75 (May 1991): 52–64.

Levine, George, ed. *The Cambridge Companion to George Eliot*. Cambridge and New York: Cambridge University Press, 2001.

Linehan, Katherine Bailey. "Mixed Politics: The Critique of Imperialism in *Daniel Deronda*." *Texas Studies in Literature and Language* 34 (Fall 1992): 323–46.

Maas, Jeremy. *Holman Hunt and the Light of the World*. Aldershot, Hants: Scolar, 1984, reissued by Wildwood House, 1987.

Macleod, Dianne Sachko. *Art and the Victorian Middle Class*. Cambridge: Cambridge University Press, 1998.

Mancoff, Debra N. *Burne-Jones*. San Francisco: Pomegranate, 1998.

———. *Flora Symbolica: Flowers in Pre-Raphaelite Art*. London and New York: Prestel, 2003.

———, ed. *John Everett Millais beyond the Pre-Raphaelite Brotherhood*. New Haven: Yale University Press, 2001.

Marillier, H. C. *Dante Gabriel Rossetti: An Illustrated Memorial of His Art and Life*. London: George Bell and Sons, 1899.

Markiewitcz, Henry. "Ut Pictura Poesis: A History of the Topos and the Problem." *New Literary History* 18 (Spring 1987): 535–58.

Marks, Arthur S. "Ford Madox Brown's *Take Your Son, Sir!*" *Arts Magazine* 54 (January 1980): 135–41.

Marsh, Jan *Pre-Raphaelite Women: Images of Femininity in Pre-Raphaelite Art.* London: Artus Books, 1987.

———. *Dante Gabriel Rossetti, Painter and Poet.* London: Weidenfeld and Nicolson, 1999.

———, ed. *Dante Gabriel Rossetti: Collected Writings.* Chicago: Ivan R. Dee, 2000.

———, and Pamela Gerrish Nunn. *Pre-Raphaelite Women Artists.* London: Thames and Hudson, 1998.

Martin, Carol M. "Contemporary Critics and Judaism in *Daniel Deronda.*" *Victorian Periodicals Review* 21 (1) (Spring 1988): 90–107.

McCaw, Neil. *George Eliot and Victorian Historiography: Imagining the National Past.* New York: St. Martin's Press, 2000.

McGann, Jerome. *Dante Gabriel Rossetti and the Game That Must Be Lost.* New Haven and London: Yale University Press, 2000.

Meisel, Martin. *Realizations: Narrative, Pictorial, and Theatrical Arts in Nineteenth-Century England.* Princeton: Princeton University Press, 1983.

Meyer, Susan. "'Safely to Their Own Borders': Proto-Zionism, Feminism, and Nationalism in *Daniel Deronda.*" *English Literary History* 60 (Autumn 1993): 733–58.

———. *Imperialism at Home: Race and Victorian Women's Fiction.* Ithaca and Cornell: Cornell University Press, 1996.

Meyers, Jeffrey. *Painting and the Novel.* Manchester: Manchester University Press, 1975.

Millgate, Michael. *Thomas Hardy: A Biography.* New York: Random House, 1982.

———. *Thomas Hardy: Career as a Novelist.* New York: St. Martin's Press, 1994.

———, ed. *The Life and Work of Thomas Hardy.* London and Basingstoke: Macmillan, 1984.

———, ed. *Thomas Hardy's Public Voice: The Essays, Speeches, and Miscellaneous Prose.* Oxford and New York: Oxford University Press, 2001.

Mitchell, W. J. T. *Iconology: Image, Text, Ideology.* Chicago: University of Chicago Press, 1986.

———. *Picture Theory and Essays on Verbal and Visual Representation.* Chicago: University of Chicago Press, 1994.

Mitchie, Elsie B. *Outside the Pale: Cultural Exclusion, Gender Difference, and the Victorian Woman Writer.* Reading Women Writing Series. Ithaca: Cornell University Press, 1993.

Monypenny, William Flavelle, and George Earle Buckle. *The Life of Benjamin Disraeli.* 2 vols. New York: Macmillan, 1929.

Moore, Kevin Z. *The Descent of the Imagination: Postromantic Culture in the Later Novels of Thomas Hardy.* New York and London: New York University Press, 1990.

Morowitz, Laura, and William Vaughan, eds. *Artistic Brotherhoods in the Nineteenth Century.* Burlington: Ashgate, 2000.

Mulvey, Laura. *Visual and Other Pleasures.* Bloomington: Indiana University Press, 1989.

Murdoch, John. "English Realism: George Eliot and the Pre-Raphaelites." *Journal of the Warburg and Courtauld Institutes* 37 (1974): 313–29.

Myers, William. "George Eliot: Politics and Personality." In *Literature and Politics in the Nineteenth Century,* ed. John Lucas, 105–30. London: Methuen, 1971.

Nead, Lynda. "The Magdalen in Modern Times: The Mythology of the Fallen Women in Pre-Raphaelite Painting." *Oxford Art Journal* 7 (1) (1984): 26–37.

———. *Myths of Sexuality: Representations of Women in Victorian Britain*. New York: Basil Blackwell, 1988.

Neill, Edward. *Trial by Ordeal: Thomas Hardy and the Critics*. Columbia, S.C.: Camden House, 1999.

Newman, Beth. " 'The Situation of the Looker-On': Gender, Narration, and Gaze in *Wuthering Heights*." *Publications of the Modern Language Association* 105 (5) (October 1990): 1029–41.

Nicholes, Joseph. "Dorothea in the Moated Grange: Millais's *Mariana* and the *Middlemarch* Window Scenes." *Victorians Institute Journal* 20 (1992): 93–124.

Nochlin, Linda. *Women, Art, and Power and Other Essays*. New York: Harper and Row, 1988.

———. *Realism*. Harmondsworth, Middlesex: Penguin, 1990.

Nurbhai, Saleel, and K. M. Newton. *George Eliot, Judaism, and the Novels: Jewish Myth and Mysticism*. New York: Palgrave, 2002.

O'Fallon, Kathleen. "Breaking the Laws about Ladies: Wilkie Collins's Questioning of Gender Roles." In *Wilkie Collins to the Forefront*, ed. Nelson Smith and R. C. Terry, 227–40. New York: AMS Press, 1995.

Ormond, Leonée. "Pre-Raphaelite Brotherhood." In *Oxford Reader's Companion to George Eliot*, ed. John Rignall, 313. Oxford and New York: Oxford University Press, 2000.

———. "Millais and Contemporary Artists." In *John Everett Millais beyond the Pre-Raphaelite Brotherhood*, ed. Debra N. Mancoff, 21–42. New Haven: Yale University Press, 2001.

Pacteau, Francette. "The Impossible Referent: Representations of the Androgyne." In *Formations of Fantasy*, ed. Victor Burgin, James Donald, and Cora Kaplan, 62–84. London and New York: Methuen, 1986.

Page, Norman. "Hardy's Dutch Painting." *Thomas Hardy Year Book* 5 (1) (1975): 39–42.

———. *Thomas Hardy*. London: Routledge, 1977.

———. "Art and Aesthetics." In *The Cambridge Companion to Thomas Hardy*, ed. Dale Kramer, 38–53. Cambridge and New York: Cambridge University Press, 1999.

Parris, Leslie, ed. *Pre-Raphaelite Papers*. London: Tate Gallery, 1984.

———. *The Pre-Raphaelites*. London: Tate Gallery Exhibition Catalogue, 1994.

Pearce, Lynn. *Woman/Image/Text: Readings in Pre-Raphaelite Art and Literature*. Toronto: University of Toronto Press, 1991.

Peters, Catherine. *The King of Inventors: A Life of Wilkie Collins*. Princeton: Princeton University Press, 1991.

Pettit, Charles P. C., ed. *Reading Thomas Hardy*. London and New York: Macmillan and St. Martin's Press, 1988.

Pittock, Malcolm. "The Dove Ascending: The Case for Elizabeth Gaskell." *English Studies* 81 (6) (2000): 531–47.

Pointon, Marcia, ed. *Pre-Raphaelites Re-Viewed*. Manchester and New York: Manchester University Press, 1989.

Pollock, Griselda. *Vision and Difference: Femininity, Feminism and the Histories of Art*. New York: Routledge, 1988.

Poovey, Mary. *The Proper Lady and the Woman Writer: Ideology as Style in the Works of Mary Wollstonecraft, Mary Shelley, and Jane Austen*. Chicago: University of Chicago Press, 1984.

Porter, Bernard. *The Lion's Share: A Short History of British Imperialism, 1850–1870.* New York: Longman, 1975.

Poulson, Christine. *The Quest for the Grail: Arthurian Legend in British Art 1840–1920.* Manchester and New York: Manchester University Press and St. Martin's Press, 1999.

Praz, Mario. *Mnemosyne: The Parallel between Literature and the Visual Arts.* Princeton: Princeton University Press, 1970.

Prettejohn, Elizabeth. *The Art of the Pre-Raphaelites.* Princeton: Princeton University Press, 2000.

Regan, Stephen, ed. *The Politics of Pleasure: Aesthetics and Cultural Theory.* Buchingham: Open University Press, 1992.

Rhodes, Kimberly. "Degenerate Detail: John Everett Millais and Ophelia's 'Muddy Death.' " In *John Everett Millais beyond the Pre-Raphaelite Brotherhood,* ed. by Debra N. Mancoff, 43–68. New Haven: Yale University Press, 2001.

Rignall, John, ed. *Oxford Reader's Companion to George Eliot.* Oxford and New York: Oxford University Press, 2000.

Robinson, Kenneth. *Wilkie Collins: A Biography.* New York: Macmillan, 1952.

Rose, Andrea. *The Pre-Raphaelites.* London: Phaidon Press, 1992.

Rosenfeld, Jason. "The Pre-Raphaelite 'Otherhood' and Group Identity in Victorian Britain." In *Artistic Brotherhoods in the Nineteenth Century,* ed. Laura Morowitz and William Vaugham, 67–81. Burlington: Ashgate, 2000.

Roston, Murray. *Victorian Contexts: Literature and the Visual Arts.* New York: New York University Press, 1996.

Rowland, Susan. *C. G. Jung and Literary Theory: The Challenge from Fiction.* New York: St. Martin's Press, 1999.

Rylance, Rick. *Victorian Psychology and British Culture 1850–1880.* Oxford and New York: Oxford University Press, 2000.

Said, Edward W. *The Question of Palestine.* New York: Vintage, 1979.

———. *Culture and Imperialism.* New York: Alfred Knopf, 1993.

Sanders, Andrew. "Millais and Literature." In *John Everett Millais beyond the Pre-Raphaelite Brotherhood,* ed. Debra N. Mancoff, 69–93. New Haven: Yale University Press, 2001.

Schor, Hilary M. "The Plot of the Beautiful Ignoramus: *Ruth* and the Tradition of the Fallen Woman." In *Sex and Death in Victorian Literature,* ed. Regina Barreca, 158–77. Bloomington: Indiana University Press, 1990.

———. *Scheherezade in the Marketplace: Elizabeth Gaskell and the Victorian Novel.* New York and Oxford: Oxford University Press, 1992.

Schweik, Robert. "The 'Modernity' of Hardy's *Jude the Obscure.*" In *A Spacious Vision: Essays on Hardy,* ed. Phillip V. Mallett and Ronald P. Draper, 49–63. Newmill, Cornwall: Patten Press, 1994.

Scott, Grant F. *The Sculpted Word: Keats, Ekphrasis, and the Visual Arts.* Hanover and London: University Press of New England, 1994.

Sharp, William. *Dante Gabriel Rossetti.* London: Macmillan, 1882.

Showalter, Elaine. "Representing Ophelia: Women, Madness, and the Responsibilities of Feminist Criticism." In *Shakespeare's Middle Tragedies,* ed. David Young, 56–69. Englewood Cliffs: Prentice-Hall, 1993.

Smart, Alistair. "Pictorial Imagery in the Novels of Thomas Hardy." *Review of English Studies,* n.s. 12 (1961): 262–80.

Smith, Alison. *The Victorian Nude.* New York: Watson: Guptill, 2002.

Smith, Anne-Marie. *Julia Kristeva: Speaking the Unspeakable.* London: Pluto Press, 1998.

Smith, Lindsay. *Victorian Photography, Painting, and Poetry: The Enigma of Visibility in Ruskin, Morris, and the Pre-Raphaelites*. Cambridge: Cambridge University Press, 1995.

Smith, Nelson, and R. C. Terry. *Wilkie Collins to the Forefront*. AMS Series in Literature and Culture. New York: AMS, 1995.

Sonneson, Göran. *Pictorial Concepts*. Sweden: University of Lund, 1989.

Sproles, Karen Z. "D. H. Lawrence and the Pre-Raphaelites: 'Love among the Ruins.' " *D. H. Lawrence Review* 22 (3) (Fall 1990): 299–305.

Spurr, David. *The Rhetoric of Empire: Colonial Discourse in Journalism, Travel Writing, and Imperial Administration*. Durham: Duke University Press, 1993.

Starzyk, Lawrence J. *"If Mine Had Been the Painter's Hand": The Indeterminate in Nineteenth-Century Poetry and Painting*. New York: Peter Lang, 1999.

———. "Tennyson's 'The Gardener's Daughter': The Exegesis of an Icon." *Mosaic* 32 (September 1999): 41–58.

Stave, Shirley A. *The Decline of the Goddess: Nature, Culture, and Women in Thomas Hardy's Fiction*. Westport and London: Greenwood Press, 1995.

Stein, Richard L. *The Ritual of Interpretation*. Cambridge, Mass.: Harvard University Press, 1975.

———. "The Pre-Raphaelite Tennyson." *Victorian Studies* 24 (3) (Spring 1981): 279–301.

Steiner, Wendy. *The Colors of Rhetoric*. Chicago: University of Chicago Press, 1982.

———. *Pictures of Romances: Form against Context in Painting and Literature*. Chicago: University of Chicago Press, 1988.

Stiles, Peter. "Grace, Redemption, and the 'Fallen Woman': *Ruth* and *Tess of the d'Urbervilles*." *Gaskell Society Journal* 6 (1992): 58–86.

Sucksmith, Harvey Peter. "Dickens among the Pre-Raphaelites: Mr. Merdle and Holman Hunt's 'The Light of the World.' " *Dickensian* 72 (3) (Autumn 1976): 159–63.

Suriano, Gregory. *The Pre-Raphaelite Illustrators*. Delaware: Oak Knell Press, 2000.

Surtees, Virginia. *The Paintings and Drawings of Dante Gabriel Rossetti (1828–1882): A Catalogue Raisonné*. 2 vols. Oxford: Clarendon, 1971.

Sussman, Herbert. "The Language of Criticism and the Language of Art: The Response of Victorian Periodicals to the Pre-Raphaelite Brotherhood." *Victorian Periodicals Newsletter* 19 (Spring 1973): 21–29.

———. *Victorian Masculinities: Manhood and Masculine Poetics in Early Victorian Literature and Art*. New York: Cambridge University Press, 1995.

Symons, Julian. Introduction. In *The Woman in White*, by Wilkie Collins, 7–21. Harmondsworth: Penguin, 1985.

Sypher, Wylie. *Rococo to Cubism in Art and Literature*. New York: Random House, 1960.

Taylor, Dennis. Introduction. In *Jude the Obscure*, by Thomas Hardy, xvi–xxxiv. London and New York, 1998.

Taylor, Jenny Bourne. *In the Secret Theatre of Home: Wilkie Collins, Sensation Narrative, and Nineteenth-Century Psychology*. New York: Routledge: 1988.

Thompson, Nicola Diane. *Reviewing Sex: Gender and the Reception of Victorian Novels*. New York: New York University Press, 1996.

Tinker, Chauncey Brewster. *Painter and Poet: Studies in the Literary Relations of English Painting*. Freeport, N.Y.: Books for Libraries Press, 1969.

Todd, Pamela. *Pre-Raphaelites at Home*. New York: Watson-Guptill, 2001.

Treuherz, Julian. "A Brief Survey of Victorian Painting." In *Art in the Age of Queen Victoria: Treasures from the Royal Academy of Arts Permanent Collection*, ed. Helen Valentine, 12–25. New Haven and London: Royal Academy of Arts and Yale University Press, 1999. An exhibition catalog.

Tucker, Herbert F., ed. *A Companion to Victorian Literature and Culture*. Oxford and Malden: Blackwell, 1999.

Turner, Paul. *The Life of Thomas Hardy*. Oxford and Malden: Blackwell, 1998.

Uglow, Jenny. *Elizabeth Gaskell: A Habit of Stories*. New York: Farrar Strauss, 1993.

Unsworth, Anna. *Mrs. Gaskell: An Independent Woman*. Montreaux, London, and Washington: Minerva Press, 1996.

Upstone, Robert. "Symbolism in Three Dimensions." In *The Age of Rossetti, Burne-Jones, and Watts: Symbolism in Britain 1860–1910*, ed. Andrew Wilton and Robert Upstone, 83–92. New York, London, Paris: Flammarion, 1997. Tate Exhibition Catalogue.

Valentine, Helen, ed. *Art in the Age of Queen Victoria: Treasures from the Royal Academy of Arts Permanent Collection*. New Haven and London: Royal Academy of Arts and Yale University Press, 1999. An exhibition catalog.

Walkowitz, Judith R. *Prostitution and Victorian Society: Women, Class, and the State*. Cambridge: Cambridge University Press, 1980.

Warner, Malcolm. "John Everett Millais's *Autumn Leaves*: A Picture Full of Beauty and without Subject." In *Pre-Raphaelite Papers*, ed. Leslie Parris, 126–42. London: Tate Gallery, 1984.

Watson, Margaretta Frederick, ed. *Collecting the Pre-Raphaelites: The Anglo-American Enchantment*. Brookfield, Vt.: Ashgate, 1997.

Weber, C. J. *Hardy of Wessex*. New York: Columbia University Press, 1940.

Wildman, Stephen. *Visions of Love and Life: Pre-Raphaelite Art from the Birmingham Collection, England*. Alexandria, Va.: Art Services International, 1995. An exhibition catalog.

———, and John Christian. *Edward Burne-Jones: Victorian Artist-Dreamer*. New York: Metropolitan Museum of Art, 1998. An exhibition catalog.

Williams, Kellen M. " 'Traced and Captured by the Men in the Chaise': Pursuing Sexual Difference in Wilkie Collins's *The Woman in White*." *Journal of Narrative Technique* 28 (1998): 91–110.

Wilton, Andrew, and Robert Upstone. *The Age of Rossetti, Burne-Jones, and Watts: Symbolism in Britain 1860–1910*. New York, Paris, and London: Flammarion, 1997. Tate Exhibition Catalogue.

Wise, T. J., and J. A. Symington, eds. *The Brontës: Their Lives and Correspondence*. 4 vols. Oxford: Oxford University Press, 1933.

Witemeyer, Hugh. *George Eliot and the Visual Arts*. New Haven: Yale University Press, 1979.

Wolf, Sylvia. *Julia Margaret Cameron's Women*. Chicago: Art Institute of Chicago, 1998.

Wolff, Janet, and John Seed, eds. *The Culture of Capital: Art, Power and the Nineteenth-Century Middle Class*. Manchester: Manchester University Press; New York: St. Martin's Press, 1988.

Wolff, Robert Lee. *Sensational Victorian: The Life of Mary Elizabeth Braddon*. New York and London: Garland, 1979.

Wood, Christopher. *The Pre-Raphaelites*. New York: Crescent Books, 1981.

———. *Burne-Jones: The Life and Works of Sir Edward Burne-Jones (1833–1898)*. London: Weidenfeld and Nicolson, 1998.

Wynne, Deborah. *The Sensation Novel and the Victorian Family Magazine*. London: Palgrave, 2001.

Young-Eisendrath, Polly, ed. *The Cambridge Companion to Jung*. Cambridge: Cambridge University Press, 1997.

Index